The Man Puzzle

The Man Puzzle

A Guide To Understanding Men
(Heart, Mind and Soul)

PHILLIP PETREE

Petree Publishing

Petree Publishing, LLC
Lighthouse Point, FL 33064
www.petreepublishing.com

Ordering Information:
Quantity sales: Special discounts are available on quantity purchases by corporations, associations, and others. For details, contact the publisher at: www.themanpuzzle.com. Orders by U.S. trade bookstores and wholesalers. Please contact:

Ingram Content Distribution:
Tel: (800) 800-8000; or visit: www.ingramcontent.com/

ISBN-13: 978-0-9964025-0-7

First Edition: July 2015

Printed in the United States of America

10 9 8 7 6 5 4 3 2 1

TABLE OF CONTENTS

"Learning is acquired by reading books, but the much more necessary learning, the knowledge of the world, is only to be acquired by reading men, and studying all the various editions of them." - Lord Chesterfield, "Letters to His Son"

"There are three kinds of men: The ones that learn by reading. The few who learn by observation. The rest of them have to pee on the electric fence." - Will Rogers

Plato knew that there are two horses in man's soul: a rebellious one and an obedient one, and that the carriage driver has great difficulty guiding his carriage because of the unruliness of the disobedient horse. Four centuries before Christ, Plato saw, with remarkable acuteness, that men were torn between what is good, but tempted by evil. The skilled woman will help a man stay true to his good qualities while displacing his rebellious tendencies.

INTRODUCTION

I HAVE ALWAYS BEEN A voracious reader and willing to read anything lying around and I've always had a particular curiosity about articles in women's magazines written about everything from finding the right man, seducing the right man, keeping him happy in bed and the list goes on and on and on. These articles are most always penned by highly educated, well meaning women who seem to have a penchant for handing out advice that, generally speaking, would, at best, provide only a modest amount of amusement for most men.

While reading these articles I would think about how frustrating it must be to try some of the things suggested just to have your man stare at you in disbelief, not respond the way you were expecting or worse, not respond at all and then I would wonder what a woman would do if she had the real inside scoop.

Much later in my life I met a truly remarkable woman. She was everything a man would want in a woman, she was smart, educated (a Ph.D.), easily one of the most beautiful women in the world, the best cook I have ever encountered, a great (but not adventurous) sex partner, and a wonderful companion. We shared the same faith, and had similar childhood events. We had every necessary ingredient for a successful relationship.

1

The Man Puzzle

We loved each other deeply, we were both intelligent and certainly, we thought, more emotionally capable than most other people we knew. But for several years, we struggled in our relationship, and we both walked away numerous times only to be swayed by one another to try, try again. Eventually we both concluded that it just wasn't going to happen.

What she and I had discussed many times and what I found to be true was that she really knew nothing about us "boys." Whether it was me, my sons, her son, her ex, you name it she was generally baffled by our species. When I would talk with my buddies about this (and yes, men do talk about these things, but more about that later), they would just shake their heads and say things like "Typical woman." or "What did you expect?"

The "typical woman" or "What did you expect?" and similar comments are heard all too often among men. So I decided to start asking men about how understood they felt by the women in their lives, and I can honestly say the vast, vast, majority do not feel understood.

When I asked my women friends what they understood about men, I would get the typical eye roll and then comments like: "No one can understand a man" or "all they want is sex, and someone to cook and clean for them."

Now don't get me wrong, great sex, a hot meal and a clean house are all wonderful things, but they're NOT the only things men want. We want so much more, but how can men get what they truly want and need with so much misunderstanding between the sexes? How can men be understood when men and women are such completely different creatures?

No two men are alike... every man is the same!

What an odd and confusing statement! But then, we are an odd and confusing species. We come in all different shapes, sizes and colors. Some of us are quiet and soft spoken while others are loud and boisterous. Some of us are rugged and outdoorsy while some are refined and prefer the ballet over blades of grass. We're Republicans and Democrats, Christian, Jewish, Muslim, Hindu, agnostic and atheist. You name a look, belief or interest and somewhere there's a man that's just like that.

With such a wide variety of men, it's no wonder that women are confused and can't seem to get a handle on who, or what we are, and certainly not on what makes us tick. Add in the "well meaning" advice found in nearly every women's magazine and romantic movie and you end up with total confusion.

The good news is that even with all the differences, there are still similarities that run through the veins of every man and while there are no absolutes there are enough threads of consistency that, with a little work, we can start to make some sense out of how and why men are the way we are.

In this book I will try to remove some of those preconceived notions, clear up some of the misconstrued advice and half truths and to dispel the myths while providing some very clear insight as to how and why we men evolve to be the way we are and, hopefully, I can supply the information in a way that is meaningful and understandable.

Remember the old adage: "Behind every good man is a great woman." Every great woman has one essential piece of knowledge, she understands her man.

Chapter 1

PHYSICAL DIFFERENCES

BEFORE WE GET STARTED, I want to be clear that some of what you're going to read will be very surprising to you and even though I will reveal some striking differences between men and women, it's important to understand that these differences do not make one gender superior nor inferior; it simply makes us different.

So imagine this, you have two souls and these souls are identical in each and every way. Now take one soul (you choose) and put that soul in a woman and take the other soul and put it in a horse. Now put those two beings in the same environment together for their entire lives. Do you believe those two souls would experience the world in the same way?

So much of our belief about men and women has been because we somehow came to believe the vessels were, other than some pesky reproductive organs, the same. This belief became so widespread that scientists only ran lab tests on males because, it was believed, that since we males didn't have those pesky female organs and hormonal cycles, the scientists had a more predictable outcome, and the test would be more accurate.

In this old school thinking, which has been prevalent over the last 40+ years, physical differences didn't matter. Now, modern science has enabled us to see differences, not just in our physical bodies, but how our organs are different and especially how our brains are actually wired and utilized differently.

In essence, those vessels that we thought were the same, are so completely different that you might conclude we have as little in common as the horse and woman. Overly dramatic? Perhaps. But if you can open your mind to the possibility, you can begin to see options and avenues that you might have never known existed and things that never before made sense, just might fall in place.

Back in the 1960's and 70's, women's study programs popped up at college and universities all across America and many of those programs were based on a view promoted by the philosopher Simone de Beauvoir which claimed: "One is not born a woman, one becomes one". This view proposed that the term "gender" should be used to refer to the social and cultural constructs of masculine and feminine and not to the physical state of being either male or female.

This view served a very important purpose and that was to level the playing field between men and women and to remove much of the false beliefs that women were incapable or inferior and thus allowed for equality to move forward. This view also created some problems and the problem is that men, by virtue of how we were raised, are somehow broken.

Now, as we move to modern times, we learn that there are, indeed, significant physical differences between the genders and that men and women have entirely different emotional processes and emotional needs. In fact, in recent years a handful of colleges and universities have began to offer Men's Study programs. Men's studies, often called Men and Masculinities, is an interdisciplinary offshoot of traditional Gender Studies programs and is devoted to topics concerning men, masculinity and gender differences. This is a new and evolving recognition of the physical, mental and emotional differences between the genders and how those differences affect the way men interact with and respond to the world around them.

None of this is to say that men and women can't be equal which is why, when doing the math, it's important to recognize that even though 2x6=12, so does 3x4!

Evolution:

When we discuss differences, do we really want to go back to the days of knuckle dragging Neanderthals and talk about how men were great hunters and how our brains became wired for hunting and conquering? Or how women were gatherers and developed different evolutionary traits? Well, actually, we do. Not because we need a history lesson but because so much of our evolution explains modern behaviors in men that many women can't comprehend. Things like our addiction to sports, our grunting responses, our desire to sit for long periods of time watching yet another rerun of a show we've seen 15 times, why we won't stop and ask for directions or even why women typically demonstrate more empathy than men. So much of it is evolutionary based.

On Average:

Before we jump into the physical differences between genders in which many averages are used, it's important to note that there are many individual exceptions to any generalization but those exceptions do not invalidate a generalization. For example, there are many women who are taller than the average man, and there are many men who are shorter than the average woman.

But the statement "Men are, on average, taller than women" is still valid. Similarly, not all men have a strong male brain, and not all women have a strong female brain, but, on average, men are far more likely to have the male brain and women are far more likely to have the female brain. So, keep in mind that when we talk averages, or generalizations, it means just that, "on average."

Basic External Differences:

Let's begin by looking at some obvious differences. These differences are averages and as I explained a moment ago, there are exceptions but the exceptions do not invalidate the average.

The average male is about 5'9" in height and weighs about 184 pounds while the average woman is 5'3" and 154 pounds.

The average length of an adult male hand is 7.4 inches (189mm), while the average length of an adult female hand is 6.7 inches (172mm). The average hand breadth for adult males and females is 3.3 inches (84mm) and 2.9 inches (74mm), respectively.

The first finger of a woman's hand is usually longer than the third. This evolved with picking or gathering. With men the reverse is true as a more stable grip was needed on tools and fighting instruments.

The average male foot is about 10.4" (26.5cm) long while the average woman's foot is 9.8" (25cm) in length. An interesting study in Australia showed that boys and girls foot sizes were about the same until around 8 years of age at which time boys' feet started growing larger than girls' feet.

The sexes also differ in skeletal structure with women having a shorter head, broader face, less protruding chin, shorter legs, and longer trunk. And, of course, women also have a wider pelvis.

Basic Internal Differences:

Men have smaller stomachs, kidneys, livers, and appendix, and larger lungs than women with the average female lung capacity being about 30 percent less than in males.

Men's blood has 20% more red blood cells. Since red cells supply oxygen to the body, men have the upper hand on endurance. During WW2, when women replaced men in factories and workdays grew from 10 to 12 hour shifts, accidents among women increased 150% while the rate of accidents among men did not increase significantly. Simply put, a woman's internal structure was simply not designed to support long days of extreme physical labor.

Do you think these differences can be overcome with training? Not so. Dr. Benjamin Levine, director of the Institute for Exercise and Environmental Medicine at Presbyterian Hospital and the University of Texas Southwestern Medical Center in Dallas, conducted research that recruited sedentary men and women and trained them to run a marathon. At the start of the study, the men's hearts and the women's hearts were the same size relative to the size of their bodies. "Gram for gram, they had the same size hearts," Levine said. "We trained them for over a year. Heartbeat for heartbeat, they had the same training." And the result? "The women's hearts did not grow anywhere near as big as the men's hearts," said Dr. Levine.

On average, men are 50 percent stronger than women in brute strength. Women who weight train can narrow that gap except when it comes to men who weight train, then testosterone gives men the upper hand as men will develop strength and build muscle mass far more quickly than women.

Those are just some general differences between the sexes. Now let's look at some specific differences that actually impact our daily lives:

Why Men Have Nipples

Have you ever wondered why men have nipples? All embryos start the same, as girls and, of course girls need nipples. In boys, at about 6-8 weeks the Y chromosome kicks in, brain changes start to occur, and fetal size and growth changes begin. By 15 weeks in the pregnancy, the testicles are fully formed and we're well on our way to producing a bouncing baby boy! But the nipples, already in place, remain.

A LOOK UNDER THE HOOD

The Heart:

A man's heart is about 25% larger than a woman's. While a man's heart, on average, will weigh about 10 oz., a woman's heart will weigh about 8 oz. A man's arteries are also larger measuring about 0.1 inches (2.5 mm) versus a woman's at 0.05 inches (1.5 mm).

Men also have sturdier valves which may account for why women are born with more valve disorders such as mitral valve prolapse, a condition that affects about 6% of women and can progress to the point where the valve between the upper and lower left chambers no longer closes properly and requires heart surgery for repair or replacement.

A man's heart also beats slower averaging about 70 beats per minute while a woman's heart rate is generally about 78 beats per minute. This faster heart rate also applies while sleeping.

In men, arterial plaque typically builds up in uneven/irregular patches or peaks while in women the plaque buildup is typically spread evenly along artery walls and normally isn't treatable using procedures such as angioplasty and stents.

Not only is the size of the heart different but the actual physiology is different, too. At puberty, the rate of repolarization (the time in a heartbeat when the heart muscle prepares for the next contraction or pump) becomes longer in females and shorter in males. After age 60, the repolarization returns to being about the same in both sexes. Researchers now know this is due to gender-related differences in the biology of the ion channels in the heart - the tiny "pores" in cell membranes that allow charged molecules to flow in and out of cells which affect the duration of repolarization. Yes, even the core biology of the heart is different between men and women.

"We all went to medical school and were taught that all hearts are the same, it's just a muscle. But, in fact, it's a hormonally sensitive muscle," remarks Raymond Woosley M.D. Ph.D., Chairman of Pharmacology at Georgetown University. "Sex hormones interact with one of the most primitive signaling mechanisms in the body, potassium channels, and this has direct consequences in terms of heart rhythm."

Gender-related differences in the heart also seem to extend to proteins in the muscle tissue itself, notably myosin, and in the overgrowth of muscle that leads to cardiomyopathy, (heart muscle disease) such as FHC, an inherited disease that causes thickening of the heart muscle which hampers the hearts ability to pump blood. In males with FHC, the heart enlarges initially, and when they become fully mature adults, these men develop features of congestive heart failure and begin to die. However, in females with FHC this is not the case; with adult females, the heart keeps getting bigger and bigger but continues to function as close to normal as possible. Researchers have no idea why this is but the suspicion is that female hormones offer some form of protection.

In his article, "A woman's heart: a mystery of science" (Baron-Faust, 2000), Dr. Michael Rosen, Director of the Center for Molecular Therapeutics at the Columbia University College of

Physicians and Surgeons, was quoted as saying "One thing is clear. We can no longer use men as a generic model for the human heart, or the human race."

By the way, when a woman receives a heart transplant, she typically receives a man's heart.

Hearing:

When born, boys and girls exhibit equivalent hearing, meaning there is nothing that genetically predisposes men to have worse hearing than women. The difference in men's hearing ability versus women, however, is the result of environmental factors. According to a study from Johns Hopkins University, men are five and a half times more likely than women to experience hearing loss as they age with loss starting as young as 20 years old.

"Basically, men have overall worse hearing than women as they age, but it's hard to isolate behavioral risk factors," said Dr. Charles Limb, an associate professor in the Department of Otolaryngology-Head and Neck Surgery at Johns Hopkins University School of Medicine.

Dr. Limb pointed out that risk factors like cardiovascular disease and smoking are more prevalent among men and could contribute to hearing loss, but that men are more likely to be in situations of high noise exposure—working in construction, for example, or being in the military—and less likely to use earplugs or protect themselves otherwise.

And the hearing problem doesn't resolve as men get older.

Aging women have better high-frequency hearing than men. But women in their sixties through their nineties lose low-frequency hearing at a faster rate than men, according to researchers from the Department of Otolaryngology-Head and Neck Surgery at the University of Washington Medical Center in Seattle.

The Man Puzzle

When it comes to communicating, "Speech consonants are high frequency, so high-frequency loss causes men to have difficulty in understanding words" said George Gates, M.D., a professor of Otolaryngology and head and neck surgery at the University of Washington. Over the course of a lifetime, "men seem to get more noise exposure than women and thus have more high frequency loss," Gates said in an interview with ABC News (Chitale, 2009).

> **NOTE:** This is extremely important piece of information because of how it ties to how men listen to women's voices, which I'll discuss shortly.

In general, the loss of lower frequency sounds is where hearing problems evolve for many women. "Vowels are low frequency," Gates said, and the reduced ability to hear these sounds is more prominent in women according to the research.

Hormones may play a role in the hearing differences between women and men. New research from Cornell University in Ithaca, N.Y., reveals that estrogen improved the hearing in female fish. And these findings may be able to be applied to human beings. "Human females have estrogen receptors in their ear," said Andrew H. Bass, Ph.D., lead researcher and professor at the Department of Neurobiology and Behavior at Cornell.

Remember though, men have hearing loss in the high frequencies which is where women speak, and women have hearing loss in the low frequencies which is where mean speak.

When men and women speak, the human brain processes the sounds of those voices differently. While most of us actually hear female voices more clearly, men's brains hear women's voices first as music. But it's not music, it's someone giving them a honey-do list. So the male brain goes into overdrive trying to analyze what is actually being said.

Bottom line: Men have to work harder deciphering what women are saying because they use the auditory part of the brain that processes music, not human voices. Men's brains are not designed to listen to women's voices. It's not the pitch of the woman's voice, but rather the vibration and number of sound waves that cause the problem.

But guys have no trouble at all hearing each other because men use a much simpler brain mechanism at the back of the brain to decipher another man's voice and recognize it as speech.

Due to differences in the size and shape of the vocal cords and larynx between men and women, the female voice is actually more complex than the male voice. Women also have a more natural 'melody' in their voices which causes a more complex range of sound frequencies than in a male voice. When men hear a male voice, they process it in the 'mind's eye.' This is the part of the brain where people compare their experiences to themselves, so the man is comparing his own voice to the new voice and because it's similar, it's easy to understand.

Because women's voices are higher, when a man's hearing starts to falter, it becomes far more difficult for him to hear the woman's voice and the high pitched sound can even become annoying. Have you ever noticed how older men have less tolerance for small barking dogs with their high pitched yaps or for crying babies? Oddly, companies spend, or rather waste, millions of dollars each year by advertising products using actors that have voices that older men either can't hear, or worse get annoyed by! (Sokhi, Hunter, Wilkinson, & Woodruff, 2005)

What this means in the classroom is that if the average boy is to hear and be able to understand as well as the average girl, female teachers may need to speak as much as 6-8 dbs more loudly than they currently do. This difference also explains why boys hear better and behave better around male teachers. They don't have to employ the same set of conversion and processing in order to decipher the words.

While women may have an advantage in regard to auditory perception, males may have an advantage in others, particularly in regard to the localization of sounds. Why? What is the point of sex differences in hearing? In their paper, "Sex differences in auditory motion perception: looming sounds are special" (Neuhoff, Planisek, & Seifritz, 2009), lead researcher John Neuhoff suggested that sex differences in hearing may have an adaptive function, i.e. they may have evolved because they had survival value.

Another important part of hearing is what happens inside the brain. Dr. Joseph T. Lurito, Assistant Radiology Professor at Indiana University School of Medicine, presenting evidence at the Radiological Society of North America's (Lurito, Phillips, Dzemidzic, Lowe, Wang, & Mathews, 2000) annual meeting said that his research found men use the left side of the brain, the side traditionally associated with understanding language, to pick up conversations. But women also used the right side. Dr. Lurito said, "I don't want to provoke a battle of the sexes. I just want people to realize that men and women may process language differently," and he went on to suggest that women were not necessarily better listeners.

Vision:

Remarkably, the physical structure of the eye is fairly similar between men and women with the primary exception being the pupil. In the average male, the pupil is about .13" (3.5 mm) wide while the average woman has pupils which are .15" (3.8 mm) wide. Of course the pupils control how much light enters the retina and this affects all kinds of things.

Physical Differences

Where it starts getting interesting is in how the brain processes things. Research discovered that the way the visual centers of men and women's brains works is different. Men have greater sensitivity to fine detail and rapidly moving stimuli, but women are better at discriminating between colors (more light).

In the male brain there are high concentrations of male sex hormone (androgen) receptors throughout the cerebral cortex, especially in the visual cortex which is responsible for processing images. Androgens are also responsible for controlling the development of neurons in the visual cortex, and males have 25% more of these neurons than females.

Researchers from Brooklyn and Hunter Colleges of the City University of New York compared the vision of men and women over 16 years of age and from both high school and college, and including students and staff. All volunteers were required to have normal color vision and 20/20 sight (or 20/20 when corrected by glasses or contact lenses).

When the volunteers were required to describe colors shown to them across the visual spectrum it became obvious that the color vision of men was shifted, and that they required a slightly longer wavelength to experience the same hue as the women. The males also had a broader range in the center of the spectrum where they were less able to discriminate between colors.

Images of light and dark bars were used to measure contrast-sensitivity functions (CSF) of vision; the bars were either horizontal or vertical and volunteers had to choose which one they saw. In each image, when the light and dark bars were alternated, the image appeared to flicker; researchers then rapidly varied how the bars alternated or how close together they were and found that at moderate rates of image change, observers lost sensitivity for close together bars, and gained sensitivity when the bars were farther apart. However when the image change was faster, both sexes were less able to resolve the images over all bar widths. Overall, the men were better able to resolve more rapidly changing images that were closer together than the women.

Professor Israel Abramov, who led this study commented, "As with other senses, such as hearing and the olfactory system, there are marked sex differences in vision between men and women."

Professor Abramov added "Since these neurons are guided by the cortex during fetal development, testosterone plays a major role in somehow leading to different connectivity in males and female brains." (The eyes have it: Men and women do see things differently, 2012)

You can trace differences in vision back to caveman days. Naturally, women developed better peripheral vision because they gathered food, watched out for children and for danger while men developed stronger straight-on vision for hunting. While the human brain can identify an image the eye has seen for only 15 milliseconds, that ability doesn't explain why most men can't tell the difference between white, snow white, floral white and why most women can. It's not that men don't care, we really can't see what the fuss is all about! On the flip side, have you ever had a man try to show you something sitting in a tree and get frustrated because you didn't see it? It's not because you're daft, it's because he can see things you can't!

Smell:

The question of whether men and women differ in their ability to smell has been the topic of scientific investigation for over a hundred years. Although conflicting findings abound, most studies suggest that, for at least some odors, women outperform men on tests of detection, identification, discrimination, and memory.

Most functional imaging and electrophysiological studies similarly imply that, when sex differences are present, they favor women.

Researchers found women whose odor sensitivity was tested many times, were able to detect the cherry-almond smell of benzaldehyde and a few other odors at progressively much lower concentrations than men. In fact, men taking part in similar tests never improved their ability to identify odors with experience.

Some of the compounds that women detect better than men include some surprises:

- Acetone (nail polish remover),
- Butanol (solvent used in perfumes and that "funny" smell in markers),
- Citral (citrus scent in shaving cream, dishwasher detergent, air freshener, colognes and perfume)
- Ethanol (Aftershave, body lotions, shampoos, suntan lotions, toilette bowl cleaners),
- Hydrogen sulfide (sewer gas – rotten egg smell, automotive oil treatments, pesticides),
- Phenyl ethanol (flavors especially in ice cream, perfumes, candy, some breads),
- Pyridine (antifreeze, fungicides and dyeing agent for textiles),
- M-Xylene (solvents used in printing/rubber/leather, aerosol paints, plastic bottles and polyester clothing),
- 1-hexanol (beer, wine, vodka, particleboard furniture and cabinets, insecticides for crawling insects, water based indoor paints such as semi-gloss, eggshell or satin and many tinting bases),

- 3-mercapto-butanol (degradation by-product of feline cat urine and a cat pheromone, also used in foods as a thickener, sweetener or flavoring agent for meats, coffee, breads, etc.).

According to research, during ovulation when estrogen levels soar, women have an even better sense of smell. Here's what's amazing, further studies suggest that pre-pubescent females also detect certain types of odors better than male children. These studies suggest that smell is not entirely dependent on sex hormones but are innate differences between males and females. (Doty & Cameron, 2009)

So what do men like to smell? There are certain smells, such as pumpkin pie and lavender that men actually find arousing. However, some of the latest research shows the aroma of breakfast is a man's favorite smell, and the phrase "wake up and smell the coffee" is truer than you might imagine. When sleeping, our sense of smell shuts down and when you wake up, the smell of coffee is one of the first smells you can detect.

Smell is such a strong sense that familiar smells are more closely linked to emotions and memory than vision. People can remember smells with 65% accuracy after a year, while visual recall is about 50% after three months. One of the most evocative smells from childhood are Crayola brand Crayons. A survey found that 85% of all people remembered their childhood when they caught the smell of Crayola crayons. Other research says that we have such a strong recall, you can smell those crayons from just having read this paragraph!

Why is it important to know this? Because smell, especially familiar smells, signifies to us at a very deep level that we're in a safe environment, that we're home and that makes it important to make sure men are surrounded by familiar smells when they're home.

But smell doesn't just work on odors and emotional recall or our feeling of comfort or discomfort; we also use it in choosing a mate. Attraction is quite literally about chemistry, and our noses have receptors for scent molecules so finely-tuned that even consciously imperceptible chemicals are detected and subconsciously processed by the brain.

While at the University of Bern in 1995 biologist Claus Wedekind conducted a ground breaking study detailed in his paper titled "MHC-Dependent Mate Preferences in Humans" (Wedekind, Seebeck, Bettens, & Paepke, 1995) in which women were asked to smell t-shirts worn by different men and to rate which ones were most attractive to them. The participants overwhelmingly selected the shirts worn by men whose MHC, a large cluster of genes that relate to immune systems, was vastly different than their own. Wedekind's study shows that women are innately attracted to partners who have different immune systems than their own because this indicates a genetically different profile and more diverse offspring which guarantees a healthy gene pool in future generations.

It seems, however, that modern science has thrown a monkey wrench into the selection process to which our sense of smell contributes. Professor Wedekind's research also showed that a woman's odor preference is compromised while taking oral contraception. Apparently, oral, patch and insertable contraceptives hormonally mimic pregnancy and a side effect is that it shuts down a woman's detection process for a suitable mate. By taking control of your reproductive cycles you're dismantling one of evolutions greatest gifts – the ability to sniff out a suitable partner.

This side affect can surface in two distinct ways: the first is that once a woman is off the contraceptive and has conceived a child, she can suddenly find herself completely unattracted to her mate. In modern society, we rationalize this away as being too busy caring for the baby, too tired from being up all night with the baby, too many new chores to do because of the baby and basically just not having time for sex… but there is a deeper cause!

The emotional, physiological and financial cost of this specific side effect from hormone-based contraception receives very little attention; yet, lives are shattered and children are raised in broken homes because a primary evolutionary mechanism has been short-circuited. After the 9 month gestation period plus the breastfeeding time a woman can find herself no longer attracted to her partner when her evolutionary mate selection mechanism reactivates.

The second way we see the side effect of contraception is that by altering a primary means by which a woman chooses her mate, we create unions with genetically weak foundations and, according to scientists, miscarriages are frequently the body's next line of defense against the conception of a fetus by partners who share similar genetic profiles, as often happens with inbred offspring for example.

So, what things can a man smell better than a woman? Actually, it's a pretty short list. Men can smell fear, and it's something we developed for defensive purposes. Not only can men identify what fear smells like in other people, but we will naturally become afraid ourselves after smelling it.

The other thing men can smell is when a woman is ready to get pregnant. In a blind study, scientists discovered that heterosexual men sniffing the T-shirts of various women would consistently label the shirts of ovulating or fertile women as more "pleasant" or "sexy" than the T-shirts of other women who weren't ready to conceive. Apparently, men can identify this scent up to a week after the clothes were worn.

If you're curious, studies have shown that women are typically more aroused by the scent of cucumber and licorice and that an adult woman's favorite smell is that of a newborn baby!

Taste:

Interestingly, taste is an area that is pretty even although women still come out ahead in key areas and behind in a few others. On average, most human adults have about 10,000 taste buds, and the number is largely genetic.

According to research by Linda Baroshuk, a psychologist and Professor of Community Dentistry and Behavioral Science at the University of Florida and an internationally known researcher specializing in the chemical senses of taste and smell, in humans, the difference in the number of taste buds can vary widely. You could have from 11 to 1,100 taste buds per square inch.

Professor Baroshuk coined the phrase "supertasters" which describe those people who have the higher number of taste buds, "regular-tasters" for those of us in the normal range and "non-tasters" for those who have a lower numbers of taste buds and who have a problem tasting or can't taste at all.

On average, supertasters have 425 taste buds per square centimeter (0.16 square inches) on the tips of their tongues, compared to 184 for normal tasters and 96 for non-tasters.

Interestingly, the number of taste buds also varies by ethnicity. For example, Asians seem to have a higher proportion of super-tasters followed by Africans, and India has the highest number of non-tasters (about 40%).

There is a chemical, 6-n-propylthiouracil (PROP), which is one of several probes used for testing genetic variations in our ability to taste bitter. An increased sensitivity to PROP means an increased sensitivity to bitter taste. Scientists have learned that genetics play a definite role in determining a person's ability to taste bitter and this genetic variation for PROP sensitivity is related to the supertaster trait, which is characterized by the ability to perceive flavors more intensely. Only about a quarter of people (25%) are supertasters, half (50%) are regular tasters and a quarter (25%) are non-tasters. When you break it down by gender, women are more likely to be supertasters than men, with 35% of women categorized as supertasters while 15% of men are categorized with this trait.

A gender difference in taste perception is seen in children as well. In a 2008 Danish study (Allesen-Holm, Bredie, & Frøst, 2008) involving 8,900 Danish school children, scientists found that girls were better at recognizing tastes than boys for all concentrations of sweet and sour flavors. On average, boys needed approximately 10% more sourness and 20% more sweetness than girls in order to recognize those flavors.

This same study found that girls preferred more muted flavors, while boys had a preference for more extreme flavors. Boys liked super sweet flavors and gave top marks to the most sour-tasting samples. Think about that the next time you cook a meal for your man and he complains that it's too bland.

So, on average, women do have more taste buds than men, which makes them more sensitive to sweet, sour, salty and bitter taste which causes women to prefer those tastes more muted. This may explain why men who're put on low sodium diets complain about the food having no taste, because, for them, it really doesn't!

Brain:

Now we get into the organ where things get really different. If you've ever wondered why we're so different, get ready to find out!

A recent study by Israeli researchers found distinct differences in the developing fetus at just 26 weeks of pregnancy. Using an ultrasound scanner, researchers found the corpus callosum - the bridge of nerve tissue that connects the right and left sides of the brain - was thicker in female fetuses than in male fetuses and that's at 26 weeks! (In a minute, I'll show how some brand new science reveals that men get something in return!)

Men have approximately 6.5 times more gray matter in the brain than women but women have about 10 times more white matter than men. What does this mean?

The real processing occurs in the gray matter while white allows communication to and from gray matter areas, and between gray matter and the other parts of the body. So, men seem to think with their gray matter while women connect more thoughts with the white matter. In this way, a woman's brain is a bit more complicated in setup, but those connections allow a woman's brain to work faster than a man's in some areas such as linguistics.

In his book "Change Your Brain, Change Your Life" (Amen, 1999), Dr. Daniel Amen says that the brains of men and women are measurably different, particularly the area called the limbic system which is the part of the brain that, among other things, feels emotion. It is also where we store highly charged emotional memories; where we tag some memories as unimportant, and therefore, are easily forgotten. Because the limbic system deals with emotionally charged memories, it filters external events through internal states, creating what is called emotional coloring. This sets the emotional tone of the mind.

Our emotional tone also effects our motivation to succeed, our ability to bond, and our libido. A happy man is going to be more successful in his work, more caring towards you and his family and more sexually interested in you. Conversely, negative, emotionally charged memories produce unpleasant feelings like fear, anxiety, hopelessness, rage, despair, hurt, and shame. If men don't have enough positive emotional memories to offset the negative ones, you can find your man getting sullen, becoming depressed, withdrawing and less interested in you.

Had a rough day? Has your man? When someone has an orgasm, the limbic brain has a mini seizure, which tends to lessen deep limbic activity. Since depression and sadness are created by an overactive limbic brain, lessening its activity with a "mini seizure" creates emotional stability.

The prefrontal cortex is commonly called the "thinking brain" and is the area of the brain that causes us to think critically about our lives, to figure things out, follow through, persevere, control our impulses, learn from our experiences, express our emotions, and create empathy for those who are less fortunate. Not only is a woman's limbic brain measurably larger than a man's and, according to Dr. Amen, it is a scientifically proven fact that women have many more neural connectors between their limbic brain and the prefrontal cortex than men do. What this means is that women are emotionally wired to think about how they feel in a way that men aren't.

Emotional Memories:

The emotional center of the brain is used by women to form far more memories than men who use the limbic system only to store emotionally charged memories. For other memories, men use an entirely different part of the brain. This is one reason why men have a difficult time remembering things like what you were wearing when you first kissed or what restaurant you ate at on your first date or even his nephew's birthday. He had a very low emotional attachment to those events. This also means he probably doesn't remember that pretty coworker he met at your company office party (no matter how many times you say her name and try to remind him); he has no emotional reason to remember her. He probably also doesn't notice that you got your haircut or that you have on a new dress or even the first time he had peas and carrots. However, he will remember when he scored his first touchdown in little league football or hit his first homerun in baseball because those were emotionally charged memories for him.

This wiring also explains why men don't tend to be as bothered by smaller emotional events nor hang on to them as long as women; our limbic system tags them as unimportant. So, while a small, off-handed remark can bug a woman for weeks, many men will have forgotten that same barb in hours or a day or two. When it is brought up, he has to retrieve it from a different part of his brain and will attach a different meaning to it than a woman.

Navigating:

The brain has a specialized region just for navigating the spatial environment. This structure is called the hippocampus and is a substructure of the limbic system and is also known as the map center of the brain. The hippocampus helps us determine where we are, how we got here, and how to navigate to the next place.

In one set of research, it was discovered that activity in the entorhinal cortex, a region of the brain which connects the hippocampus (navigation) to the cerebral cortex (memory, attention, perceptual awareness, thought, language, and consciousness) played a key role in navigation and memory and was sensitive to the straight-line distance method when first working out how to get to a destination. Once underway, the posterior hippocampus, also known for its role in navigation and memory, became active when keeping track of the actual path needed (turn left at the corner, right turn after jumping over log) to reach the destination.

What happens next is really interesting; several studies have demonstrated that men and women use different strategies when trying to navigate. A study from the Netherlands asked men and women to find their way back to their cars in a crowded parking lot. As a result, men tended to use more distance terms when describing the route while women mentioned landmarks more often. A professor at Utrecht University, Albert Postma, claims that a man's brain is better suited to precise distances while women focus more on the relationship between objects.

Another study asked a group of men and women in a Mexican village to gather mushrooms. The researchers fitted them with satellite positioning devices and heart rate monitors. The study found that the women expended less energy and seemed to know where to go. The women were also more likely to recall their routes using landmarks and retraced their paths to the most productive areas. Although men are usually better at reading and using maps, women usually get to their destination quicker because they are better at remembering landmarks. Consequently, women are less likely to get lost.

Other studies demonstrate that men and women develop different methods of navigating and orienting themselves to the spatial environment because of differences in roles as hunters and gatherers. This could explain the reason why men get lost in supermarkets while women can find their way around in minutes. Research done at Queen Mary, University of London demonstrated that men are better at finding hidden objects while women are better at remembering where objects are located. In addition, Frank Furedi, a sociology professor at Kent University, found that women were better at making judgment calls when it came to basic navigational tasks while men tend to overcomplicate those tasks.

Before you start feeling all smug about your directional capabilities, during the navigation process, men and women fared differently in the MRIs. When it comes to performing activities that require spatial skills, like navigating directions, men generally do better. According to research by David Geary, Ph.D., Professor of Psychological Sciences at the University of Missouri (Geary, 2010), when navigating, women use the cerebral cortex, or problem solving area of the brain while men use an entirely different area, mainly the left hippocampus - a part deep inside the brain that's not even activated in the women's brains during navigational tasks! The hippocampus, Dr. Geary explains, automatically codes where you are in space and, as a result, women are more likely to rely on landmark cues: they might suggest you turn at the 7-11 and make a right at the church, whereas men are more likely to navigate via distance reckoning—go east 1 mile, then west 2 miles.

David, an Atlanta executive, explains his sense of satisfaction in finding his way after getting lost:

"Anytime I get lost my wife immediately starts in on me to stop and ask for directions while I steadfastly refuse. I actually enjoy trying to find my bearings. It's like some primitive sense takes over and I can feel the space around me and if I just take one or two more turns it will all click into place and I'll know where I am. When I finally do find my destination there's this great sense of satisfaction that seems to envelop me... its primal... I don't know how to explain it other than to say it feels like something I have always known how to do, like it was a primitive test that I just passed."

From an evolutionary standpoint, there is a real, practical reason for this: Early humans worked in groups or tribes with very different roles between the sexes within those groups. When men went off hunting and chased prey through the forest, the journey would often require running down hills, around bends, leaping fallen trees, crossing streams etc. and without a portion of the brain to track this geospatial activity, men would become lost and unable to reunite with their tribe. On the other hand, the women of the tribe would need their ability to remember landmarks as a way to steer the group back to fertile feeding grounds.

One way of navigating isn't better; they just have different reasons for existing and is further evidence of not just the differences between our genders but also how much each gender relies on the other.

How Brains Define Our Interactions With Each Other:

Simon Baron-Cohen of the University of Cambridge is one of the leading researchers into the differences between the "male brain" and the "female brain," and one key finding from his research is that male brains are typically characterized by a tendency to "systemize".

"Systemizing" is the drive to analyze, explore, and construct a system for understanding something. The "systemizer" intuitively figures out how things work, or extracts the underlying rules that govern the behavior of a system. The purpose of this is to understand and predict the system, or to invent a new one.

By comparison, the female brain is characterized by a tendency to "empathize". "Empathizing" is the drive to identify another person's emotions and thoughts, and to respond to them appropriately. Empathizing occurs when we feel a fitting emotional reaction in response to the other person's emotions. The purpose of this is to understand another person, to predict his or her behavior, and to connect or resonate with him or her emotionally.

What's comical is when we men try to apply systemizing to understanding women. In some ways we can be very successful and learn very quickly that when our woman does 'X' that 'Y' is going to follow. However, things go awry when we try to systemize a woman's emotions like you were a toaster with logical moving parts; if you push this button with this knob turned this way, you get dark brown toast. Of course anytime you try to systemize emotions and feelings, it's a hopeless cause but at least you can now look at a man and know, that for him, he's trying to build or modify a system for understanding why you are upset over something.

Many of these gender differences emerged out of need during our human evolution. Systemizing is useful for making tools, building processes, understanding hunting, war and developing tactics for those needs. Empathizing was useful in raising children, building consensus within the tribe or community and moving humanity along. Empathy was something that men didn't want or need because it's hard to fight and kill someone who you have empathy with and certainly it's hard to eat an animal you cared for. What's weird about this is that children typically learn empathy from their fathers, not from their mothers! (I'll tell you more about that later and it will really surprise you!)

Another reason women have higher empathy abilities is because women were often uprooted and moved to neighboring tribes as part of the marital process as this kept inbreeding at a minimum. One of the key survival skills a woman required was the ability to empathize and understand the feelings inside her new tribe.

Remember earlier when I said female fetuses show higher connectivity between the hemispheres of the brain but that men get something in return? While women have greater connectivity between the two sides of the brain, men have more connections within each side allowing us to process the data specific to that side of the brain more efficiently than women.

Using a special brain-scanning technique called diffusion tensor imaging, which measures the flow of water along a nerve pathway, researchers were able to establish the level of connectivity between nearly 100 regions of the brain, creating a neural map of the brain called the "connectome".

In one of the largest studies looking at the "connectomes", or wiring of the brain between the sexes, Dr. Ragini Verma, Ph.D., an Associate Professor in the Department of Radiology at the Perelman School of Medicine at the University of Pennsylvania, and colleagues (Ragini Verma, 2013) found that men have greater neural connectivity from front to back and within one hemisphere of their brains which suggests that men's brains are structured to facilitate connectivity between perception and direct, coordinated action. In contrast, in females, the wiring goes between the left and right hemispheres, suggesting that women better facilitate communication between the analytical and intuition parts of the brain.

The connectome research was carried out on 949 individuals - 521 females and 428 males - aged between 8 and 22. The brain differences between the sexes only became apparent after adolescence, the study found.

This difference in the way the nerve connections in the brain are "hardwired" occurs during adolescence when many of the secondary sexual characteristics such as facial hair in men and breasts in women develop under the influence of sex hormones, the study found.

This research clearly shows that, in women, most of the connections go left and right across the two hemispheres of the brain while in men, most of the connections go between the front and the back on the same side of the brain.

The maps showed a stark difference in the architecture of the human brain that helps to provide a potential neural basis as to why men excel at certain tasks, and women at others. Not that one gender is superior or inferior but again, is another example of how our brains are complementary.

"It's quite striking how complementary the brains of women and men really are," said Rubin Gur of Pennsylvania University, a co-author of the study.

After reading this you may conclude that men's and women's brains, taken as genders, have little in common and that's not the case. Men and women do have lots of brain areas that are semi-functionally the same; moreover, members of both sexes excel at skills that are commonly labeled gender specific with all things having some overlapping distributions. There are many women with better-than-average spatial skills, and plenty of men with superior verbal skills and, as several researchers have noted, our brains have evolved to be complimentary, not competitive!

When you start adding up all the physical differences of the body and mind, it's really no wonder that we perceive the world around us so differently. We see and hear differently, we use different parts of the brain for communicating, storing memories, navigating and on and on. Even though we can share the same experience that experience will be perceived differently just because of how we see it, hear it, smell and store it.

None of this is to say that one gender is better or worse, more capable or less capable, just that we're very different, and we actually evolved differently to offset the other gender's weaknesses and that interdependency is what makes us need each other.

Chapter 2

HOW BOYS BECOME MEN

ONE COMMENT THAT I'VE FREQUENTLY heard is that it's no big mystery how boys become men, they just grow up! Oh, if it were only that easy! There's actually an entire process that goes on that most people are completely unaware of. The obvious part, the part we can see, is the physical growing up part. What we don't see is how boys develop their idea of masculinity and the challenges and risks that come with integrating that idea into their emotional and intellectual beings.

In this chapter I'm going to explain the masculinity development process and the risks that come along with it. Like everything so far, this chapter is based on new research and tends to expose the male maturity process in ways that most people (male and female) are oblivious to.

Whatever preconceived beliefs you may hold, it's important to set those aside in order to understand this process because by understanding this process you will understand how the men in your life (bosses, brothers, boyfriends or husbands and fathers) came to be the way they are.

Testosterone:

Physically speaking, during our mother's pregnancy, boys are covered up in testosterone, which is why newborn boys have constant erections. Within a few weeks or so of birth, our testosterone levels drop off and are close to the same levels found in similar aged girls. Right around age 3-4, boys will see a big increase in testosterone and suddenly take an interest in action figures, toy trucks and make believe adventures. By age 5, both girls and boys are, on average, about 42" tall. Once school starts, a boy's testosterone level drops back and stays at this lower level thus explaining the girls are "yucky" stage. This testosterone level stays on par with girls until puberty which starts as early as age 11 and as late as age 17 but on average around age 14 and boys will again gain the size advantage over girls and find those "yucky" girls to be quite interesting!

It's also important to point out that regardless of the culture, race, religion or any other social barriers, all men essentially go through this same process, only some of the messages they receive differ.

THE MALE MATURITY PROCESS

Starting from birth, a little boy is completely dependent on his early caretakers for feeding, touch, and shelter as well as the equally important love and support needed to mature into a healthy and responsible man. We learn to crawl, walk and fall down with the help of others and when we cry, there's always someone there to pick us up, kiss our boo-boos and assure us that we're okay and then send us on our way. During this time we learn that expressing our needs is acceptable, that it's okay to be cranky when we're hungry or tired and that depending on others for emotional support and encouragement is a good thing. Our worlds are looking mighty good!

At some point around kindergarten or first grade boys experience that first major pain in life where we're told "big boys don't cry", "shake it off", "pick yourself up" and "stand on your own two feet" and other such reprimands that deny boys their feelings and tell them to begin suppressing any outward expression of their emotions. This period marks the beginning of a long road of inner conflict and turmoil that all males must travel.

What's happening at this early age is that young boys are starting to be confronted with messages that men are strong, men are self reliant, men don't cry, men don't show their emotions, and that no matter what life throws at us, we buck up and move on. We're told that dependency and emotional neediness we relied on and which provided us with fulfillment those first few years is contrary to masculinity and that to accept satisfaction and fulfillment from the dependency we experienced in those first few years is unmanly. For the mothers, aunts, sisters and babysitters reading this, you would have experienced this as the little boy getting hurt but when you came to comfort him, he pushed you away and told you to leave him alone. The young boy has already started grappling with cultural and familial definitions of masculinity.

As boys begin to build their core male identity, they must decipher how their peers, their family, the influences of school, outside activities such as sports and the media (movies, music, news, sitcoms) view certain aspects of masculinity and then learn to interpret these views and figure out how each piece fits into their own evolving definition of masculinity. Our ability to navigate this development period and our ultimate success is highly dependent on the adult male role models in our lives. Our fathers, uncles, older brothers, teachers, ministers, coaches and most every other male we encounter teaches us something about how to be a man.

We learn to spot kindness, toughness, warmth and anger, but how we assimilate this into our own code is highly dependent on the men closest to us and how we see the women around us respond to these men.

So, on one hand mom teaches us to want and need dependency while society teaches us that such dependency is a sign of weakness and that this dependency is contrary to the male's understanding of masculinity. Wow! What a tough card, women are dealt! It's no wonder you can't understand what's going on inside of us! You're constantly trying to decipher these mixed messages, and sometimes it's like trying to hit a moving target!

The importance of having adult male role models that teach boys to tend to the poor, to help the people who're broken down on the side of the road, to express emotions, to control their anger and let it out in constructive ways just can't be underestimated and, unfortunately, boys will not learn these things from their mothers; not because mothers are incapable of teaching them but because boys look to grown men for guidance.

In the second half of this chapter, I'll talk about derailing the male maturity process (a must read section) and the consequences of not having strong male role models. But before we go much further, I want to point out that boys who lack strong male role models will, around middle school age, start looking towards their peers as role models. Think about that, 12, 13 and 14 year old boys learning about masculinity from each other. This is the blind leading the blind and generally they lead each other off a cliff!

As boys mature into men, they try, accept and reject many definitions of masculinity. You may have a boy whose father takes him hunting and after his first kill, he decides that he'd rather take piano lessons. Or, you may have a boy who plays hooky from piano lessons to go hunting. One boy may secretly write poetry while another will listen to hard rock. The writing of poetry may be a phase or may become permanent. It may get pushed aside for many years and revisited. His musical interest may jump exclusively from one genre to another. He may try fighting, get into stunts on his skateboard, bicycle or motorcycle. The choices are limitless and some will stick, some will be rejected and parts of some may be integrated while other parts are casts aside.

To further add to this inner conflict, we live in a society that idolizes famous men or men in powerful positions and this reinforces society's expectations of achievement, strength, and toughness and teaches us that independence is an essential aspect of masculinity while dependency is to be avoided because it exposes a man's neediness and vulnerability.

By the time he becomes a grown man, he's tested many aspects of masculinity and decided what works for him and what doesn't. He has an idea of the type of man that he is and how he wants to proceed in the world. What he values in himself, what he values in others and what he has little tolerance for.

Sounds good, right? You've found this great guy and you think he might be "the one" and you step up and ask him to be more open and emotionally available and he looks at you like you have two heads and internally he's thinking "Do what?" Remember, starting at around 3 or 4 years of age boys are taught that being open, vulnerable and dependent is counter to masculinity! So in his mind, he's being as open and vulnerable as he dares and you're asking for MORE!?!? For him, alarms start sounding, horns are blaring and he has no idea what's wrong but he does know it's not good!

In his book "New Psychotherapy For Men" (Pollack, 1998) coined the term "Defensive Autonomy" to describe how men distance themselves in close, interpersonal relationships so that we can avoid appearing needy or dependent and certainly to avoid showing emotional intensity. For women, this "Defensive Autonomy" becomes what you may experience as him not caring or being fully engaged in the relationship.

Because the traditional male role requires men to hide our more vulnerable emotions, we often have few outlets for emotional expression. This is shown, in comparison to women, with men having higher rates of alcoholism, drug addiction, violence, and successful suicides which suggest that many men internalize their emotional pain versus seeking healthy ways to share what they're feeling.

As if that wasn't enough, look back over the last 40 years and the enormous changes in the roles of women and we find many of our traditional definitions of masculinity and the male role are no longer accepted. However, this hasn't changed the message that men receive defining masculinity which still tells us that we're to take charge in our relationships, in our roles as fathers and husbands and at work. We're still expected to earn more, know more about cars, dishwashers and baseball than the women in our lives. In the mean time, when we're called upon for cooperation and dependence or emotional flexibility to resolve disagreements, we often experience internal conflict that surfaces as frustration and confusion.

As women, you often see our closed posture, hear our harsh or terse language, experience our unwillingness to share and lack of emotional expression as uncaring, unfeeling, uncommitted or, as we commonly hear it described as "intimacy issues" while the reality is, we really do want to be intimate with you but we must guard against being vulnerable or exposing our neediness as this runs counter to the definitions of masculinity.

If you're starting to realize there might be more to a man's soul than you originally thought, you're right! The soul of a man runs deep and it takes as much courage for you to let him reveal his soul as it does for him to reveal it. The rewards for women who can navigate through this, is an immense love, dedication and openness from men who were previously distant.

The Message of Masculinity and Cultural Differences:

So the question becomes, what are some of these messages of masculinity and how do men incorporate these?

There are some messages of masculinity that I call "meta-messages" because they transcend cultural boundaries. These meta-messages are the most prominent and stem from societal beliefs. These meta-messages define the core, or basis, of our definition of masculinity.

One such meta-message is independence. Independence is a requirement for masculinity and this message is conveyed in numerous ways, such as our society's admiration of the "self-made" man. In order to be manly, a man must be independent, self reliant, and self sufficient. The message of independence is so strong that it causes enumerable conflicts within intimate relationships. Women experience this as a man making a major decision such as purchasing a new car or buying that 60" big screen TV without consulting her. Sitcoms make jokes about it, and men chide each other for not being able to stop for a drink after work by calling those who can't stop "hen pecked." Every time you hear these types of messages, your man is being told to be independent and you're being told that an independent man is masculine.

Some other meta-messages transmitted include: men are tough, heterosexual and the breadwinner. Meta-messages also tell men that driving fast and doing dangerous things are manly behaviors. To show how men adopt and reject certain aspects of these messages, consider skydiving. Skydiving is regarded as high risk, dangerous and manly. However, there are many men who wouldn't consider jumping out of a plane and no amount of cajoling would change that. These men don't consider their unwillingness to skydive as something that detracts from their masculinity; instead they call those men who do jump "idiots." Another example is the meta-message on toughness. Just look at men being injured in movies or on TV and refusing to see a doctor; the meta-message that you "must be tough" is reinforced. Ever wonder why men don't go to the doctor? That's why.

Meta-messages related to masculinity you don't hear are ones of sensitivity. You don't hear "real men cry" messages or anything that tells a man that it's "okay to care and show feelings" beyond a minimal degree.

In addition to meta-messages are cultural messages. Cultural messages can be regional, ethnic or religious. For instance Latinos receive a message that their "machismo" is essential and must be protected at all costs. Black men are told that drugs and violence are a normal way of life. Jewish men are told they must be successful (How often do you see a movie or TV program that shows a homeless Jewish man?).

The regional cultural messages define masculinity for a specific region. In the southern U.S., you're expected to be able to chop firewood, hunt, fish and camp. If you can't do these things you're just not very manly. However, the ability to hunt and fish are not requirements for men raised in large cities. There, you find value placed on the ability to navigate tough parts of town, to hail a taxi or get a reservation in a highly desirable restaurant.

Now, take a man raised in an environment or culture where one set of messages are transmitted as part of the definition of masculinity, and transplant that man into another environment or culture where those definitions don't apply. This happens in the military, corporate relocations and other forms of transplanting. Men, in these situations, are forced to fall back on the meta-message of masculinity until they can learn and incorporate the new cultural requirements.

Besides the meta-messages and the cultural messages, boys and men also absorb masculinity messages from the other males in their lives. I call these local messages. Boys receive messages from their dad, uncles, male teachers, coaches (their role models), cousins, neighbors and their peers. A boy who witnesses his mother being physically abused absorbs the local message that "it's okay to hit women." A boy surrounded by men who are community givers will learn that "it's good to be of service."

Men receive messages from their boss, peers, neighbors, friends and, even the other guys on the softball team. All of these messages require men to constantly monitor and adjust their own definitions of masculinity.

Following are quotes from some of the top bloggers and writers on men and masculinity (Michler, 2015). These are their definitions of masculinity and you can see how they've integrated meta, cultural and local messages of masculinity into their own definitions.

"A man is comfortable in his own skin; he is confident without arrogance and strives to impact the world in a positive way."
- Aaron Marino

"Being a 'man' doesn't have anything to do with drinking your coffee black and your whiskey straight. Being a man means striving towards the best possible version of yourself, every day.

Are you strong but compassionate? Do you give back as much as you take? Are you willing to shed social pressures and lift those up who others may believe they don't deserve it? Lifting weights is easy – the real question is, are you strong enough to be the man you know you can be?" - **Andrew Snavely**

"A man should be courageous, committed, hard-working, honest, thrifty, kind, a leader, passionate, positive-thinking, respectful, tolerant, and have initiative. Every day, I try to be a man." - **Antonio Centeno**

"Being a man is having the integrity to own your truth, and that means fully embodying and living it." - **Dilan Prema**

"A true man must be courageous when he is scared, dutiful when he is needed and honorable when no one is looking." - **Kyle Boureston**

"It would be convenient to define manhood by simply listing a series of "manly" traits (a full beard, big muscles), skills (chopping wood, fixing a car), interests (beer, sports), or accomplishments (earning a lot of money at your job, having kids).

But to me, being a man means being bold enough to pursue what you're passionate about and confident enough to live as your authentic self. Real men take responsibility for themselves and their actions, and they act as a source of strength and protection to those around them. Most importantly, they constantly seek personal growth and strive to be better men." - **Nate Lewis**

"Being a man means existing as a male of self-determination. Men are self-sufficient, strong, courageous, males who shape the world around them and invite others to participate in the creation of that world." - **Tanner Guzy**

"A true man is rugged, resilient, and strong. In many ways he is self-made and claims his own victories but he understands what it means to be a member of the team. He understands the strength that comes from his tribe. He is stronger when he is beside his men and his men are stronger because he is one of them." - **Ryan Michler**

Loss And Grief:

Another major facet of a boy's development process is in how we're taught to handle loss and grief and this "teaching", has a lifelong impact, not just on how we learn to mourn losses but on how we form attachments in our adult lives.

While women are often thought to be more comfortable with the feelings surrounding loss and grief, men seem alarmed by them and, more often than not, we dissociate ourselves from these feelings and "stuff them down deep into the inner parts of our core where we keep them hidden until we can process them in teeny-tiny bits over a longer period of time.

Throughout our entire lives, men go through a process of making and breaking intimate attachments with others. When we never learn how to express our feelings or that expression is taken away from us, our normal process of grieving is derailed and what develops in its place are other defense mechanisms such as anger, shame and control issues. All of this combines to create conditions ripe for self-medication via alcohol and drugs or acting out to relieve the discomfort caused when these emotions threaten to break through into consciousness.

During one interview session with a group of women, as we were discussing this part, one woman said "Oh boohoo! Buck up and get over it. Everyone has loss and men don't need to cry about it!" The room fell silent for a moment as the other women looked to each other and then to me for an answer and I looked back at them and finally said "Well? Is that the way it is?" In truth, what this woman had expressed is the same thing that society expresses to men every day; You're not to express your feelings. You're not to be vulnerable. And, most importantly, you're not to make me uncomfortable because I have no idea how to deal with a crying man!

One of the most important skills a male can learn, and inversely, the one we're the worst at, is in understanding our own wounds. Some of this is because those early "cry baby" years sent us on a course that eliminated the language of emotional expression (unless you consider "screw off" or "kiss my ass" as complete emotional expressions) and proper expression of our emotions is essential in dealing with any kind of loss.

One gentleman I interviewed, named Dave, had a buddy at work that he had lunch with once or twice a week and played golf with most every weekend. The buddy was one of Dave's best friends. Dave's wife had met Dave's buddy once or twice over the previous two years but never gave the connection much thought beyond "it's just a golf buddy from Dave's work." One evening while sitting in bed Dave told his wife how his buddy had just gotten a transfer and would be moving away. Dave had just expressed the first piece of grief. His wife asked if Dave's friend was getting promoted. How far he would be moving and other logistical questions but not once did she ask how Dave was feeling about his loss. As Dave recounted the experience he said he realized at that moment, that he was "alone in handling his feelings."

In the male mind, wounds challenge our basic sense of self because the wounds attack our very own, self developed sense of masculinity, they make us aware of our shortcomings and our perceived inability to live up to societies definition of masculinity. We tend to incorporate all of this into an umbrella known as "failure".

Rejection in an intimate relationship is an obvious wound to our "self". Men who are rejected by their partners generally have no complete understanding of what went wrong so they feel confused, hurt and angry. Our sense of adequacy as a partner, both sexually and socially, has been challenged and we must now reconcile our sense of self and what we thought our world was with how our partner sees us. This realignment of how we perceive ourselves versus how another perceives us is frequently a painful one for many men.

Work related failure, whether a temporary setback on the job, a lost promotion, a firing or a business closing are similar wounds that men must deal with. For example, a man who is fired or laid off from his job experiences a sense of failure and inadequacy and a process of realignment, similar to that which occurs with rejection in an intimate relationship, takes place and wherein the man must reconcile his perceptions of himself as a worker or boss with those of others. In addition, not only is his identity as a provider challenged but again, his self built definition of masculinity is attacked. Even lost promotions are taken very personally because of the perceived attack on a man's sense of self.

More importantly, all these outer definitions of masculinity often conflict with our inner needs, wishes, and values and it's only when a man can be supported in his natural state that he can live a happy and fulfilling life.

Obviously, it takes a great deal of effort to raise a boy into a fully functioning, adult male and it takes a lot of understanding and empathy to be able to look at an adult male and unwind certain behaviors and responses and figure out what led him to incorporate that piece into his definition of masculinity. Those women who undertake this process are generally rewarded with an understanding that allows them to maintain a much greater sense of peace, happiness and harmony in the relationship.

NOTE: *As I have shared this chapter with my male and female friends, both sides have said that the following section is VERY difficult to read. Not because of the content but because of the emotions it stirs up. Men say they're forced to look at their own upbringing and to question their own parenting and women say they don't like the idea of understanding why a man may be weak or wounded and they certainly don't like the idea of thinking they may have failed as a mother. I simply cannot stress enough how important it is to push these feelings aside and work through this section.*

DERAILING THE MALE MATURITY PROCESS

There are a number of things that can partially or completely derail the male maturity process and those include: Physical and emotional abuse, sexual abuse, alcoholism, drug abuse, absentee or no fathers and/or no significant male role models. Because each one comes with its own significant set of problems, I'll cover them each individually.

Physical Abuse:

There are about 686,000 cases of child abuse reported each year and that includes cases of neglect (withholding food, medicine, school etc.) with about 10% of all cases reported being physical violence against boys by a supervising adult - that's about once every 7 minutes a boy is physically abused. According to a study published in the American Journal Public Health (Thompson, Kingree, & Desai, 2004), men were more likely than women to have experienced physical abuse during childhood.

Since physical abuse tends to devalue a human being, boys find their self worth essentially shattered and, opposite from girls, boys tend towards a more outward exhibition of their problems. Psychological and behavioral problems that have been found to be associated with physical abuse in childhood include poorer academic performance, less likelihood of completing higher education, lower intellectual outcomes, post traumatic stress disorder, depression, drug and alcohol abuse, personality disorders, suicidal behavior, and aggression towards others.

Emotional Abuse:

There are many forms of emotional abuse from outright verbal abuse and belittling to neglect. Regardless of the type of emotional abuse, boys interpret the abuse as rejection. Some of the most common forms of emotional abuse are:

Verbal abuse: yelling, insulting or swearing at a boy

Rejection: pretending not to notice the boy's presence, ignoring his attempt at conversation, value or contributions to the household

Put downs: name calling, at home or public embarrassment, calling someone stupid, blaming them for everything

Inducing fear: causing a boy to feel afraid, intimidated or threatened ("if you ever touch that again, I'll cut your hand off!)

Isolation: restricting the child's freedom of movement, stopping the child from contacting other people (like friends, family or an estranged parent)

Bullying: purposely and repeatedly saying or doing hurtful things to a boy

Passive/Aggressive: saying or promising one thing and doing another.

Although physical abuse is often seen as the more damaging, it's not true. Emotional abuse can have the exact same consequences but actually be longer lasting and harder to repair through therapy. Psychological and behavioral problems that have been found to be associated with emotional abuse of boys include poorer academic performance, less likelihood of completing higher education, lower intellectual outcomes, post traumatic stress disorder (PTSD), depression, drug and alcohol abuse, personality disorders, suicidal behavior, and aggression towards others.

Another form of emotional abuse, is when a son has to watch his parents fight. Sons grow up with the idea that this type of love and drama is normal, and this belief lasts long after they leave their dysfunctional home and enter the adult world.

When a boy is exposed to parents who are continually arguing, he develops a poor definition of self (remember, he's incorporating this into his definition of what a man is). Witnessing such emotional abuse between parents makes a boy feel confused, powerless and helpless. Many boys blame themselves for the anger between their parents further lowering his self-esteem. His self-esteem can be damaged even further by the inconsistent responses from both parents as they try to curry favor or compensate for guilty feelings. Boys raised in this type of environment often grow up to be bullies, criminals and abusive toward women. The cycle of abuse continues with their children witnessing this behavior. The cycle goes on through one generation after another. Wash, rinse, repeat.

Parents who learn to argue and resolve conflicts in a healthy way relieve their sons of the emotional burdens of feeling confused and powerless. Instead, their sons feel happy and secure and learn that couples can stay together and resolve their differences. More importantly, sons learn conflict resolution skills which they can then carry forward into other aspects of their lives.

Sexual Abuse:

One man, Dave Atkins, who leads a team of prison volunteers, observed that the phenomenon of childhood sexual abuse destroys the foundation of the male essence and is "likely root cause of upwards of 80 percent of habitual criminal behavior" (Koehler, 2013) — "and no one's listening."

Think about that for a moment, "Childhood sexual abuse destroys the foundation of the male essence." Unfortunately, Dave Atkins isn't the first one to draw that conclusion as there's probably nothing more destructive to a male than to be sexually molested and the consequences last a lifetime!

A 2003 national study (Briere & Elliot, 2003) of U.S. adults reported that 14.2% of males were sexually abused before the age of 18. That's roughly 1 in every 7 boys. The next time you're around a group of boys, look around the room, the ball field or the classroom. Odds are that ONE or MORE of those boys is being or has been sexually abused. The next time you're at work, look around the conference room or in all the cubicles or at the male customers and patients that come through your door and odds are one in seven has been molested.

Amazingly, one would think that molested boys are mostly found in the lower classes but just like domestic violence, sexual abuse knows no societal boundaries. It happens equally to the rich and poor, to the educated and uneducated. And it happens close to home. Check out these nationally verifiable stats:

- 90% of juvenile sexual assault victims know their molester; this means that "Stranger Means Danger!" is a complete hoax! It not only teaches your children to beware of the wrong people, it lulls parents into a false sense of security!

- 33% of attackers were family members, usually older siblings or adult males with only 14% of attackers being women

- 57% were acquaintances, friends of family including neighbors, clergy, coaches, music teachers, tutors etc. This is why many boy based organizations prohibit one male from being alone with one or more boys and why many modern music studios have teaching rooms with large windows

- Only 10% of the perpetrators were strangers to the victim boy!

An interesting statistic is that in cases where child protective services confirmed that childhood sexual abuse had occurred, only 14% of boys realized (or admitted) they had been sexually abused while 64% of girls recognized they had been abused.

Sexually abused boys have significantly more emotional problems, behavioral problems, suicidal thoughts and suicide attempts than boys who were not abused. Various studies show the experience of sexual abuse carried far more consequences for boys than for girls regarding the use of drugs and alcohol, aggressive and/or criminal behavior, the amount of truancy or behavioral incidents while at school, as well as regarding suicidal thoughts and behavior. For example, where 2.6% of the non-sexually abused boys reported a former suicide attempt, with sexually abused boys this percentage was 13 times higher at 26.5%.

In terms of absorbing this abuse into their male psyche, boys (and grown men) demonstrate a number of repercussions from having been molested. Some common things therapists see are these:

- **Guilt and self-blame:** Boys not only feel incredibly guilty over the abuse, they often blame themselves for not being "male enough" or "not running away" or "being too afraid". Of course, in a young boys mind, these are rational and reasonable thoughts and once planted, these become a belief that follows a man his entire life

- **Negative self-image, self loathing:** this includes a viewing of themselves as a monster, horrible, girlish, incapable, inadequate etc.

- **Intimacy issues:** the ability to accurately identify and maintain intimate relationships, the ability to regulate trust (either over or under trusting) inside of an intimate relationship, the ability to have a normal sexual experience

- **Sexual problems, compulsions, or dysfunctions** – one study found that upwards of 70% of child molesters were themselves molested

- **Depression and drug and alcohol abuse:** Boys tend to internalize their pain and externalize their behavior

- **Macho behavior:** young men and adult males will attempt to "prove" their masculinity by having multiple female sexual partners, sexually victimizing others, and/or engaging in dangerous or violent behaviors which can include an obsession with guns, martial arts or fighting and extreme masculine behaviors

- **Sexual identification:** This includes confusion over their sexual orientation. Am I straight? Gay? Bi ?

- **Feelings of inadequacy:** There is an innate sense of brokenness that prevents them from reaching the self or societal standard of what a man is

- **Sense of loss:** Abused males have lost, or rather been robbed of, their personal power and of their ability to control their own destinies

Although all or most of the above will be present, the degree to which they are present is fully dependent on the love, support, belief and validation that boys, young men and adult males receive when they come forward. A young boy walking up to his mother or father and telling her/him that "Uncle Joe" has been making him "do things" has taken a huge personal risk and, unfortunately, most parents have the initial reaction of not believing the child which, essentially, is telling the boy it's OKAY for the abuse to continue. What should be happening, is the parents need to quiet the sense of fear, shame and anger they're feeling and sit down and get the facts. Keep Uncle Joe away until things can be properly investigated and the appropriate authorities consulted. Once these things happen, then support MUST be given in terms of both restoring the male to whole AND helping him reclaim his sense of self. Odds are that once the molester is outed, there will be other victims come forward and even other victims within the family!

One important warning: most victims of child sexual abuse don't understand why or how one or both parents didn't know what was happening and this creates a tremendous sense of anger in the abused boy towards the parent.

Alcohol And Drugs:

Many parents are shocked to learn their son drinks, smokes pot or does other drugs and some parents are simply in denial. After all, they raised "good kids who're smarter than that!"

Teenagers abuse a variety of drugs, both legal and illegal. Legally available drugs include alcohol, prescribed medications, inhalants (fumes from glues, aerosols, and solvents) and over-the-counter cough, cold, sleep, and diet medications. The most commonly used illegal drugs are marijuana (pot), stimulants (cocaine, crack, and speed), LSD, PCP, opiates, heroin, and designer drugs (Ecstasy). The use of illegal drugs is increasing, especially among young teens.

The Man Puzzle

In April 2012, The Partnership at Drugfree.org released the latest results of an ongoing study (The Partnership Attitude Study, 2012) where researchers gave anonymous questionnaires to 3,322 teens in grades 9-12 that they filled out at school from March to June 2011. What researchers found may shock you!

The average age of first use marijuana among teens is 14 years old. Nearly half of all teens (47%) have used marijuana, a 21% increase from 2008. Additionally, 2 out of every 5 teens (40% of all teens) have tried marijuana in the past year up from 31%. Past month use has increased 42%, up from 19% in 2008 to 27% in 2011. Heavy monthly use (20 or more times) is up 80% from 5% of all teens to 9% of all teens. <u>Teen boys are primarily responsible for the increase in usage – their past month usage is up 38% and heavy monthly use is up 57% since 2008.</u> 73% of all teens report having a friend who smokes marijuana. Still think you're immune? Half of teen boys (51%) say they have tried marijuana in their lifetime.

Use of harder drugs - cocaine and methamphetamine - has stabilized in recent years, the group's survey showed. But past-month usage of marijuana grew from 19% in 2008 to 27% last year. Also alarming, the report says, is the percentage of teens smoking pot 20 or more times a month. That rate went from 5% in 2008 to 9% last year, or about 1.5 million teens smoking pot that frequently.

One in 10 teens report using prescription painkillers - Vicodin or OxyContin - in the past year, down from a peak of 15% in 2009 and 14% in 2010. Just over 50% of Hispanic teens, 39% of Caucasian teens and 42% of African American teens report using an illicit drug, such as Ecstasy or cocaine, in the past year.

One quarter of all teens had their first drink by the age of 12 and by age 15, 6 out of 10 teens have had their first drink. The age of first use is critically important: research has shown that more than 40 percent of those who start drinking at age 14 or younger developed alcohol dependence, compared with 10 percent of those who began drinking at age 20 or older.

Warning signs of teenage alcohol and drug use may include:

Physical: Fatigue, repeated health complaints, red and glazed eyes, and a lasting cough. The cough could be from "huffing" or inhaling aerosols, paints and other toxins or from smoking pot and cigarettes.

Emotional: personality changes, sudden mood swings, irritability for no reason, irresponsible behavior, low self-esteem, poor judgment, depression, and a general lack of interest or motivation

Family: starting arguments, breaking rules, or withdrawing from the family and that includes spending most or all of their time in their room.

School: decreased interest, negative attitude, drop in grades, many absences, truancy, and discipline problems.

Social problems: new friends who are less interested in standard home and school activities, problems with the law, and changes to less conventional styles in dress and music.

Some of the warning signs listed for drug and alcohol use can also be signs of other problems. If you look closely, some of the signs for drug and alcohol use overlap between sexual abuse, physical abuse and emotional abuse so the drug and alcohol abuse can be the result of other things happening in your son's life.

According to the American Academy of Childhood and Adolescent Psychiatry, if you recognize these signs of trouble and possible use of alcohol and other drugs with your child or teenager, you should consult a physician to rule out physical causes of the warning signs and then follow this with a comprehensive evaluation by a child and adolescent psychiatrist or mental health professional who specializes in children.

No Or Absentee Fathers:

Before we start this discussion, we need to examine our beliefs and see where our beliefs fit within societies and then look at the absolute facts backed by dozens of studies. The following question was asked as part of a research project commissioned by the National Fatherhood Initiative (and if you think, considering the source, this will be one sided, think again!):

"If a child does not have an involved father, a mother can adequately substitute for the absence of a father, essentially being both a father and a mother"

strongly agree | agree | disagree | strongly disagree

And

"If a child does not have an involved father, a male role model, such as a friend of the mother, can be an adequate substitute for a father."

strongly agree | agree | disagree | strongly disagree

The responses of the mothers to the replaceability questions are incredibly disturbing. The "agree" percentage was 55% for the replacement-by-mother statement, and 66% for the replacement-by-other-male statement. Mothers who did not live with the father of the boy were more than twice as likely to agree with the replaceability statements. For men, when asked similar (but not identical questions), the answers were 53% that the mother would be a suitable stand-in father and 57% thought another male would be a suitable stand-in. Apparently, the majority of both men and women believe fathers are replaceable and provide no value to a child's life (Glenn & Whitehead).

This might be acceptable if it weren't for the tons of independent, peer reviewed research that contradicts all of our current beliefs. In fact, raising a boy (or girl for that matter) without an active and involved father puts the child at so much risk that it should be a criminal offense and after learning some of the following facts, I think you'll agree!

Some Facts About Fatherless Children:

- 71% of all high school dropouts come from fatherless homes – 9 times the national average. (National Principals Association Report)

- Fatherless boys are more likely to commit crimes or to behave antisocially and in some studies 80% of imprisoned criminals come from fatherless homes

- 85% of all children who show behavior disorders come from fatherless homes – 20 times the national average. (Center for Disease Control)

- 82% of pregnant teens come from fatherless homes

- 75% of all adolescent patients in chemical abuse centers come from fatherless homes – 10 times the national average.

- 63% of youth suicides are from fatherless homes (US Dept. Of Health/Census) – 5 times the national average. While girls are more likely to make suicide attempts, boys are four times more likely to complete a suicide attempt

- 90% of all runaway and homeless children (children

living on their own on the streets) are from fatherless homes – that's 32 times the national average

- 80% of rapists with anger problems come from fatherless homes – 14 times the national average (Salisbury & Department of Criminal Justice).

Let's look at some of the educational benefits of having an active and involved father.

- Children with Fathers who are involved are 40% less likely to repeat a grade in school.

- Children with Fathers who are involved are 70% less likely to drop out of school.

- Children with Fathers who are involved are more likely to get A's in school.

- Children with Fathers who are involved are more likely to enjoy school and engage in extracurricular activities.

According to research by Caroline Wolf Harlow, Ph.D. for the U.S. Bureau of Justice (Harlow), 68% of all state prison inmates have not completed high school and only 26.6% of all Federal and State inmates have completed all 4 years of high school.

"Not having a father figure makes teens more vulnerable to mental or emotional problems, teen pregnancy, criminal behavior, and drug abuse" this, according to a study conducted by Magellan Health Services. Magellan Health, is one of the largest managed behavioral health care companies in the nation and manages mental health plans, employee assistance, and work/life programs serving more than 58 million members through contracts with insurance carriers. If you think the problems are related to teens, you'll find the problems actually start early on.

Is This Wiring Or Emotional?:

What's going on inside all these boys? Scientists have been trying to figure it out and one group of researchers led by Dr. Gabriella Gobbi, a researcher of the Mental Illness and Addiction Axis at the McGill University Health Center and an associate professor at the Faculty of Medicine at McGill University in Canada used the California Mouse, a species of mouse similar to humans in that it displays monogamous bonding and two-parent child rearing, carried out research to determine the effects of fatherless childrearing on adolescent mice. In the resulting report Dr. Gobbi said: "Although we used mice, the findings are extremely relevant to humans. Growing up without a father could permanently alter the structure of the brain and produce children who are more aggressive and angry. This is the first time research findings have shown that father deprivation during [early childhood] development affects the neurobiology of the offspring with the main impacts seen in the prefrontal cortex - the part of the brain which controls social and cognitive activity."

In another study (Howard, Burke, Borkowski, & Whitman, 2006) examining father involvement with 134 children of adolescent mothers over the first 10 years of life, researchers found that father-child contact was associated with better socio-emotional and academic functioning. The results indicated that children with more involved fathers experienced fewer behavioral problems and scored higher on reading achievement. This study showed the significance of the role of fathers in the lives of at-risk children, even in case of nonresident fathers.

Children in father-absent homes are almost four times more likely to be poor. In 2011, 12% of children in married-couple families were living in poverty, compared to 44% of children in mother-only families (Children's Living Arrangements and Characteristics, 2011).

Before anyone starts blaming the "deadbeat dad" issue, it's important to know that when fathers are the sole custodial parent, the percentage of "deadbeat moms" is almost double that of "deadbeat dads." The real culprit lies in the economic opportunities that single mothers have vs. mothers with spouses.

Absent Father Factor In Child Abuse:

A study using data from the Fragile Families and Child Wellbeing Study (CPS Involvement in Families with Social Fathers, 2010) revealed that in many cases the absence of a biological father contributes to increased risk of child maltreatment. The results suggest that Child Protective Services (CPS) agencies have some justification in viewing the presence of a social father (non-biological) as increasing children's risk of abuse and neglect. It is believed that in families with a social father figure, there is a higher risk of abuse and neglect to children, despite the social father living in the household or only dating the mother.

Some Lasting Effects:

In a study conducted by Associate Professor Melanie Horn-Mallers, Cal State – Fullerton, boys who grow up without fathers are much more likely to have difficulty in coping with stress as it relates to daily activities such as sitting in traffic or dealing with normal work activities. Why is this important? Other studies have shown that the most successful men are those who can handle day to day stress.

Her colleague, Dr. Matt Englar-Carlson, Ph.D., Professor, Department of Counseling (also at Fullerton) and director of the Center for Boys and Men, told me in a phone interview that he frequently sees young men who have grown up without fathers and, these men are always working on understanding their own manhood. One's definitions of masculinity are often hard won and just as easily lost. What this means is that many men may decide "this is my definition of masculinity" and work hard to earn and maintain their preferred model of masculinity, but as soon as he hits a stumbling block and his standing is challenged or lost, that definition would be abandoned. This happens because his definition of masculinity hasn't been accumulated and integrated over a long period of time- and because masculinity itself is constantly in flux in relation to society.

Dr. Englar-Carlson, also noted there are a few common things these men grapple with such as "Who am I without a father to show me?" and "How will I know how to be a father?"

What Fatherless Looks Like In The Real World:

Following are three adult men who've volunteered to share their deeply personal and hurtful experiences of growing up fatherless or with an uninvolved father. I share these because they typify what's seen across the fatherless male spectrum.

In this example, Lionel, had a father but the father was, in the mother's eyes, less than desirable and she made this known to her son and his method of coping was to adopt a female persona (so that he would be less bad like his father and more good like his mother).

Lionel

My father didn't really set himself as a role model for me even though he and my mother were married till I was in my early 20s. He went to work, came home, ate dinner and went drinking with his friends. Rinse and repeat. My father was rather charismatic and a ladies' man. He always had women and cheated on my mother all through their marriage. A recurring refrain from my

---

mother all through my childhood and into college was "don't be like your father." As a result, I was really close to my mother and my younger sister even though I went out and hung out with my male friends. Along with this, I had a lot of influence from my aunts and other females around me. So, early on (7 or 8 years old) I began to steal clothing from the women around me and dress up for very brief periods. I even went out to play with panties on without anyone knowing. But I was always attracted to females to the point of kissing girls and trying to peek under their skirts. Anyway, I did not have a good love life in my teens and twenties. I had girlfriends (a few) but really ended up in the friend zone a lot. I met my wife in my mid-thirties and got married. She, I believe, has some of the same issues as I except in reverse. She is very strong-willed and vocal. I have always been attracted to strong women. If there is a downside, it is that, now that I am middle aged, I wish I could have had more sex when I was single. I really enjoy sex but my wife does not have the same sex drive or interest in it. To be honest, there is a lot that I want to do sexually but she just isn't into sex that much and I am lucky to get it every three months or so. On the other hand, she has been accepting of my cross dressing. In any case, to answer your question, yes, it affected my love life... my life. Only now am I mature enough to take charge of my life and assert myself and understand that my needs and wants are legitimate and not silly.

The following story is an example of what happens when some form of male role model does exist but it's not active or is a weak role model. The boys grow into men who lack confidence and knowledge about themselves. Their integration of masculinity takes many, many years and, as was stated earlier, is often fragile.

Vishel (age 34)

"I never knew my biological dad and my stepfather wasn't introduced into my life until I was 10 years old. Even then, we weren't close. I was raised mostly by my mother and her sisters, but I also had a grandfather and a few uncles around from time to time. In my teens/and early to mid 20's, I would identify very well with women, but up to the point where they saw me as a brother, not a boyfriend. My personal thought on that issue is that I always empathized with females, but never fully disagreed/contradicted with anything they said. I was simply a listener. They were very comfortable with me, but it also meant that I was family to most of them. I never had much confidence with women, but as I grew older I learned more about myself. I learned to stop being a 'yes man' and have my own opinions about things. I also learned to make decisions properly and take charge when needed. This lead to finally seeing some traction in the dating world and I'll actually be married in May of this year. I think that once I learned more about myself, I was able to become a person of confidence. It's very cliché, but it's true. Nowadays, I still have female friends but I can actually distinguish the line between 'friend' and 'more than friend'. When I was single, I could steer the relationship to 'more than friend' and now that I'm almost married, I can keep my relationship with other women in the friend zone."

In the following story, we have an example of what happens when a well meaning mother decides that she will spare her son the pain and agony of having another "bad example" of a man in their life and so she doesn't date. This is a story that I've heard repeated so often that I'm surprised there hasn't been a social stigma created against single mothers who don't date.

> **Sorta (age 21)**
>
> My mom left my dad when I was a kid. When they were together I had no example of a healthy relationship, at least [not] on a daily basis. Since then my mom has never been with anyone else. 16 years later and it has affected my love life, in that I don't have one, because I don't know how...

Do Fathers Really Teach Empathy?:

Remember earlier when I said that children learn empathy from their fathers? Studies have shown that small children learn how to how to get along with others as well as how to solve problems from their father (Civitas, 2009). In fact, most of the things that we learn about the world when we are little come from our fathers, not our mothers.

According to Dr. Matt Englar-Carlson, Ph.D., Professor, Department of Counseling, who, among other contributions, teaches therapists how to counsel and treat men, had this to say: "Traditionally, mothers have taught children how to live inside the home and to process internal feeling states while fathers have taught children how to navigate outside the home and, in general, how the world works."

There was a study done which "found that primary school children scored higher on tests of empathy - the ability to see a situation from another person's viewpoint - if they had secure attachments to their fathers during infancy. These children were able to recognize how other children felt and took steps to make them feel better" (Civitas, 2009).

Apparently, there's something to be said for fathers crawling around on the floor, playing with their kids and playing dead or faking other injuries. Not only are your children being entertained, they're learning valuable life skills!

Is not having a strong male role model an automatic sentence for a lifetime of pain, suffering and possible failure? Of course not. So much is highly dependent on the individual boy, the strength of the mother and how she adapts to both roles. There are mothers who take their sons fishing, play ball with their sons and even help their sons work on cars. There are mothers who encourage their sons to play sports and spend countless hours sitting in camp chairs or on hard bleachers so that their sons can play football, baseball, basketball and soccer. These moms understand the importance of being involved, being present, keeping their sons active and safe. Also, one benefit of boys being raised by their mothers is that mothers typically raise more emotionally aware men.

So what happens if you're in a relationship with a man who was raised fatherless and who is grappling with certain aspects of his masculinity? Does that mean you should dump him and start over? Absolutely not! What that means is that you have an opportunity to be supportive in ways that most women won't have.

What Kind Of Role Models Did He Have?

If you want to truly understand your man, it's key to understand what kinds of male role models he had growing up. Was his father there? Who were his primary role models? Were his role models kind? Compassionate? Did they have extreme political, religious, racial beliefs? Did they volunteer with the sick or poor? Did they yell and scream or were their tempers always under control? Were they sports nuts? Fishermen? Hunters? Conservationist? I think you can see where this is going: learn about your mans masculine role models and you'll start seeing which pieces he has integrated into his definition of masculinity and which ones he's discarded.

The Man Puzzle

I want to give you some examples of what happens when it's done right. In this first story, this is what happens when a man learns how to be a compassionate father.

Dale

While growing up in the 60's and 70's, I watched my father bring countless homeless kids in to our house and feed them, clothe them and give them a safe, supportive home with good boundaries (no drugs, attend school, attend church, play sports, etc.) so after I was grown, married and my own kids were teenagers, I found myself meeting one homeless kid after another and bringing them home. Some didn't stay long, a few just didn't like the "rules" but a few more found a place where they could thrive, grow and succeed. One I put through college, one joined the Air Force, and one is in Los Angeles trying to become an actress.

This next story is my own personal story and it happened when I was about 16 and the lesson was about being in charge of your own emotions.

Phil

For some reason my mother was on the warpath, she was yelling, screaming and just being completely intolerable. I'm not sure how, but I became her target and she was yelling at me, calling me names and just saying some awful things. I tried escaping to my room but she followed me there and continued on her tirade and about 5 minutes into this I started yelling back. The meaner she got, the more hurt I was and the meaner I got. Finally I went back downstairs and she followed me there and we had a heated exchange going in the kitchen. I vaguely remember hearing the kitchen door open and then my dad appeared in front of me and ordered me "OUTSIDE!" Being a retired military

---

an, when I say he ordered me, I mean he ORDERED me and his orders were meant to be followed. Now my dad had never raised a hand to me and rarely ever raised his voice. He didn't need to. He got what he wanted by respect and love, not by fear. So I was doubly shocked when he yelled at me. So, outside I went and I was standing in the yard dreading what was coming. After a minute or two he came outside and walked up to me and just pointed to the barn. It was then I knew my life was over. I was going to get the beating of a lifetime for yelling at my mother like that. My shoulders dropped and I walked to the barn like a prisoner to the gallows. Once inside the barn, he closed the door and I remember looking around at the light streaming through cracks in the wood thinking "this is it!" and my dad walked up to me, placed his hand on my shoulder and very sternly said "Son, don't you ever, EVER again let anyone manipulate you in to losing your temper like that! The moment you raised your voice, she was in control of you and your emotions. That's not a place a man needs to be. Are we clear?" I replied with a "yes sir!" and he told me to stay out here awhile and straighten things up. He turned and left the barn and that was all that was ever said about it. Now, does that mean I don't get angry? Of course not. What it means is that in that one lesson, he taught me the difference between reacting versus responding and the difference between feeling ashamed of my behavior versus pride in my actions.

As I've told this story countless times women have often asked why my dad didn't punish me for yelling at my mother. I was in my late 30's and dad had been diagnosed with a terminal condition and we were talking one day and I asked him that very question. His response was simple and loving: "Because I didn't want you to think for a minute that you deserved to be spoken to like that by anyone, not even your own mother." So, here he was, months away from dying and still teaching me what it was to be a man.

The Evidence:

Do you now, still, believe fathers can be replaced? Even bad ones have a role and play an important part in your child's ability to grow up strong and healthy. No matter what your personal beliefs are about the man himself, the children deserve to have their fathers in their lives.

Gender Neutral Child Rearing:

The entire concept of gender neutral child rearing is based on the underlying belief that there is something inherently wrong with males and that if we can just eliminate some of their maleness they will grow up to be better people. This is just about as close to child abuse as one can come without actually physically abusing the male child. As I've shown, boys are wired to seek out masculine role models and, given a void in that input, these boys risk growing up with incomplete identities and the ability to fully engage with their male counterparts.

An adult male without a fully developed sense of masculinity is nothing more than an empty husk waiting to be filled with a lifetime of pain and disappointment.

Combining The Influences

Now that we've looked at the masculinity process, how do you apply this to your man?

It's essential to understand which parts of the meta, cultural and local messages on masculinity your man has integrated into his definition and which parts he has rejected or only partially integrated. There are millions of black men who have rejected the message of "violence and drugs" and gone on to be successful business men, lawyers, judges, doctors, politicians and entertainers. Not every man accepts every message.

Next, you need to consider your man's natural personality. Is he shy or gregarious? Is he art-oriented or mechanically inclined? Is he a nurturing soul who was forced to hunt and kill deer by a well-meaning father who wanted to "toughen up the boy" or, perhaps, he was a boy more interested in fixing cars who was forced to take ballet lessons by a well-meaning mother who wanted to "soften him up a little." Boys who were forced into activities against their nature will suffer a lifetime of pain (in the form of shame - from being told their natural personality is somehow flawed).

Lastly, look at how those things that derail the masculinity process have influenced your man's definition of masculinity. Has he always had good role models and is what we call "a solid, stand up guy?" Was there a point where he was a "wild child" and later found his way back? Perhaps he still carries the wounds from his childhood and those force him to struggle with life. Is there a part of his masculinity that was lost and he has reclaimed?

Once you understand how your man has integrated these influences into his own definition of masculinity you then have the basis for understanding him on a deep, emotional level.

> **Note:** If you watch sports programming, most commercials are targeted at men with women portraying traditional or background roles while men are represented favorably. However, outside of sports, almost every commercial with a couple shows the man as a bumbling idiot. How do these messages affect how we view each other?

Where Do We Go From Here?:

Regardless of which types of men you have in your life, the key to healthy and successful romantic, work and friendly relationships is being able to communicate with us. Like everything else so far (and as you've probably already gathered from your life experience), we do that differently as well. In the next chapters, I'll teach you how we communicate and how you can use good communication skills to get closer to us.

Chapter 3

COMMUNICATING WITH MEN

THERE IS ABSOLUTELY NO DOUBT that without communications, no relationship can exist. Business cannot be conducted, understanding cannot occur and peace accords cannot be reached. Every man knows this. If men know this, then why is it so difficult to communicate with us? Why don't we just open up and share our feelings like women do?

If you remember from the previous chapter, we talked about how boys start off expressing our needs and, as we grow into men, how we learn to mask expressions of vulnerability because sharing those feelings is a sign of weakness and how vulnerability goes against cultural definitions of masculinity. I didn't say that men stopped sharing their emotions altogether, we just learned a whole new and different way to communicate those feelings; a way which is accepted within the confines and definitions of masculinity.

It's incredibly important to understand how men communicate differently and I don't mean with primal grunts and smoke signals (although those are very useful tools), I mean that the way we communicate feelings is so fundamentally different than the way women communicate their feelings that trying to understand us or to get us to share our thoughts and feelings by using the same ways that you talk to your girlfriends, simply doesn't work. In fact, those ways leave us men feeling shut down, unheard, and not understood.

One of the first things women ask me is "Why does this have to be so difficult?" or "Why can't he just talk to me?" and my response to both questions is quite simple: It's really not hard and he does.

Well gee, if my man is already communicating, isn't the problem with his primal grunts and smoke signals? Can't he just be normal? Why do I need to bother learning something new? Honestly, the answer to that is just like the answer to anything else, new ways are not necessarily bad ways. Look at it this way, if you take a new job with a new company you may be hired to do exactly what you were doing in your old job, but the new company will have some new ways of doing that same job. Some will be better, some not; but in order to be good at and to keep your new job, you still have to learn the new ways. The same applies to communicating with men. Learning a new way isn't a bad thing, and if doing so allows you to grow your relationship and increases your happiness, it's worth doing!

Men Don't Talk About Their Feelings:

Despite what you hear in the break room at work or what you read in magazines or even what other women say, I'm going to let you in on a little secret, but before I do, you have to promise not to throw this book across the room (or a plate or your wine glass or anything else). Not just SOME men but ALL men talk about their feelings and we ALL do it every single day.

What? You think I'm crazy, right? This can't be! Every woman knows that men don't talk about their feelings! Well, really, only some women believe that old myth and there is an entire group of women who have mastered the secret of unlocking their men and getting them to talk. In fact, I bet you can look around at most any woman whose been married to the same man for 50 years and see a woman that knows exactly how to hear, understand, fight with, push, comfort, encourage and accept her man. And she will flat tell you that men DO talk about their feelings.

So, yes, we men do talk about our feelings and we share on a constant and ongoing basis. What you need to ask yourself is this: If my man is not talking to me, then who is he talking to and why them and not me? Before you throw this book down and go running in with insane arm waving and interrupt the game your man is watching and demand he tell you who he's talking to, you need to continue reading and learn a little more and perhaps get him to talking with you.

What I'm going to teach you in this chapter will make communicating with men quite easy, joyful and you'll be amazed at the results. After all, without communications there would be no first date. Without good communications there will be no second date, no relationship and no marriage. When communication fails, there is only separation, breakups and divorce. I think you can agree, learning a few new skills is far better than facing preventable bad outcomes.

Before we get to the actual how-to, whys and actual tips and tricks for communicating with men, we need to do a little housekeeping and the first part of that is to make sure that you're in a good mind space. This is important because if you're not, then nothing else will work. Trust me, when you see how simple this becomes, you'll have lots of head slap moments and more than a few "oh damn!" moments so it's worth working through this process.

4 Skills Needed In A Relationship With Men:

There are 4 key components you need to have in place within yourself in order to make any relationship work with men:

1. The ability to compromise without hurt or anger; if you feel that making a concession or finding a way to cooperate means you lose, then your communications will alienate your man to the point where, eventually, they stop caring, stop communicating and sooner or later they walk away.

2. The ability to express your feelings and needs in constructive ways; there have been volumes of books written on this topic and later in this chapter I'll cover one of the most useful methods of expressing your feelings in a way that will help you get understood and without making matters worse.

3. The ability to forgive and let go of past hurts; once an issue has been resolved, you absolutely must be able to let go and move forward. If you're still bringing up past hurts, then it either hasn't been resolved or you've not let it go. If you're arguing over the same things, then you're not arguing over the right things, neither of you are being heard and the problem is not being addressed or any compromise reached.

4. The ability to show empathy and compassion; without being able to put yourself in your partner's shoes and to understand his feelings, you make it next to impossible to allow your partner to feel heard, understood, accepted and loved. If your response is to tell him he's wrong or to blame him, then he's going to feel criticized and eventually he'll stop communicating with you.

These are all essential elements to building and maintaining healthy communications with any man and these are all things that start within you. So, what if he doesn't offer these same things to you? Charity begins at home. When these behaviors become a core part of how you communicate with your man, watch how quickly these same qualities are reflected back to you.

How Men Communicate:

In general, men communicate in order to relay information. We are more topic focused (think car, football or hobby), and generally avoid discussions relating to feelings and emotions. When we talk, it's normally about solving problems and not about the feelings associated with those problems (this book is topical and is about solving a problem). Think of it like this, how often have you heard a man say "If my team doesn't win, I will cry my eyes out!" Instead, what typically happens after a loss is the game gets dissected and turned into a set of problems that need solutions. "This player is too weak in that position, we need someone stronger." Or "The defense is having problems handling speed on the right side; they need to shift players to compensate."

While many "experts" believe that men communicate out of one-upmanship and power and control, what is really happening is that men communicate to build or maintain alliances. Alliances are formed for mutual benefit and interests and as such, they typically don't work well when they are not perceived as equal. This means that power and control are typically not valid tools.

Alliances constitute most of our work, neighborhood, charitable and non-intimate relationships and fringe friendships. These are not our close, intimate relationships.

Kevin in L.A. tells this story:

"My wife was always asking me why I spent so much time getting to know all the people in the neighborhood. I speak to everyone I see. After an earthquake in 2014, our neighborhood lost power and everyone was scrambling and trying to help ourselves and each other. I was the one who could connect people who had with those who needed. My wife remarked 'I had all the power' and I told her, it's not about power, it's about using all the alliances I'd built in the neighborhood to keep everyone safe. While I don't think she understood what I said, she certainly understood the results and never again questioned my connections with my neighbors.

While men are more information and alliance focused, women are typically more connection and relationship focused. Relationships require discussing and sharing of feelings and emotions, something women excel at.

Unfortunately, when it comes time to have an intimate relationship, men find the expression of feelings in ways that women want is not natural for us and puts us at a disadvantage. Not only do we not like participating in things where we're at a disadvantage, we have to fight the societal beliefs about masculinity which discourages men from expressing feelings and, often times, it's just too many battles to fight. Your job is to level the playing field by making it safe for your man to ignore the limiting definitions of masculinity so he can grow and participate openly with you.

Since men grow up learning to communicate to build alliances, and since society frowns on men expressing their feelings, men develop a separate framework, or shorthand, for communicating feelings.

Shared Experiences - The Shorthand

Several times so far I have mentioned that men talk but not just about sports or work, they share feelings and they do this using a shorthand or secret language. When men speak to each other, to the casual observer it seems as though nothing relevant was said and no real information was exchanged. But to a man, a lot of significant information was exchanged. Understanding shared experiences is a key step in having conversations that have deeper meaning.

Let's take this example: First thing in the morning your man has a meeting with his new boss and the new boss has been described as very detail oriented. On the way to work, your man has a flat tire and is late for the meeting. When he gets home from work, you ask him how his day went and he says "I had a flat tire on the way in. What's for dinner?"

Okay, you think, a flat tire was inconvenient but obviously he doesn't want to talk about it so you let it drop and start talking about dinner.

Let me tell you what I heard. His boss is new so your man is feeling some apprehension about the meeting because he doesn't know how his work environment will change or how what's expected of his performance will change. His boss is detail oriented and therefore more than likely doesn't like people being late. The flat tire caused him a lot of stress, he didn't want to show up for this meeting dirty but changing a tire is dirty work. He arrived late, dirty and then had to deal with his boss and the whole ordeal threw his morning off if not his entire day. What's for dinner means "I've had a rough day, and I need some serious down time."

What are shared experiences? Shared experiences are experiences that all men have gone through and all men understand the steps, pitfalls, challenges and glory. A new boss, we've all had them. A flat tire, we've all had them. Being late for an important meeting, it's happened to all of us. Combine all these things into one morning and you can bet someone's stress level is going to be high. So what would someone who has had a stressful day want? He'd want a nice quiet dinner, a cold beer, a decent movie or a game and his woman next to him.

As a man, I can easily understand his experience because I've had all of them as had most every other man in existence. We all know how we felt with each of those experiences so we "get" what your man experienced. If you were in the hall at work after lunch when one of your man's work pals asked him "How'd the meeting with the new boss go?" and he heard "I had a flat tire on the way in." You would have seen his pal wait for any additional info and if none were forthcoming, the pal would have said "Man, that sucks!" followed by pat on the shoulder as the two walked in different directions. The work pal would have validated your man's experience and let him know he understood.

The Prairie Vole and Stress:

In research, Prairie voles, a small rodent which is highly monogamous and typically mates for life, have a similar response to stress as do humans. When the male vole is under stress, he runs to his female partner for comfort and support while the female vole runs to the females they were raised with.

How can you use this shared experience to start conversations? The first requirement is empathy. Being able to understand the pressures associated with the new boss, the meeting, flat tire and being late and learning how to apply feelings to these events. When your man told you about the flat tire, how would you have handled it? Would you have recognized the question about dinner as a statement about his needing some down time or would you have taken it a different way? I bet you could even see how his question about dinner could have led to a huge argument.

Imagine the different ways you could handle this situation. If you had plans to go out you could say "It sounds like you had a really bad day, would you rather stay in and order a pizza?" How about just opening the door to the fridge and handing him a beer with a little wink to let him know you "got it?" How about during one of the commercials acknowledging that he had a frustrating day by saying something like "That flat tire came at a really bad time, how did you handle the frustration?"

It's important to understand just how significant shared experiences are in how men communicate about their feelings and it's important to know that when you ask your man how his day went and he says "fine" that he's not blowing you off but actually giving you tons of information.

Expressions Of Vulnerability:

When I have described the following conversation to women, hardly any in nearly 1000 recognized this for what it is: how men express doubt and vulnerability. However, just as soon as I described it you could hear the forehead slaps and statements "Oh my! I hear this all the time!"

Remember, society frowns on men being vulnerable but obviously we are, and because we are, we need safe ways to express that vulnerability. Take this conversation:

Bill: I'm not sure how this will work out. (an expression of doubt and vulnerability)

Jack: What options do you see and do you have a plan for those? (inquiry into the type of support being asked for)

Bill: I think A & B are the most likely and …

Jack: When I went through that I ended up experiencing option C and I had to ... (providing new information without judging Bill's options of A & B).

What happened was a complete dialog of vulnerability and support without Bill exposing his soft underbelly. It's cleverly masked and happens every day in all manner of male/male relationships.

Interestingly, this approach has its own hidden defenses. Had Jack said "You're just being insecure, you've got this!" Bill had a defensible position and could have denied his insecurity. Or, Jack could have replied "I've never been in that spot, I have nothing to offer." Which could mean "I'm not willing to help you." Or, it could be an honest statement. Either way, Jack's response can't be attacked.

If you pay close attention to HOW men speak you will find your own examples in your own work and home environments each and every day. In fact, you may have heard your own man, your brother, father or co-worker use that very statement and not realized what he was asking.

GETTING MEN TO TALK

Encouragement:

The absolute easiest way to encourage communications between a man and a woman is by acceptance. But, aren't most of us pretty accepting? I think by and large, yes, we are, but "pretty accepting" isn't going to encourage your man to communicate with you in a deep and meaningful way.

The key to acceptance is to recognize that acceptance is the complete opposite of judging, and when you judge someone you are applying your beliefs, values and experiences to their situation.

It might help to understand the three most common reasons we judge others and how these might play out in our intimate relationships:

1. **You wouldn't tolerate the same behavior in yourself:** For instance, your man might be contemplating taking a risk at work and you are very risk averse. Your internal dialog might go something like this: "We're so stable and happy right now, I don't understand why he has to take this risk and what if it doesn't work? What will happen to our family?" Once you've had that internal dialog, what would your external words be? Because you are risk averse, your own fears might cause you to speak in ways that let your partner know you're not supportive. How many times will he be met with judgment before he stops sharing with you?

2. **The fault you see is your own:** How many times have we sat listening to a friend complain about something and then realize that our friend does the very thing they're complaining about. It's like a smoker complaining about smokers or a gossip complaining about someone who gossiped. Maybe what your man is discussing is a shortcoming we find within ourselves and one which makes us very uncomfortable. Perhaps the conversation goes like this: "Honey, I really want to sign up for the Greek classes at the library" and because you've tried and failed to learn a foreign language several times you judge your man for your short coming. How would your own shortcoming cause you to respond to his request? Would you opt out? Would you discourage him? Would you withhold support?

3. **You become jealous of those who have what you want:** Your partner has obtained an opportunity that

you have long strived to attain or have in some way coveted and his achievement or opportunity reminds you of your own lack of success in this area. You may resent their higher degree of accomplishment and then find something wrong with him in order to avoid your own feelings of inadequacy.

Now that we have a better understanding of why we judge, let's look at some ways that we can actively demonstrate being accepting:

The best place to start is by recognizing that no one is perfect. Each person has their own weakness and faults, just as they have their own skills and strengths. We all have lessons to learn and challenges to face; it's through these opportunities that we grow and, believe it or not, men do like to grow!

When your man is talking, remember that everyone has their own path that is right and true for them. We all have a way of living and approaching each day that works for us. It's natural for us to want those we love to follow our path and to do things the way we would do them. After all, that's not only what works for us, but it's also what we're most comfortable with. However, allowing your man to choose and walk his own path is truly accepting.

Many of a man's decisions are framed inside his definition of masculinity so no matter how much you may disagree with your partner's path, you can still show love, respect and honor to him. Just because we don't agree with how someone else lives their life, it doesn't mean we have to change how we interact with them and whether or not we extend love and care towards them. In fact, when we disagree is when it's most necessary to show love otherwise, our partner feels like they're alone on their journey.

Another part of accepting your man is to understand that you can't change him. All you can do is focus on yourself, and by doing so, you shift attention away from what you disagree with and allow yourself to develop ways to be supportive.

A part of not attempting to change your man is to not give advice unless asked. Giving advice is not accepting; in fact, no matter how badly we want to help, unsolicited advice is often received as criticism. How often do women have this very complaint about men?

When you not only accept but truly believe that your man is doing the best he can under his circumstances and that he wants to be happy, be successful and to make you happy, you'll find it more difficult to judge.

GETTING YOUR MAN TO OPEN UP

Opening The Lines Of Communications:

Men have a lifetime of training that's gone into teaching us to not be vulnerable, to not share our feelings and to "be the man". But wait, just a few pages back didn't you say that men do share their feelings? Yes, yes I did. I also said that there are things you need to understand about men so that you can get your man to share those feelings with you. Right now, I want to cover the reasons why men avoid intimate conversations with their girlfriends, fiancés, wives and yes, even mothers.

Over our lifetimes, despite women telling us that it's okay to be vulnerable and it's okay to for us to share our feelings with them, experience has taught us that it's really not. We have learned that it doesn't pay to share our deepest thoughts & feelings and that doing so is a sign of weakness. Every man knows that when you are weak and vulnerable your woman will lose respect for you and once she loses respect for you, the relationship is over. As if losing a relationship with the woman you love isn't bad enough, you are also now a failure because you couldn't keep a woman because you were a sissy. Yeah, that's just exactly what every man wants to experience and carry forward with him.

We all, both men and women get our hearts broken and go through some horrible learning experiences. For men, these experiences only serve to enforce the cultural message which tells us that we men don't share our feelings, we don't "do" expressions of love and we absolutely do not make ourselves vulnerable. How fortunate that this fits so nicely with society's definition of masculinity.

So, you end up fighting society's definition of masculinity plus the parts of masculinity that he's incorporated in to his own definition and a lifetime of experiences that have reinforced all of that learning. Believe it or not, there's a way to break this down and get your man to be vulnerable, or at least vulnerable with you and to share with you what he's really feeling.

One of the most common complaints I hear from women is "my man will not talk to me about his feelings" and each time I hear this, I can guarantee the outcome. No matter what I say or how I say it, she will not hear the message. Somehow, women have been brainwashed into believing that men don't talk about their feelings, about their day or even about what's wrong with the lawnmower.

The truth is, men and women communicate differently. No earth shattering news there, but what is earth shattering is that you can learn how to get your man to talk and the rewards of getting him to open up is a deeply intimate and satisfying relationship that will go far beyond your wildest dreams.

That's a pretty heady claim right? But isn't that really what you want, a deeply intimate and satisfying relationship? The kind of relationship about which movies are made?

What I'm going to teach you is to understand how men communicate and how you can change how you communicate with men to create an environment where your man will open up.

Why Men Stop Talking:

There are three reasons men stop talking. They don't feel like you listen. They feel judged. They feel blamed. If any one of those reasons are present. Your man will stop talking (and maybe start arguing).

Learning To Listen:

Listening is the most tremendous gift you can give anyone and learning to listen to a man opens doors you never thought possible. Listening allows your man to think more fully, connect with you more deeply and show you who they are and what their challenges are.

"But I listen!" you say. Yes, I'm sure you do and I'm sure all your friends agree with you. What I learned is that men and women have different expectations for conversations. When you watch a group of women sitting around talking, what you see is an exchange involving a lot of give and take. Women interrupt each other, ask questions, learn the details and explore every nuance of the experience. There is an ebb and flow to the conversation. A group of women can go back and forth and take 30 minutes to get everything out. How women talk to each other doesn't work with men.

The Three Interruption Rule:

In one group setting after another I found that most men stop talking AFTER the third interruption (some men say two is their limit) and when they've hit their interruption limit, they've determined that you really don't want to hear what they have to say and that it's pointless to continue, and we stop talking. When this happens, what you'll find is that your man feels unheard, misunderstood and uncared for.

Men inherently like things simple. Trying to talk when your partner is unwilling to listen is frustrating and no man will waste his breath trying to keep a conversation going when he keeps getting interrupted. This single difference in how we communicate is probably responsible for generating more relationship problems than society recognizes.

One of the really odd things you will learn about men and how we communicate is that if you stop talking, stop asking questions and listen truly intently, more often than not, he'll fill in all those pesky details as he goes along and ultimately, he will end up telling you more than you ever thought you'd hear.

Does this mean you can't ask questions? Absolutely not! What it means is that you need to keep a mental note of things you need to have clarified and you ask those things only after he's exhausted his story and you still need to ask those questions. It is absolutely best to ask your questions while the conversation is still in play because once the conversation is closed. He will have put the story behind him and not want to revisit it. That doesn't mean the topic is dead; it just means he will probably need a heads up before jumping back in, and the more time that passes, the harder it is to revisit a topic.

Building Trust:

Communication is an integral part of a trusting relationship and trust is an essential requirement of a relationship with communications. Communications is not just the foundation upon which successful relationships are built, communications is a part of a strong friendship and a strong friendship will sustain you during difficult times.

If your man doesn't feel safe opening up, a part of your trust has been eroded and this needs to be restored first and restoring trust needs to be your number one priority.

Once you are open to building/rebuilding trust in communications, don't expect overnight miracles. Your partner will naturally be suspicious because, as the old cliché goes, it takes eons to build trust and it can be destroyed in a moment. However, once your man sees a change in you and starts recognizing the trust, it won't be long before he becomes open to reciprocating.

So what are some of the ways that trust gets destroyed? Well since we're talking about communications let's focus on communications based trust factors and not cheating or domestic abuse (those are covered later in this book).

There are 3 core destroyers of communications trust: Lying, Criticism and Invalidation.

Lying:

Trust is the most important asset you have in your relationship. Trust is slow to build and can be destroyed in a single careless act or statement.

There are many reasons to lie to a partner, none of them good. I've heard both men and women list off a litany of reasons as to why they lie to their partner and usually it comes down to personal or emotional safety. As one person said, "I will lie to avoid an argument."

Lying invalidates your partner by sending the message "you are not worthy of the truth."

The Man Puzzle

Here's the news: Most all men know when we're being lied to. I can't begin to tell you the number of times I heard a man say "I knew she was lying but I didn't care because _____" and the because is generally it didn't matter such as "she spent a little more on my birthday than we agreed" or because he's getting something out of it as in "she can lie about where she goes on Tuesday nights all she wants just as long as I have dinner on the table and the kids are taken care of".

Where lying gets really ugly is when the man doesn't know you've told a lie and then finds out later. Lying is never about love, it's about avoidance.

During interviews with one group of men one of the older guys told this little story:

My Favorite cologne:

"I had a favorite cologne that I had worn for years and I remember asking my wife several times if she liked it and she always said she did. After about 10 years of marriage I overheard her telling her sister how much she hated the cologne I wore and I remember thinking to myself 'If she has lied about this all these years, what else has she lied about? Does she like the way I dress? Does she really think my jokes are funny?' Basically, she called in to question everything she had ever told me. I didn't know what to believe. I know it sounds crazy but if she would lie to me over something so silly as cologne, what else would she lie about?"

Most men, even knowing it's a little white lie, still prefer being told the truth because each little lie is like the blade of an axe chopping into the trunk of the tree of trust... enough chops and eventually the tree will fall.

Criticism:

Criticism is a bad way to make your point and an even worse way to make a request. Often, when we criticize someone, it is because they are not doing something we would like them to do or they are doing something we would like them to stop doing or because we have contempt for the person or their actions.

For the most part, criticism isn't just about what was said but also about how it was said and by who said it. Criticism will only be accepted if it is perceived that the critic has the right to make that judgment. A slob criticizing someone because their house wasn't clean enough for a dinner party would be an example of a critic who didn't have the right to make a judgment and the criticism would not be well received. A woman with no kids telling a woman with four small kids that her children are out of control would be another example of a critic who didn't have the right to make a judgment and the criticism would not be well received.

Criticism is an attack form of communications and if you're using criticism as a way of making requests or changing a behavior, rather than attacking, it would be much healthier and much more effective to simply make your request. Especially since men respond much better to healthy, polite and direct request. "I can't believe you folded those towels like that! They look horrible!" is an example of criticism used to change behavior while "Honey, would you please fold the towels more neatly?" is an example of a direct request. Now which one do you think a man is more likely to respond to?

Criticisms come in two forms, overt which is obvious and covert which is hidden. An example overt criticism is, using our towel example, "I can't believe you folded those towels like that! They look horrible!" while covert criticisms are just as dangerous and have the exact same effect as overt criticisms, they are simply much more difficult to uncover.

Covert criticism is far more difficult to uncover and understand. It's usually veiled under some form of compliment such as putting your partner down with seeming kindness: "Honey, that's okay, you never have been much of a cook" or even using what seems like encouragement: "It's not much of a promotion but it's better than nothing!" While covert criticism often sounds like you're being the nice person and the person on the receiving end may not immediately hear the criticism, you can bet that the message gets received loud and clear!

Invalidation:

Emotional invalidation is when one partner denies the feelings of the other by rejecting, ignoring or judging their thoughts and feelings. Invalidation is especially destructive because it tells your partner they don't matter to you because your feelings and beliefs are the only feelings and beliefs that matter. With men, this is particularly damaging because a man will simply stop sharing anything meaningful because the pain they experience is too great.

Most women would deny that they invalidate the internal experience of their man but the problem is, most are generally unaware when they do or unaware as to how they're doing it. However, if you were to ask a man who's not talking, he'll tell you: It's pointless. (Pointless is man speak for my feelings don't matter.)

The problem is, most people don't understand what it means to validate someone. They believe if they validate they are agreeing with your feelings or acknowledging that they have done something wrong. Validation doesn't mean agreeing, it means acknowledging. Everyone is entitled to their own feelings, beliefs and experiences and to acknowledge your man's feelings validates his importance as a human being and as your partner.

A person can state, "I understand and I'm sorry that you feel that I lied to you," and not agree with you. Validation is not agreeing. But because they want to reassure you they invalidate by saying, "I'm an honest and trustworthy person, I can't believe you think I lied to you!" This not only invalidates your man but actually turns this around into an attack on his feelings!

Invalidation comes in many forms so I'm going to cover the more common forms: Blaming, Judging, Ridicule, Minimizing and non-verbal invalidation:

Blaming:

Blaming is an aggressive form of invalidation. "You always get jealous when I talk to other men." "It's your fault we're going to be late!", "It doesn't matter if I'm late getting ready, we have to stop because you didn't put gas in the car before you got home" Blaming is always invalidating as it's the exact opposite of taking responsibility.

How do you know if you're blaming? If your response to your man contains the words "You" or "Because" then most likely it is a blame statement.

Judging:

Have you ever said something like "You are so overreacting," and "That is a ridiculous thought!"? These are examples of invalidation by judging. Ridicule is also particularly damaging: "Here we go again. I talk to one man and you think I'm leaving you!" Instead of addressing the issue and reassuring your partner, you're actually invalidating them and making the problem worse.

Denying:

Denying is a form of invalidation where you tell your man he doesn't feel what he said he's feeling: "You are not hungry, you ate all those snacks during the game." We invalidate the other person by saying they don't feel what they say they are feeling or that their feelings are based on bad data.

Minimizing:

"Don't worry, it's nothing," and "you're just going to keep yourself awake tonight over something silly" are usually said with the best of intentions. Still the message is "don't feel what you are feeling". This is called minimizing.

Dismissing:

I once had a girlfriend who had asked me a question along the lines of "have you ever…" and I started to tell her a story and she stood up and started dancing and with a wave of her hand said "I've already heard that story" and completely dismissed what I was going to say. What she didn't know (and doesn't know even today), is that when I originally told her the story, I gave her the edited version. Had she not dismissed me, she would have heard lots of juicy details that would have given her insight into my past. Dismissing a conversation, or something your man has to say, even if you've heard it before, is invalidating!

Silent Treatment:

The silent treatment is invalidating. If you want to tell a man he's meaningless to you, give him the silent treatment.

A young man named Jason told me this story:

"My wife of 4 years was forever giving me the silent treatment. Sometimes it would go on for days. In the beginning I would go crazy trying to figure out what I had done wrong and do all sorts of things to win back her favor. After about two years of this, I just stopped! I would come home and just ask 'Still not speaking?' and then call one of my buddies and go hang out with him. Right at the end of the 4th year she started in on another silent treatment, and I dropped divorce papers in her lap. Suddenly, then, she wanted to talk but I didn't."

Just remember when he's dying to talk and you're not willing to listen, you are creating an opportunity for him to be understood somewhere else.

Nonverbal:

Nonverbal invalidation is as powerful as verbal invalidation and includes such things as rolling your eyes or drumming your fingers in an impatient way. Even checking your watch or your phone while your man is talking with you is invalidating. Regardless of your intent, your actions can be as invalidating as your words.

Are you surprised by these examples? Can you find yourself having said these things to your man?

Of course the opposite of invalidating is validating or acknowledging your man's right to feel what he feels. When you validate your man's feelings by responding in a sincere and empathetic way, it says that you care. Well actually it says more than that, it says you care enough to really listen and try to understand. Validation is a powerful tool that you can use to reduce frustration, conflict and anger as well as to create that friendship that leads to deep intimacy.

HOW TO TALK TO YOUR MAN

How To Bring Up A Conversation

One of the most important aspects of talking to a man is knowing when and how to bring up a conversation. If you want your man to be open to talking to you, it's best to learn the art of bringing up a conversation.

Honey, We Have To Talk:

There is probably no single sentence that will strike fear into a man's heart as quickly as "Honey, we need to talk." What you're telling him is "something has come to a boiling point and I need to talk about it NOW!" What he hears is "you have screwed up and I want to spend 30 minutes ripping into you and telling you what a horrible man you are and trust me buster, this is gonna end in a fight!" Hardly a way to encourage a man to engage in a meaningful dialog so my advice is to avoid that sentence at all costs, in every situation.

Honey, I'd Like To Find Time To Talk About…:

So, how do you approach a conversation with a man? You give warning! "Honey, I'd like to find time to talk about what you said about my sister at dinner last night. Can we plan on tomorrow after we put the kids to bed?" This does three things: You have given your man a topic (remember, we are topical creatures), you have given him time to think through what he said and what he was feeling when he said it and you have established the topic as something important to you and that you need to discuss in the immediate/near future. What you have not done is to turn this into a threatening conversation.

Types Of Conversations:

Obviously, there are several types of conversations which range from the mundane to the emotionally charged. Does it matter how you approach each conversation? Absolutely! Men respond best to topical, factual, straight forward conversations.

Learning To Ask The Right Kinds Of Questions

I always find this such an interesting topic. I watch some of my best guy friends struggle with trying to understand what his woman is asking of him. Even in my own personal experience, I often have to stop and think in order to try and understand what's really being asked of me and how, if at all, I want to respond and there have been many a time that I have apologized for not participating in a conversation because I took what was being said as my partner venting and not her asking for participation. For this reason, it's vitally important to learn how to ask your man questions that are both meaningful and will get you a response that you can use to move things forward.

I think most men have an adverse reaction to many questions and when we hear them we immediately put our defenses up and look for ways of abandoning the conversation. The one I hear guys make the most jokes about is "How did that make you feel?" This one question, almost universally, will end any meaningful conversation you might have been having or might have had with your man.

Traps:

For as long as men have been males, we have been conditioned to watch for traps. Do these pants make my butt look big? Do you notice anything new about me? Do you like my new dress?

The Man Puzzle

After awhile, we males learn that one of the first things to do is evaluate what's been said to see if there's a trap. Any question that has two possible answers is a trap and when men experience a trap we have three possible responses 1) do nothing, say nothing and wait for the woman to ask the question again so that we know how we're supposed to answer; 2) lie like a dog (your butt looks great in those pants) or 3) ask for clarification. I can hear it now, "what exactly do you consider big?" Now, how often do you hear a man asking for clarification? Rarely right?

The first thing you have to do is to remove the traps from your communications. But, you say, "I don't ask those kinds of questions!" and I think you might be surprised. For a week or so, I'd like you to write down all the questions you ask your man over the course of the day. Write down your exact words and what information you wanted from him along with what information you actually got. Don't over think what you're doing, don't change how you're asking questions (you may be doing it right), just write down the questions and a few days later look at your list and honestly evaluate your questions for traps.

Sometimes, a question can even make matters worse. Want an example? While your man is swearing and hopping around after just banging his finger with a hammer, just look at him and ask "Are you okay?" and see if that doesn't get ranked up there among the dumbest questions of all time! On the other hand, try asking this question: "What I can do to help?" and you'll notice an immediate change (de-escalation) in his frustration level. Your question was asked out of concern and caring but had an adverse effect while the second question, one which would not occur to very many women, would work on your man on so many levels.

What Do You Want For Dinner?

One of the greatest questions ever asked a man is "Honey, what do you want for dinner?" That question evokes so much hope and joy in a man we almost become giddy. So why do men answer with "I don't care"? There are two reasons: 1) We're grateful for any meal that anyone wants to cook for us, and if you're grateful you don't want to impose on the food gods by making special request; 2) It's a question that generally ends in an argument, disappointment or both.

During my research I asked men "how they liked" this question and, after being met with chuckles, the general consensus was that it's a pointless question to answer because it seemed that no matter how hard they tried, there was no correct answer.

Lee, in Montgomery, Alabama put it this way:

"I only answer this question when I'm given a choice. 'Do you want burgers or pork chops for dinner?' If I'm given an open ended question I might say 'fried chicken' and get an answer like 'I don't feel like cooking that' or 'That takes too long' or 'That's not good for you' all of which means to me, that no matter what I ask for, I'm not going to get it which makes this a pointless question to answer."

Negotiating:

When you ask a man a question such as "What do you want for dinner?" or "Would you like to eat out tonight?" Men don't recognize this as an opening of a negotiation, we think it's a straight up question, so we answer it as such!

You: *Would you like to eat out tonight?*

Him: *No.*

Conversation over. You don't feel heard or understood and he has no clue that you didn't want to cook. He hasn't been privy to your internal dialog and doesn't realize that you're too tired to cook or that you've thought about dinner all day and just can't decide what you want for dinner or that you forgot to take the chicken out of the freezer last night. By asking if he wants to eat out tonight, you're opening a negotiation and he has no clue that's what's happening.

When you want to get an answer to a question, keep it simple and offer options otherwise, be prepared to handle answers you weren't expecting or answers that are less than useful.

You: *I'm too tired to cook, do you want to eat out or order in?*

Him: *I'm too tired to go out, let's order in.*

Good Questions:

Now that we know some of the bad ways to ask a question, let's look at some of the good ways. First, we need to understand there are two types of questions: There are requests for actions, and there are requests for information.

When asking for information, you really want to ask opened ended questions and avoid yes or no questions (and certainly traps). Let's pretend your man was hosting the end of season BBQ of the company's softball team and he asked your help. In order to avoid misunderstandings and fights, you would need to know what your duties would be so you might ask "What are your expectations are for me?" or "What part do you need me to do?" If you were to ask "Do you want my help?" that would be a closed ended question which would result in the yes/no answer.

An example we used earlier involving the flat tire was "How did you deal with all that frustration?" This type of answer requires more than a yes or no answer and should illicit more than a shrugged shoulder.

Obviously, these were two simplistic examples but they accurately demonstrate how to ask opened ended questions in order to get a conversation started.

The other type of question is the request for action or help. Men want to see their women happy and that means doing things for you, but there's a right way and a wrong way to ask for help. A man will have great sympathy for a woman who expresses herself gently. It's hard to be sympathetic or want to help someone who's angry or screaming. For that reason, learn to ask good questions in an assertive but kind way. Some examples are:

"I need you to _____."

"It would be meaningful to me if you would _____."

"So that I don't get upset with you later, before you paint the room, I want to make sure everything is covered so if paint spatters it's not a problem."

One important note that, if you're going to tell us how to do something, make sure you do it so that you are taking responsibility for WHY you want it done that way.

"I go crazy if the towels aren't folded this way and I would just end up refolding them all and I would get frustrated and angry so if you would please learn my way on this."

This is only going to work so often... it's powerful, it's simple and if you over use it, it will lose it's meaning.

Examples Of How To Say Things:

Bad: "It's so sweet you want to help me _____, but I can do it faster myself."

Insult: "I can do it faster/better/____ myself." You're basically incompetent.

Better: "I got this, but if you want to help you could do _____."

Bad: "I'm amazed you were able to fix the _____."

Insult: "I'm amazed." I really thought you were incompetent.

Better: "Nice Job!"

Bad: "I do _____ this way, but thanks for trying without me asking."

Insult: "trying" denotes failure. If you want him to keep doing, you're far better off to encourage him by being appreciative. So what if he folded the towels differently or doesn't put the trash can liner in how you do. Lighten up!

Better: "Thanks for doing _____. I appreciate your help!"

Bad: "You're the only person I can talk to."

Insult: "You're the only person" frightens most men and honestly, you don't come off as emotionally whole.

Better: "Thanks for being my best friend and listening."

Bad: "You're so cute!" "Your dimples are cute." "Your butt is cute."

Insult: "cute" Cute is demeaning, and avoids deeper intimacy.

Lump a guy in with babies, puppies, kittens and new born marmosets and you'll do a number on your intimacy and chemistry.

Better: "You're so handsome!" "Your dimples make you more handsome." "Your butt is amazing!"

Bad: "This gift isn't quite my taste, but it's the thought that counts."

Insult: He doesn't know you or he has bad taste. Criticizing what he bought is a sure fire way to make sure he doesn't buy you anything else. Instead, just wear it on occasion and when the next holiday nears, take him out and point out things you like... and let him point out things he likes. You might learn something about why he chooses what he chooses.

Better: "Thank you for the present. I really appreciate your generosity!"

Bad: "No man ever got my taste like my ex."

Insult: He can never measure up to your ex, why bother trying.

Better: Keep your mouth shut. Don't say anything.

Bad: "Sometimes It's like you're another one of the kids, but I love you anyway."

Insult: "but" is really passive/aggressive. Break the sentence into segments and positive up the criticism.

Better: "I really like that you're so playful with the kids. Right now though, I need you supporting me while I'm trying to get the kids in bed."

The Man Puzzle

Bad: "My husband did the most romantic thing ever."

Insult: You tell your friends, they tell their husbands and their husbands will give your man a hard time about being "whipped" and how "he made them all look bad." That doesn't endear your husband to you and it makes him wonder what else you tell your girlfriends that they in turn tell their husbands. This creates a huge trust violation and de-motivates your husband to do nice things for you.

Better: Keep your mouth shut. Any bragging about your man's efforts should be to the man, not your friends.

Bad: "I love your paunch!"

Insult: Just yesterday you were talking about buff body builders or the lifeguards. Why would he believe your comment about his paunch? This creates another trust violation.

Better: "I really appreciate that you're such a good husband and father." or "You're such a caring and thoughtful man and I appreciate you for that."

Bad: "You're the best I've ever had."

Insult: Compared to who? Compared to how many? Do you really want to make your man insecure and cause him to start thinking about your past?

Better: "When you do _____ it just drives me insane!" or "I love how it feels when you _____."

Bad: "Men are like coffee, the best ones are rich, warm and keep you up all night."

Insult: Yes, for women this is funny but when the woman we love says these things or shares them on social media, it sends a very bad and degrading message. This is very much one of those "cake and eat it too" scenarios. Women don't want men saying these things but feel it's okay for them to say it. It's not okay.

Better: Don't say or share these things and speak up when others do. It lets your husband know you value him and men.

Things To Absolutely Never Say:

Why:

With men, the most dangerous covert criticism comes in the form of a "Why" question. Why questions are, simply put, the most inflammatory questions you can ask and they immediately put your man on the defensive. Why questions are criticisms in disguise. "Why did you fold the towels like that?" "Why did you bring us to such an expensive restaurant?" Your goal should be to seek understanding and to do that you can easily replace why questions with questions that allow for a dialog.

Let's look at the following exchange:

"Why did you bring us to such an expensive restaurant?" and he responds *"Geez, I can't do anything right for you can I?"* and before you know it, you have an argument on your hands and you have no idea why it started.

Now look at the exchange this way:

"Wow! This is an expensive restaurant, is there a special occasion?" "No, nothing special going on, I just really wanted to treat you to a nice dinner." and before you know it, you have

*a loving and romantic dinner on your hands and you've built
another wonderful memory.*

Don't Ask Why

While working on this book I was invited to visit an extremely
successful friend at his ocean front home.

My friend has founded several medical companies, taken one
public and sold the others for $100's of millions of dollars. He
is a venture capitalist and frequently speaks at conferences all
over the world.

Over wine one evening, my friend's fiancé was questioning the
progress of my book and challenging my assertion that women
should never use the word "why" when conversing with men.

My friend had been in the kitchen pouring some wine and had
not heard the exchange between his fiancé and myself. Upon his
return I asked him if he ever used "why" in business and he said
"No!" and his fiancé immediately asked "Why not?"

My friend's response was exactly on point: "There are easier
ways to get the information. Asking 'why' creates an adversarial
position where one doesn't need to exist."

After another sip of wine, I asked my friend's fiancé how often
he used the word "why" with her and she thought quietly for a
moment and said "I can't remember a time and that might be a
reason why he's so easy to talk to."

By simply asking the question differently, you changed the
tone of the conversation from adversarial to loving and kind. You
were able to get all the information you wanted while keeping the
conversation positive and the moment happy.

But:

"But" is the destroyer of all things kind. It negates everything said before it and men only hear what was said after it. Let's look at a few common uses of "but":

"Thanks for folding the towels but I don't like them folded that way" – Your man heard *"you did a crappy job and it doesn't please me"*

"I really appreciate your bringing me roses but I wish you would get the nice ones that last longer and not the ones from the grocery store." – Your man heard *"I don't appreciate your gift and to make me happy you need to spend more money on me."*

"I love our Friday night dates but sometimes I wish I could go out with my girlfriends." Your man heard *"This relationship is in trouble. I don't like spending my Friday nights with you anymore, I want to start hanging out with my girlfriends instead."*

The word "but" negates anything positive you may have said. If you have a complaint or need a change in something, those are two different conversations. The gratitude expressed needs to stay as gratitude and the change request needs to come in a different conversation.

"I really appreciate your bringing me roses." Period. Stop there!

At a later time you can drop hints about how you bought flowers at the local florist and you were amazed at how long they lasted. You can even take him along when you pick up flowers and when he asks why not just get them at the grocery store you can tell him that you found the ones you get at the florist last longer. A smart man will get the hint. (He may not change where he buys your flowers but he will get the hint!)

The Man Puzzle

Honey We Need To Talk:

We've already covered this one in a previous section but it's worth repeating. When a man hears "Honey, we need to talk!" what he really hears is "Honey, you screwed up and I'm mad!"

Are You Ok?

It's funny sitting around listening to a group of guys talk about things that women say that really "set them off" and I can't begin to tell you how often this one comes up. Imagine this scenario: Your man is hammering away at something and then you hear a bunch of loud cursing and you rush to find him hopping up and down with his hand tucked between his legs and screaming obscenities. What's the first thing you would ask? Of course the question is "Are you okay?" and that one question just made the problem 10 times worse!

Let me take you through the process: First, he's not okay, this is obvious by the screaming, the hand between the legs, the hopping around and the purple face. Second, asking if he's okay takes his already feeling stupid about his accident and raises it to a whole new level. Third, when in pain, answering an absurd question just makes most men even angrier. Fourth, you stand the risk of making yourself the target of his obscenities.

A far better question would be "What can I do?"

"What can I do?" a simple question that completely changes the context and direction of the conversation.

What Happened?

This question, like the one above, is one of those questions that's seemingly innocent and well meaning but actually adds to the male frustration level.

Your man arrives home and is covered in grime and you ask "What happened?" and that's a fair question and it will get answered. "I had a flat tire on the interstate and had to stop and change it" and you're off and running. Good conversation coming up!

Now let's change it around just a bit. Your man arrives home and is covered in grime and you look at him and he says "I had a flat tire on the interstate and had to stop and change it" and you ask "What happened?" – and now we have a problem starting. This is when he gives you one of those dirty looks like you didn't hear what he said. He just told you what happened. He had a flat tire and had to stop and change it! But obviously you know that. What you're asking isn't about what happened, it's perhaps about how it happened? Did a truck dump a bunch of broken glass on the road? Did he run over a nail? Was it a bad tire? What you really want to know is "What caused the flat?"

Bossy Bessy:

It doesn't matter how you say it, when you're giving orders you're being bossy. Sometimes, it's okay to be bossy. If you're trying to get the house ready for company and your man is your laborer, he fully expects some "put this there", "move that", "carry these to that room". We get it. That's what you need and frankly, most of us are thankful for the *polite* direction.

When things turn bad is when you become bossy about how he thinks or behaves. If you find yourself saying "you need to do this/you need to do that" or "you need to stop being like that/you need to be more like this" then you're being judgmental and a Bossy Bessy.

Bossy Bessys typically end up in arguments without a clue as to how they got there. Those judgmental comments are criticisms and every man recognizes them for what they are: Mean, ugly comments. That means it's only a matter of time before you have an argument.

At this point, you probably have figured out that men hear and process the same words and sentences differently than you do. What can be a normal conversation among a group of women can cause a man to shut-up and walk away. That's why it's important to pick your words wisely and to pick the timing of conversations carefully.

GETTING HIM TO LISTEN

There is nothing more gratifying than being truly heard and understood, and there's nothing worse than having a partner that doesn't listen.

In all the research I've conducted for this book, one of the top complaints women seem to have about their men is, "He doesn't listen!" I am going teach you some surprisingly simple techniques that will help you get heard.

Time And Place:

I'm sure you've heard the expression "pick your battles" and not only is that extremely good advice but so is "pick the time and place for your battles." When you're out running errands together, on a date, have friends over, he's watching the big game or finishing a report for work, these are NOT the times or places to have a discussion. You want your man to be in a mental place where he can hear and pay attention to you without constant interruptions, people over hearing or any other distractions. Also, if either of you are upset, tired, overwhelmed or hungry, you're bound to be a bit snippy and snippy can turn in to an argument very quickly.

Get Rid Of The Distractions:

Speaking of which, men typically don't multi-task nearly as well as women do and most of us certainly have a difficult time listening to two things at once. If the game is on, music is playing or we're surfing the Internet, these are all big distractions and these need to be eliminated before you can get his full and undivided attention. Remember, we have to run your voices through our music processor first and then try to make sense out of it. It's nearly impossible to do that with background noises going on.

If I'm talking on the phone, I, like many other men, actually stop talking when an announcement comes over the P.A. on either end. Why? Because many men simply can't process two conversations at once and this is especially true as we get older and our hearing starts to deteriorate and we have to focus our listening skills on just one set of voices.

One lady told me that when she speaks to her husband while they're watching TV, he actually hits the pause button and turns toward her. After years of this, she asked him why he did that and his reply was simple: "I can listen to you OR the TV but I can't listen to both."

Other women talk about how their husbands can be watching sports on TV and not hear a bomb going off. Yep. Where our focus goes, so goes our listening.

Position And Posture:

Sometimes, it's the little things that make the biggest difference. In the male world, head-on, face-to-face is a sign of impending aggression and a sign confrontation is near, men shut down and get ready for a fight or flight. This is not what you want! Instead, choose a quiet place to sit, position yourselves side by side or at a slight angle to each other and touch! Always be touching because it's nearly impossible to get mad when you're touching. Hold hands. Intertwine your arms or legs but keep physical contact. Choosing the correct position allows you to bypass millions of years of evolution!

Think that's hooey? It works on you the same way. In an experiment we did in college, women who were approached head-on by strange men were not at all receptive to anything the men had to say, while women who were approached from a 45 degree angle were 5 times more likely to be helpful. Add in a gentle touch to the forearm or shoulder before making the request and the number doubled to 10 times more likely to be helpful!

Your posture is equally important; if you're slouched over reflecting a "I don't care" attitude, then don't expect your man to apply the same importance to the topic as you do. Likewise if your posture reflects one of anger or rage, your man is just as likely to be a non-participant in the conversation.

Research has shown that men will stay in a conversation longer as much as twice as long if you are not facing each other directly. There must be a slight offset in your positioning. For instance, stand facing him, take one normal step to the side and then turn slightly towards him.

Visual Clues:

One of the most interesting things about traveling around and interviewing countless groups of men and women is in how the different genders listen.

With women, you see much more active listening with a focus on the speakers face with brief glances away (generally around the room at the other participants). Men, on the other hand, would be focused on some object (paper on the table, water bottle, etc.) and have brief glances at the speakers face.

While interviewing the groups of women, if I focused on an object while listening (this allowed me to concentrate entirely on her words and not be distracted by such things as the lipstick on her teeth), I would often be asked if I heard what was said. I was never asked this when I was looking directly at the woman doing the speaking.

With men, if I stared at their faces their responses would be shorter, sometimes even trailing off. Sometimes, when I would explain a complex concept or when one of the men in the group has just shared a complex feeling, I would wonder if one guy or another had heard anything which had been said. Generally, it was from this "disconnected" guy that the most profound and insightful observations would come.

This means that just because your man is not looking at your face, it doesn't mean he's not listening. As long as he's not watching TV, he's probably very focused on the conversation.

Know What You Want:

It is completely impossible to get what you want if you don't know what that is. Do you just want to vent about your day at work? Do you need some emotional support for something you're facing? Perhaps you need help in addressing a problem? Whatever it is, you need to first get clear in your own mind exactly what you want and then to make it clear to him. Once you tell us what you want, you're much more likely to get it. Why? Because, as you know, we like fixing things and if just listening is the fix you need, then diggity dang! We can do that!

On the other hand, if you don't know what it is you want, not only do we have to try and listen to you but we also have to try and figure out what you want. How many times do we hear comments about men trying to fix things when all you want is to be heard? The reason is because we don't know what we're supposed to do and fixing is what we do and is our automatic go-to response.

Just The Facts Ma'am:

Nothing causes a man to mentally check out of a conversation quicker than unnecessary information. He really doesn't need to know what color shoes your boss's wife had on nor does he need to know that your best friend Sally ordered the salad for lunch. The more information you throw in that isn't relevant, the more likely he is to check-out and start thinking about other things.

Take this conversation as an example:

"Today I had lunch with Velma and she wore that hideous dress that makes her look 10 sizes bigger and 20 years older... I don't know why she doesn't throw that thing away. Anyway, it took us forever to decide what where to go, she wanted Chinese but I really just wanted a nice salad. We finally decided on the Asian House of Salad and the service was just horrible! So after the food came we talked about her new boss and we decided that it's been forever since the four of us have had dinner together and she's not sure if she wants to keep working there and anyway we're going out to dinner with her and her husband on Friday and I'm sure by then she'll have made up her mind about her new boss."

Seriously, every guy out there has had this VERY conversation and you know what? When Friday comes around he has no recollection of the conversation and has no desire to go to dinner with you, Velma and her husband. You're mad and convinced he doesn't listen to you and he thinks you're insane because you NEVER had a conversation with him about going out to dinner with Velma on Friday night.

Get Acknowledgement:

When you need us to acknowledge what you've said, then ask us to tell you what we heard and understood. What you'll find is that many times, what you say and what we hear are two different things and that more conversation needs to take place in order for us to understand what it is you're truly trying to tell us.

If it's a task you're asking us to complete, like picking up milk on the way home or junior from little league, ask us to repeat back the time or to call from the grocery store.

While this is a good technique for getting your feelings validated, I'm not a huge fan of this method for confirming to-do list items because, it can, depending on the man, be quite destructive. The risk is that no one likes being treated like a child. You need to find out how your man feels about this. If he's overly forgetful, this might be the solution and he may be agreeable while other men may be offended.

Write It Down:

A majority of men respond better to something concrete, like a note, a list, or even a drawing, than they do to something they hear so if we see what you need done in writing, we're more likely to remember to do it.

For many of us, a to-do list is pretty easy to accommodate as long as it's clear, concise and complete. Writing things like "paint the fence" may not get much done because we don't know what color you want and just saying "white" isn't much help. Solar white? Off white? Remember, to you there are huge differences in these things but to us, not much, if anything at all. So be clear, concise and complete.

In the end, there are some logical reasons for how and why we men communicate the way we do. How we express feelings and share emotions is easily explainable and now you can apply some new information and open communications and build a deeper understanding of your man.

Downplaying Is Supporting:

You've just poured your heart out and shared some great fear you have about your upcoming business trip, the presentation you have at work tomorrow or some family event and you hear one of these familiar phrases:

"You've got this!"
"It's no big deal, why are you so worried?"
"Don't worry, it'll be ok."
"Don't sweat the small stuff."

And you wonder "Did he hear ANYTHING I just said?" You feel hurt. Your feelings were discounted. You get mad.

Of course, he has no clue what you're upset about because he heard you! He was supportive! He was encouraging!

In guy speak, what we tend to do is support by minimizing the problem. We downplay it as "no big deal." It's the old saying "Don't make a mountain out of a molehill" put into action. We do this as an extension of those "shared experiences" I talked about earlier but in this case it's the short form of "You're the smartest, most capable woman I know and of course you're nervous about the presentation, anyone would be, but if anyone can pull it off and make it out like the world champ, it's you!"

Of course, you'd rather hear the long version but that's not really how we communicate. The next time your man, your boss, your dad, your brother or the barista at Starbucks gives you some "downplayed support" just parrot it back to him in the long version with "what I heard you say is that I'm smart, I'm capable, I have a right to be nervous and you believe in me and you're confident I'll do this well." and watch the guy stand there and smirk like he'd just been caught with his hand in the cookie jar.

Chapter 4

RESOLVING PROBLEMS – HOW TO ARGUE

"An argument is about who is right, a discussion is about what is right." ~ Unknown

ONFLICT IS NORMAL AND DIFFERENCES between two people of the opposite sex guarantee that conflict will occur. There is no need to fear conflict because, when it's handled right, it's not only healthy but you can both learn from each other and both learn where you need to grow.

Arguing does not mean screaming and yelling and if that's how you argue, you're doing it wrong! Resolving conflict does not mean that you need to fight with your partner. Ever.

Having a conflict is not a problem and it doesn't mean you have a bad relationship. What conflict means is that you have something that needs to be resolved. All couples have disagreements and your ability to stay together is determined by how you handle the disagreements.

When you look at relationships which have lasted 3, 40, 50 or more years you find that most arguments are long forgotten. If one is remembered, it's one that left deep, emotional scars. Causing your partner emotional pain or scaring is not what you want and if you follow the rules below you are far more likely to resolve the conflict, build a deeper understanding of each other and a stronger relationship.

Arguing is such a complex topic, not because it's hard to argue but because most people don't understand exactly why they argue and when they do argue, so much emotion gets dragged into the process that nothing constructive happens and, ultimately, it becomes impossible to have a positive outcome. As a result, things are left unsaid and resentment builds to the point where the relationship fractures. Not at all what most people want for their relationship.

What Is Arguing:

Argue
ar·gue
/⬚ärgyo⬚o/

verb

1. To give reasons or cite evidence in support of an idea, action, or belief with the purpose of persuading your partner to share your view.

2. To exchange or express diverging or opposite views to persuade your partner to do (or not do) something by giving your reasons in a compelling and thoughtful way.

Just like anything else with men, there's a right way and a wrong way to argue and I want to teach you some methods that allow you to have constructive outcomes. But first, let's understand why we argue.

Arguments are typically conducted in a heated or angry way and that heat and anger makes arguments unproductive. The purpose of the discussion should be to try to explain your position to your partner so that you are understood and a resolution to the conflict can be reached. The purpose is not make your man defensive. Good communication inspires compromise and changed behavior and is more likely to win the day which is far better than alienating your man and making the problem worse.

Arguments are not about venting or nagging. You must have the intent of seeking resolution to a definable problem by having a discussion. It's not getting something off your chest by dumping a barrage of built up "stuff" on your man.

Why We Argue:

Inside every relationship we all have expectations as to how things will go. You have expectations about how your boss will treat you; about how your co-workers will treat you; about the type of service you'll receive at a restaurant or when checking in to a hotel. You certainly have expectations about your relationship with your man just as he has expectations about his relationship with you. When one of you doesn't meet an expectation held by the other then a conflict arises. Depending on the severity of the "violation," things quickly escalate into an argument.

If expectations were only about how we were treated in one area, life would be so simple. Unfortunately, our expectations cover the entire scope of our relationship, and these expectations can be broken down in to areas which I call "Subjects" because they're really what you should be talking about and "Incidents" which are the actions that we end up arguing about.

Imagine the Subjects are the limbs on a tree. You have the main limbs and off of each limb you have branches which are your expectations. No matter what the argument is about, which expectation was unmet, the argument can be traced back to one of the main limbs, or Subjects.

The Subjects most commonly fought over are: Money, Sex, Religion, Chores, Power and Control, Family and Parenting. Every argument can trace its branch back to one of these limbs.

The triggers for arguments are generally some action or "Action." For example, as a couple you have an agreement that you not spend any money above $100 without consulting one another; therefore, you both have the expectation that you will talk and be in agreement before any major money gets spent. You come home and find that your man has just spent $600 (the Action) on a new big screen TV. In most cases, this turns into an argument that goes like this:

You: *"How could you buy that?"*

Him: *"I've told you for weeks I wanted one!"*

You: *"We never had a discussion about you buying a new TV!"*

The entire exchange is caused by a violation of an expectation in the Subject of Money. The argument, however, ends up being about the Action of purchasing a new TV when it should be about the Subject of Money and the agreement you had in place. You can argue over the Action until you are blue in the face and ready to end your relationship, and it will do no good. If you're not addressing the Subject, you will continue to fight over the Action and nothing will ever be resolved.

If you find yourself having the same arguments over and over and over, it's because you're arguing over Actions and not having discussions about the actual Subject.

Another example is in the Subject of Parenting. You have an

agreement that your man takes the kids to the park every Sunday for two hours. At noon, his mother pulls into the driveway with the kids in the backseat and proudly tells you that she took them to the park while your man went to play golf with his boss.

Yes, of course there would be a conversation when he gets home! But what would the conversation look like? Would you launch in on the golf? Or would the discussion be about him dropping the kids off with his mother without a discussion? What is the actual Subject that gets discussed? Can you define and separate the Action from the Subject?

Obviously the Subject is Parenting but what is the Action? There are actually several and I'm sure you can imagine how this could turn into an argument that could go all over the map. From too much golf, to dumping his kids off on Grandma, to not keeping his agreement, to him being a bad parent, to you not being properly dressed when his mother showed up to any number of other things.

The longer we're together as a couple, the more familiar we become with our partners limbs and the branches that grow off those limbs. If you've gotten anything from this book thus far it should be that with good communications you should be starting to understand your man's limbs and branches and how those came to be.

One Argument Or Two?:

I'm going to share a dirty little trick that some men use as conflict avoidance. If a man knows that what he's going to do will cause an argument, more times than not he will say one thing just to avoid an argument in that moment, go do what he wants and take the argument later. The logic is pretty simple, why have two fights (one before and one after) when you can just have one (the one after)?

In the above Parenting example, your man knows on Wednesday that he's going to go play golf with his boss on Sunday. He knows that you will be upset about it and he knows that you will be angry from the moment he tells you on Wednesday evening all the way through when he gets home on Sunday.

For some men, the question becomes: One argument or two? Does he want you to be mad at him all of Wednesday evening, all day Thursday, spend a miserable Friday night, arguments on Saturday and another fight on Sunday morning before he leaves OR would he rather not say anything, drop the kids off at his mother's and fight with you when he returns on Sunday? From the male perspective, the 2nd fight is usually easier because he's already "committed the crime" so he says "You're right! I did a bad thing!" grabs the kids and takes them to the park and on the way home picks up some flowers.

Gary in Atlanta tells this story:

"Back when I was a newlywed, I was invited to a bachelor party at a 'gentleman's club.' Now, those types of places had never been my idea of fun, but for a close friend's bachelor party you make exceptions. So, I dutifully informed my new bride and she said "Oh, no. I don't want you to go to those kinds of places." I studied her for a minute and then told her "There are two kinds of husbands, those who are honest with their wives and those who lie." And I then asked "Which kind do you want me to be?" She thought quietly for a few minutes and then said "I want you to always be honest with me" to which I replied "I will be home by 10 p.m." After that, we had a very honest relationship and I felt like I could be open and tell her anything and it would be O.K."

Whether or not a man employs this or other methods of argument avoidance depends a lot on how you handle conflict. If you stay mad for days, your man is more likely to employ argument avoidance but if you're the type to discuss and compromise, then your man is much more likely to be open and honest with you.

You can't dictate your man's behavior; you can only dictate your own. What you have to do is get your man to agree to a set of conditions such as I will not play golf on Sundays because it's family day nor will I play on days where we have family commitments like birthdays, weddings, etc. All other times are fair game as long as he's meeting your needs, the needs of the family and he gives ample notice so that you can make your own plans. Once that agreement is in place, you also have to honor your side of the agreement.

How you choose to handle conflict dictates the relationship you have with your man.

The Clown Scarf Of Arguments:

We've all seen the clown with the magic scarf. He starts pulling on the tip of the scarf in his pocket and then keeps pulling and pulling and pulling as one scarf is connect to the next is connected to the next.

Some arguments are the same way. So many issues get pulled into the argument that neither of you can tell what you're arguing over, and nothing gets resolved.

You absolutely have to keep to the topic and not drag other issues into the discussion. It's hard to do, but by limiting the topic to just what was agreed upon, you can keep things civil and the argument will end much quicker with both of you being happier.

Verbal Aggression:

"Verbal aggression" is when you name call, threaten, taunt, make nasty remarks, insult, accuse, demand your partner sleep on the couch or threaten to leave the relationship unless you get your way. Verbal Aggression is intended to cause emotional pain to another person and can be active or passive, verbal or non-verbal (slamming doors, smashing plates, punching walls).

The person who is verbally assaulted will either withdraw or retaliate with their own brand of Verbal Aggression. Sound bad? Studies of domestic violence have shown that verbal aggression is a predictor of physical aggression.

"Oh come on, it's just a good yelling argument, what could be wrong with that?" Verbal Aggression destroys trust, communications and intimacy. Living in an environment of Verbal Aggression prevents both parties from growing personally, learning about each other and growing as a couple. When you can't resolve conflicts, you keep tension, pain and conflict at the forefront of your relationship. It becomes like "living in a minefield" because you never know when your next step will set off another fight.

When you intentionally inflict pain on your man, you're essentially telling him "You are not safe with me. I would rather hurt you than lose an argument to you."

What's The Goal:

Know what you want before going into the disagreement. If you don't have a goal in mind, you won't know when you've achieved it and therefore when to quit. Learn to focus on the result and stay away from the distractions.

The primary goal of every argument should be to solve a problem; not to be right or to inflict pain, but to learn to relate to each other and to resolve the conflict. You can either be right, or you can learn about your man and you can work together to resolve the conflict, but you can't do both.

In a real sense, neither person is right nor wrong; there are only differences in beliefs, experiences and perceptions. Both win when the conflict is resolved. That's why your primary goal should be: Resolve the conflict and both win!

The secondary goal is to pull enough new information and insight from an argument to grow and learn so that the same problem doesn't get repeated. This only happens when the Subject and beliefs behind the Action are discussed. Arguing over the Action solves nothing.

Remember you are fighting FOR your relationship; you're not fighting for the sake of fighting or fighting to win.

Timing:

Don't let little things that bother you build up until one of you explodes and the conflict turns into a large, uncontrolled fight. That's not fighting fair in your relationship.

Don't insist on an argument when your spouse is tired or unable to handle the strain. A fair fight requires two ready participants.

If your spouse doesn't want to discuss the matter, set an appointment within the next 24 hours to have your discussion. It is okay to go to bed angry. You both need your sleep. Just make sure that the issue is addressed the next day.

Agree on a time limit ahead of time. Some experts recommend no more than 15 minutes and, if at the end of that time you have not resolved the problem, call a truce and set a time to discuss the problem again.

Grab A Snack:

In 2014, Ohio State University researchers asked 107 married couples to test their blood sugar each night and morning, and to stick pins into "voodoo dolls" that represented their spouses, based on how angry they were with them. The lower their blood sugar over the course of 21 days, the more pins they stuck in their dolls. The reason? Low blood sugar can cause people to feel hungry—and therefore cranky and irritable. The lead author of the study, Brad Bushman, Ph.D. said "It's simple advice but it works, before you have a difficult conversation with your spouse, make sure neither of you are hungry."

Know When To Let It Go:

Every successful couple will tell you that you need to pick your battles. That means learning when to let things go.

If you are angry about something and don't try to talk about it within 48 hours, let it go. Otherwise, you are not fighting fair.

It is pointless to condemn someone for a fault they refuse to recognize, cannot change or when it's something they like within themselves. If your man is sloppy, always late, always watching sports, it will do you no good to point this out, not even once, let alone over and over. He was either that way before you married or he has become that way for a reason. If he was that way before you married, then you will never change him. If this started after you were married, fix the reason and the behavior will fix itself.

According to Myers-Briggs 60% of males and 40% of females are not feelings oriented so going into long rants about how you feel will result in nothing. Try responding with 5 word sentences "That doesn't work for me." "I cannot agree to that." "Don't do that to me."

Discuss vs. Fight:

A man will have great sympathy for a woman who expresses herself gently. It's hard to be sympathetic with someone who's angry or screaming like a crazy woman. In fact, when you're angry your behavior, posture and tone of voice become very confrontational and create an adversarial position, and with men, this invokes the fight or flight response.

The louder someone yells, the less likely they are to be heard. Yelling only escalates things. Even if your partner yells, there's no need to yell back. Taking the volume down, starting with yourself, makes it possible for people to start focusing on the issues instead of reacting to the volume level.

How To Stop Him From Screaming At You

The first thing to understand is that when a man is screaming and yelling, he's not being objective and has entered the flight or fight response part of his brain and obviously "FIGHT" is his position. Telling him to "stop screaming" is only going to make matters worse because, let's face it, no one likes being told what to do, especially an angry person.

So, what do you do? You need to shift him from his emotional brain back to his problem solving part and this requires two steps:

First, you have to slow things down and this requires getting him to stop yelling. Do this by stating two things: 1) you can't understand him, and 2) you want to understand him. Hostage negotiators will use something similar to: "I want to understand you but you're talking too fast. Please slow down so I can help." It's almost impossible to yell when you're speaking slowly. Simply telling someone to speak slower will escalate the fight because they feel like they are being told what to do.

Second, you need to engage the problem solving part of his brain and you do this by asking him a question such as "How can I help?" or "What do you need me to do?" By asking questions you're showing him that you're not in attack mode and that you really want to understand what the problem is and help solve it.

Another option is when he stops for a breath is simply to not acknowledge that you're interested in hearing more. Avoid the "uh huh" or "yeah" or other comments that tell people you're listening. We do this automatically but you can teach yourself to not respond and after about the third breath your man will say "Are you listening?" and at that time you can ask him a question.

Keep in mind that yelling can be subjective and what is yelling to your spouse may not be yelling to you. Some people are raised in families where voices are never raised while others come from families where a normal tone is never heard. If your man feels like you're yelling, then you're yelling. How he perceives your tone and the words dictates how he will receive your message. Chose to lower your voice and if you can't because you're too upset, then it's probably best to take a time-out.

A discussion is always better because the outcome is not pre-defined. Heated arguments and screaming fights are non-productive. Discussions become productive.

Starting The Argument:

As was discussed in the last chapter, learning how to start a conversation is important, learning to start an argument is even more so and starting an argument is very different from picking a fight. People pick fights when they're cranky or they don't know what's bothering them.

Depending on how upset you are and what's going on in his

life, your man may be keenly aware that you're upset or he may be completely oblivious. Men are not mind readers so just because you're pouting doesn't mean you're mad at him or even that you want to talk. Most men learn that when a woman is ready to talk, they'll say something and until then it's best to leave well enough alone.

When you're ready, you know what the Subject is, you have your goal, you then need to give your partner the same opportunity to prepare. You do this by asking for the conversation like this:

Honey, 'x' has been bothering me and I would like to set aside 15 minutes or so within the next day so that we can talk about 'x' because I need: a better understanding / a way for us to compromise / a solution.

Once he's agreed to a time and before the discussion begins, find a calm moment and agree that neither partner should "win" an argument. If one of you wins, the other loses and that builds resentment in the losing partner. The end result being that you both loose because the relationship is damaged. Even when your man is wrong, it's important to allow him to keep his self-respect intact.

Own Your Complaint:

You are in charge of your own world which means that you own your own feelings, thoughts, beliefs and pain. In order to keep confrontation out of the conversation, you need to use "I" statements in the form of the X, Y, Z method which is a widely taught technique of communicating grievances.

If you've never heard of the X, Y, Z method, it's really quite simple. Each letter stands for one piece of the sentence: X is when the Action that you need to discuss occurred, Y is what happened and Z is how you felt.

There are lots of ways of saying this same thing but something along the lines of:

"Honey, (X) _____ when you did/said (Y) _____, I felt (Z) _____."

In a real complaint it would look something like this:

"Honey, last night at dinner(X) when you said you didn't like these shoes(Y), I didn't feel good about myself and I didn't like that feeling.(Z)"

Using this method, you avoid blame and accusation. You take ownership of how you felt and you communicated when that feeling occurred and what caused it.

It may seem easier to analyze your partner than to analyze yourself, but interpreting your partner's thoughts, feelings and motives will distract you from identifying your own thoughts, feelings and motives and will likely invite defensiveness from your man. Besides, telling your man what he thinks, believes or wants is controlling and presumptuous. It is saying that you know your man's inner world better than he does, and no one is a mind reader or that capable.

Instead, work on identifying your needs, feelings, and ways of thinking and describe these needs and feelings to your man in constructive ways that he can process.

Stay On Subject:

Write down the Subject at the beginning to insure you stay on topic, clarify the issue and stay away from the Action. Fighting fair means you both know what issue is being discussed.

Fighting fair means you don't bring up past history. Going into the past puts the focus on being right more than creating change for the future. Remember, you're there to discuss the Subject so don't throw in the kitchen sink. Dragging up all of your past hurts and anger does not help the argument proceed. Most men would find it impossible to respond to every single past insult in one disagreement. If the Subject is money, bringing up the fact that he's not done any of his agreed upon household chores in the last two weeks does nothing.

When the number of problems seems to be accumulating, as will happen in busy relationships, bring them up one at a time. If you have not resolved issues behind past Actions, break them into their Subjects and put them on a future agenda.

Communicate Without Blame:

Most people don't realize they use blame as a strategy when they express their feelings or defend against a spouse's anger. Blame places the responsibility for what you feel, think or did on someone else. Not only is this untrue, it prevents you from resolving the issue.

Anytime you use the words "you" or "because" and certainly "because you" then you are blaming. For example, *"You do that too!"* is a blaming statement. Blaming is a form of Verbal Aggression. It is a form of emotional abuse. As soon as your man feels blamed, things will either escalate into a fight or he'll shut down and walk away... either way you have created distance and the conflict will go unresolved.

An interesting note about blame is that men, by and large, want you to be happy and when you're not happy and you share this feeling the wrong way, your man will interpret that as blame. Since blaming is very toxic and is used for power and control you really have to be careful as even simple statements can be interpreted as blame and lead to big fights.

Listen. Listen. Listen:

Remember the three interruption rule from the previous chapter? No interrupting! Listen. Once your man has finished speaking, repeat back what you heard. Not in his words, but the message you actually received. This will let him know that you understood him and if you didn't, it will allow him to clarify what he meant. It's only when you understand what he says can you step towards solving the problem and your goal. Before you can refute the argument – or even that you disagree with his position, you have to know that you understand his position and he needs to know that as well.

Let one person speak at a time. When one speaks, the other should be listening—really listening, not just planning their rebuttal.

Have you ever tried to work through a difficult issue when your spouse was talking over top of you and interrupting you? How did you feel? Consciously remind yourself about this when you feel an overwhelming urge to interrupt or speak your mind.

When people feel strongly about something, it's only fair to hear them out. Respectful listening means acknowledging their feelings, either verbally or through focused attention. It means never telling someone that he or she "shouldn't" feel that way. It means saving your point of view until after you've let the other person know you understand that they feel intensely about the subject, even if you don't quite get it.

Take turns speaking and listening so that you both have a chance to say what you need.

Ask For Specifics, State Specifics:

Global statements that include the words "always" and "never" get you nowhere and most likely are not true. Besides not being true, "always" and "never" are considered fight escalators. "You never take out the trash!" or "You always forget the dry cleaning!" are comments that are just certain to escalate the argument.

When your partner has complaints, ask to move from global comments of exasperation to specific examples so you can understand exactly what he or she is talking about. When you have complaints, do your best to give your partner specific examples to work with. That's why the X, Y, Z method works so well. It gives a very specific time, place and feeling to discuss.

Disagreements are really great opportunities to understand your man. But in order for that to happen, you have to set being defensive aside and become curious. When you defend yourself you turn the argument into a fight by escalating the anger. Being curious shows your man that you really want to understand his point of view and resolve the conflict.

Find Points Of Agreement:

No matter what Subject you're discussing and how strongly either of you feel about the topic, there almost always are parts that can be points of agreement. If the Subject is Parenting, you can both agree that you love your children and want what's best for them.

Finding points of agreement help you find ways to overcome the area where you disagree. Points of agreement are the foundation of the bridge that connects you both to a solution. When you both know you have things you agree on, it makes the problem seem much smaller.

Seek Resolution:

What is a HUGE problem for you can seem like a minor problem to your man and visa-versa. Something he considers HUGE can be a non-issue for you so it's in your best interest to get a read on how big the problem is. You can ask comparison questions like: "Is this better or worse than the time we had a flat tire on the way to your sister's wedding and couldn't get a tow truck?"

You've already found the points of agreement, now find out exactly where you disagree. Use a phrase like "Please help me understand where you're coming from because I'm confused and I want to understand you."

Make sure your man understands you're there to find a solution so put the focus on him and ask "What can we do to make things better right now?"

Keep Conflicts Private:

Arguments are when you and your man are the most vulnerable in your relationship and because of that, you should never have your arguments in public, in front of friends, family and certainly not in front of your children.

Snide remarks, taunts, inappropriate teasing are all things to avoid. Doing these things in front of others puts your man in a position of either defending himself or appearing weak, and men don't want to experience either.

Airing your dirty laundry in front of others is a sure way to derail a conversation, embarrass your man, break trust, destroy intimacy and ensure that you receive zero cooperation in resolving the conflict.

No Foul Language:

Many people use foul language to make a point or emphasize something they feel strongly about, and there is no doubt that cussing has an impact. In several studies where groups of people were given a message with the only variation being the use of cuss words, the people whose message contained swear words measured the message as "more convincing" than the people whose message contained no swear words.

Having said that, now I'll tell you this: In surveys I did for this book, the vast majority of men thought that when their women swore during an argument she was "extremely angry." When arguing with your man, cussing has the opposite effect, it doesn't make your point, it makes you seem "extremely angry" and that will escalate the argument to fight level.

When arguing, foul language is considered a form of attack. Cussing is designed to keep one from being challenged and is a barrier to productive conversations. Creating a barrier to resolving conflict is not what you want.

No Over-Dramatization:

Women cry. Men know this and understand it. Even knowing this, many men feel completely helpless, speechless and at a total loss as what to do when a woman starts crying. If you're reaching a point where you're ready to cry then things have escalated beyond a point where you should be talking and it's time to take a time-out.

Intentionally using tears and/or crying is manipulative and while it may work once or twice, your man will ultimately feel tricked, used and resentful. This is simply a bad tactic when well spoken discussions will get you far, far more.

No Use Of Force:

This should go without saying, but you would be surprised how often women hit men. I've actually heard women say "He's big, I'm small, it's not like I'm going to hurt him" and "Stop whining, I didn't hurt you!"

To be clear, the use of force includes pushing, shoving, scratching, slapping, hitting, punching a hole in a wall, throwing or breaking things, spitting at/on. Even throwing a pillow is physical violence.

When you use force (and women do), you threaten your man's boundaries and sense of safety and create an environment where your man will not want to have discussions for fear of those discussions escalating out of control, him getting hit, the police getting involved and your and/or his careers being ruined.

You should never, ever use force of any kind during an argument. You should also never tolerate force being used against you.

No Talk Of Ending The Relationship:

Although I said this earlier, talk of ending the relationship is manipulative, abusive and hurtful. It creates anxiety about being abandoned and undermines your ability to resolve your issues. Your man will very quickly lose faith in your commitment to the relationship.

Once that type of trust is broken, it makes a solvable problem seem far bigger than it is and gives your man the sense that he's in the relationship alone. Men will only work under those conditions for a very short time before concluding it's time to move on.

Time Outs:

When things get out of hand and you or your man start breaking these rules or you feel the discussion is, or already has escalated into an argument, then it's time to call a time-out in order to calm down, get perspective and reorganize your thoughts. Depending on both of your needs, time-outs should be at least 30 minutes long and no longer than 24 hours.

Start with a 30 minute time-out and see if you can come back together peacefully. If you can't, then your conversation needs to be about how long you each need and not about why you are so mad. Once you've determined how long you need, established a time, then skip ahead to "The Ending" which is several pages ahead.

During the time out, walk away from each other. Go to different rooms and do whatever it is you need to do to regain calm.

> Don't just get up and walk away or, during the time-out don't leave the house without saying to your partner, "I'll be back."

Take the time during the time-out and try to understand why you feel the way you do and what's making you angry. Come up with a plan for expressing how you feel and why you feel that way using the X, Y, Z method. Think about your man's feelings and try to understand why he may be feeling the way he does.

When you're both ready to continue, come back together and pick up the discussion with your goals and fresh perspective in mind.

When you or your man gets angry, a lot of things start happening inside your bodies. These are physiological changes and are driven by the more primitive parts of your brain. Your brain triggers the release of stress hormones, your heart rate goes up, your adrenalin levels rise, self-preservation kicks your fight or flight response into overdrive and you become more hostile. All of these changes override the rational part of your brain and everything said gets magnified and taken out of context and the argument escalates out of control.

Warning!!!

Never, ever, ever follow a man who has walked away from you in anger! Most men walk away because they're getting ready to lose their temper so following them and continuing the fight is escalating the fight towards physical violence and makes you the aggressor.

It takes at least 30 minutes away from the threat in order for your body's physiology to return to normal and for your brain to click back over from defensive to rational.

Avoid Negative Interpretation:

There are two ways to interpret anything your man says or does. You can either believe that he has good and honorable intentions or you can believe there is some negative hidden meaning behind his actions.

If you believe his intentions are negative, you create an environment where, no matter how hard he tries, he can't be good enough. How long do you think a human being can last in that environment before he stops trying?

Truthfully, when you believe he had the best of intentions, the odds are in your favor that you will be right. Even if you're wrong, your giving the benefit of the doubt is better for resolution than taking the antagonistic approach of thinking the worse.

Men Are Problem Solvers:

A part of ending a fight is solving a problem so it's crucial to look for options and to help him look for options. When you can start cooperating on finding a solution, the fighting will end. Politely asking for suggestions or options invites collaboration as a team. Once options are presented, both parties should give each option careful consideration in order to show that you're respectfully trying to resolve the issue in a meaningful way. Be willing to offer options of your own so that your man knows that you're willing to try new things and the compromises are not all on him. When men perceive things as too one-sided, you'll start to see us become more difficult to deal with.

Make Concessions:

Small concessions can turn the situation around. If you give a little, it makes room for the other person to make concessions too. Small concessions lead to larger compromises. Compromise doesn't have to mean that you're meeting each other exactly 50-50. Sometimes it's a 60-40 or even 80-20 agreement. This isn't about scorekeeping. It's about finding a solution that is workable for both of you.

Be clear on what the new agreements/improvements are. For example, it could be agreed that whenever he seems tense, she will encourage him to tell her about it, instead of their old pattern of retreating into silence.

Resolution:

If you have your goal and have kept it in mind, it should be easy to recognize when you're where you want to be, but resolutions must go both ways. Just because your goal has been met, it doesn't mean your man's goal has been met.

Make sure your man understands that you're where you need to be, but that you want him to feel like the issue is resolved and that you're there to make sure that happens. You do this by putting the focus on him and ask "I have what I need to feel this is resolved, what can I do to make sure this is resolved for you?"

The Ending:

How the two of you end an argument is crucial to how you will view the success of your efforts and how you will view each other in the future. You want this phase to be as kind, supportive and loving as possible.

If your man screwed up and forgot your birthday or anniversary or whatever it was, allowing your man a graceful exit is one of the kindest things you can do and the surest way to make sure he's willing to participate in future problem resolution discussions.

Recognize when he's extending an olive branch. Perhaps he'll make a joke, or apologize. Regardless of what he does, it's essential you recognize the peaceful gesture and that you accept it gracefully. Both people need to be able to walk away with their dignity.

Avoid trying to get the last word in. Having the last word can take away all of the good ground you have gained and leave your man walking away feeling like the conflict wasn't really resolved.

Reconnect with a kiss. Not a peck on the cheek or lips but a real, lovers kiss. If you don't feel like kissing, then the problem is not really resolved for you.

Be grateful and express that gratitude with a "thanks for working through this with me, you're a great partner and I love you."

Circle back around the next day and thank your man for being your partner or remind him how good it feels to resolve problems with him and how it makes you love him more. He will feel deeply appreciated and you're reinforcing that strong bond.

After The Fight:

Once the conflict is resolved, it should never be brought up again. If the same Subject comes up again, then you've either not resolved it or you were talking about the wrong Subject.

If it's resolved, put it in the cemetery and leave it buried.

During these conflict resolution discussions, each of you will reveal vulnerabilities to each other and it's incredibly important that you protect your man's vulnerabilities. If you find that he has an insecurity about something, you never, ever, ever share that with anyone. His vulnerabilities should always be kept safe and private.

Chapter 5

NAVIGATING THE TROUBLE SPOTS

WHAT ARE TROUBLE SPOTS? TROUBLE spots are what messes us up in relationships; it's the mine field we must navigate together. While some spots can be a couple's strength, it's usually the stuff that we argue about and the stuff that ends relationships. This is the stuff that people talk about when they say "we had different values" or "our expectations didn't sync up."

BELIEFS

Have you ever wondered where you get your beliefs? From the moment we're born, we start absorbing information. It comes at us from all directions. Our parents, the most powerful and trusted of all people we'll encounter, give us many of our beliefs; Our teachers impart knowledge but also apply beliefs to that knowledge (girls really are bad at math and science and boys are not as good in writing).

The Man Puzzle

Let's examine a basic belief. When you're a small child, your mother and father held your hand when crossing the street. Why did they do that? Because they didn't want you to get hit by a car! As you grew a little older, they taught you to look both ways before crossing a street and even then to only cross at street corners. Why? Again, they didn't want you to get hit by a car. In reality, that didn't make sense to you because your car was a comfort. It was where you rode, sang songs, played games and spent time with your family. Why it was no more dangerous than your living room. Then, one day you're bigger and dad takes the training wheels off your bike and you're riding up the driveway swerving all over, you can't stop and you crash into the car and get hurt. All of a sudden, you understand that cars CAN hurt you and the belief is born, instilled and becomes fact.

That same process would happen over the hot plate set in front of you at the restaurant. Everyone tells you the plate is hot but it's not until you touch it that you get burned - just like you did with the burner on the stove. When our parents teach us about cars, hot things, running on a wet floor and, through experience we turn their words into beliefs and then into facts, it also makes sense to also turn their other words into beliefs. We learn to believe in God (or not) from our parents, we learn the core of our political beliefs from dad's comments about the news he's watching on TV. If mom taught us the stove was hot, she must also be right about us being bad at math.

As we grow we learn that some things simply aren't true - people don't really walk and make that accordion sound when a piano gets dropped on them like we saw in the cartoons and despite your mother's claim that the "math gene" skipped your family, you're actually pretty good at math. Through studies at school you may learn that some beliefs your family holds are not based on real facts. You may change your beliefs but keep those to yourself or you may learn facts that reinforce a long held family belief.

We also acquire beliefs about how relationships work from watching the adult couples in our lives. We watch our parents, our aunts and uncles, the neighbors when we play at their house or the parents of our friends. We learn from movies, fairytales, from playing with the kids at school, from our first loves to our high school romances. Every romantic encounter adds to our beliefs.

Now the big question, what if one or more of your beliefs aren't true? Could a false belief be preventing you from getting what you want? For instance, what if you've always believed "men don't talk about their feelings" and because of that belief, you've never really tried having deep conversations with men about their feelings? Or what if you have tried and the few times you did, the men closed down and reinforced your belief so you stopped trying?

Here's where it gets really interesting: Researchers have found that the more we defend a belief, the higher our emotional invest-ment is in that belief, and the higher our emotional investment, the less ability we have to change that belief.

You particularly see this played out in politics where one political party says something which is complete rubbish but that party's "true believers" buy into that statement and it becomes one of their beliefs. When the other political party attacks the belief, the "true believers" defend it and the more they defend it, the more entrenched that belief becomes.

The same thing happens with you and your beliefs about men and relationships. The more emotionally invested you are in a belief, the less likely you are to change that belief. Your man feels the same way about his beliefs. This is why arguing with a man about his beliefs is completely counterproductive. The more he has to defend his belief against you, his trusted confidant, the more emotionally invested he becomes in that belief, the more entrenched that belief becomes and less likely he is to change that belief.

Some beliefs are wrong. Believing that your pants will turn invisible when you have to speak in public is wrong. But just because a belief is wrong doesn't mean it's not serving a purpose and that purpose is usually protection from some emotion such as, in public speaking, the fear of failure which would lead to embarrassment and shame.

What happens when one of our beliefs gets destroyed despite our best efforts to keep that belief in tact? What if we had the belief that our man was the most moral man in the world and we walked in and caught him kissing Jennifer, the hot little divorcee from two doors down? We'd not believe our eyes, we'd question if what we saw was what we saw. We'd look to his excuses for ways to believe him. Our whole world would come crashing down because so many of our beliefs had just been shattered. Even our own belief about our beliefs gets brought up for examination and we get angry. We get angry because our whole mind was just sent into turmoil.

What if you believed that your man was the least romantic man on the planet and in order to get flowers for you on your birthday he'd call his sister for help and then one day you find that he, all by himself, planned an extraordinarily romantic trip? Would your belief change or would you continue to believe he was the least romantic man in the world and this was just a lucky shot or that he was doing this because of other reasons (i.e. he's feeling guilty about something)?

Who and what we are is because of what we believe. All of our actions and fears are based on those beliefs, so the thought of changing a belief can become very frightening. This is why it's crucial to understand your beliefs, they drive everything else.

EXPECTATIONS

When you expect something, it means you're looking forward to the probable occurrence of something that you want or think is due or required. Your favorite aunt hasn't missed calling you on your birthday your entire life and you always look forward to talking with her. You expect her to call.

In relationships, an expectation is derived from a strong belief that something will happen, should happen or should have happened.

If you were raised in a single parent house where the parent went from one failed relationship to another, you may have developed a belief that no matter how hard you try, the other person will leave you. Therefore, your expectation when you date is that your date won't hang around for very long. Can you imagine how your beliefs and expectations would dictate your behavior? It may come out as your being emotionally unavailable or, your being extremely clingy and jealous.

On the other hand, you may have been raised in the idealistic two parent house with a mom and dad that were truly loving and supportive of each other and of you. Your father may have always opened doors for your mother, helped her with her jacket and been the perfect gentleman. Growing up like this would lead to you have the belief that all gentlemen are "good guys" or the expectation that a gentleman should always open your door.

And if you were raised in a house with two alcoholic parents who screamed, yelled and threw things at each other day and night and you never experienced what true love is, your beliefs, expectations and behavior would be driven by what you experienced. You may think that a man who drinks, yells and throws things at you is what a loving relationship looks like (it's not!).

Whatever your beliefs, those beliefs generate an entire subset of expectations. Using the tree metaphor again, think of beliefs as the limb and the expectations as all the branches that grow off the limb. Some branches even have smaller branches growing off them. There are a lot of expectations on any grown tree and all those expectations are designed to reinforce our beliefs. When expectations are met, our belief is reinforced but when they're not met, it means the other person has done something to call into question our belief and this leads to trouble.

The Trouble Spots:

Now that we have a basic understanding of where our beliefs originate and what expectations are, let's get in to the "trouble spots" and look at how we choose (or should choose) our partners and the arguments we have with them.

Arguments in relationships occur because expectations have been violated. Either you violated one of his or he violated one of yours. When this happens, the belief associated with that expectation gets called into question then one of you gets angry, something gets said and, well, you know how it plays out. As we discussed in the last chapter on "Resolving Problems: How To Argue," these arguments occur in areas I call "Subjects" and the violation of the expectation is called an "Incident."

What we're going to look at are the Subject areas that men say are the most common causes of arguments in their relationships with women, and what I want you to do is to write down your beliefs and expectations for each of these.

Dating:

Dating is the first trial because you know so little about your man and he so little about you. At this stage, about all you know is that you're attracted to one another and you can have some form of verbal interaction. But where does it go from there?

Who asks whom out? Is it okay for the woman to ask the man out? What if you're a self-assured woman and you don't stand on convention but he's a traditional male who does? Who pays? What does it mean when you ask and you pay? Is he less of a man? What if he doesn't earn nearly as much as you do, do you still expect him to do all the asking and paying?

What about dating etiquette? Does he hold doors open for you? Hold your chair? Help you with your coat? Most every man who's dated in the last 10 years will tell you there are some women who like all these things and other women who will "take your head off" the first time you do something they consider "sexist." (As a side note, the next time you're at a busy coffee shop, watch how many times one man will hold the door open for another. Being polite has little to do with being sexist. This is one of those great examples of beliefs and expectations.)

It's important to sit down with pen and paper and write down your beliefs and your expectations. Do you believe the man should always ask? Do you know where this belief came from? Do you still hold that belief? Make a list of everything that happens on a typical date and write down your belief about that AND your expectation. Do you believe it's okay for your date to eat off your plate? How about for you to eat off his? Is it something you only do after a few weeks or months of dating? Where did that belief come from? If you're against that form of sharing, what is your expectation for when your date does it? What if he does it after you tell him that it bothers you and then winks at you and laughs? What if your date is chronically late? Obviously, there are a lot of details to write down and examine. But if you don't examine these things, how will you know when things are going off the tracks or when you might hold an old belief that you can update?

Bruce, a 50 year old man in Knoxville said this about dating: "It should be kept simple and easy. I don't like going out with women who place a lot of demands or have a lot of expectations. A good date can be a free outdoor concert or grilling burgers in the backyard."

What does that mean? Can anyone wrap their heads around what Bruce was saying about dating? I couldn't until I asked more questions. "Bruce, what does 'simple and easy' mean to you? Bruce was married to a tyrant for 26 years. Bruce's belief about dating is that demanding women are control freaks.

Power And Control:

You often hear conversations about who wears the pants in the house. Wearing the pants is about power and control. The beliefs run from "I'm the queen of this castle and I determine what goes on inside my castle!" to "A man's home is his castle and I'm the king of this castle!"

A lot of men say they're willing to abdicate day to day decisions because, well, we're guys and we just don't want to get involved in all the details. Then, their partner (the woman) believes she's wearing the pants and is off making decisions and then one day "BOOM!" There's a huge fight, and she finds out she's not exactly at liberty to make all the decisions she thought she was. Many men are willing to let the woman take the lead on most things, right up to the point when you suddenly cross a line (violate an expectation) and then he draws a line. The power and control structure has been upset.

Some couples have very balanced power and control structures. One partner takes the lead on some predetermined areas such as bill paying while the other partner takes the lead on managing the investments and they have monthly or quarterly meetings to update each other and review everything.

What are your beliefs about power and control? If you were raised in a devout Christian home you may have the belief that the man is in charge and all decisions he makes are final, or you may have been raised by a dominant mother who ruled with an iron fist. What are your beliefs? How did your parents manage power and control? What about your grandparents? Uncles and aunts? What are your beliefs? Do those beliefs fit with modern times? How do you think power and control should be managed in a marriage? What would be a deal breaker? How would you find out your date or spouse's belief about this?

Religion:

Religion is the greatest example of beliefs and expectations. None of us were alive during the time of Jesus so none of us "know" whether he was the son of God, a good preacher or just a really nice guy. But, based on how we were raised, we have our BELIEF about Jesus. People raised in a Jewish household do not believe Jesus was the son of God, while people raised in a Christian household don't understand how he could be anything less. People raised in agnostic households don't know what to believe, while people raised in atheist households think that anyone who believes in religion is a kook. With each one of those beliefs comes an entire lifetime of emotional investment which makes those beliefs nearly impossible to change.

From each one of those beliefs also stems a whole slew of expectations and those expectations can lead to some terrible, terrible fights when couples come at religion with different beliefs.

147

First, you have family issues around holidays. Where will you spend Easter or Christmas? Whose mother will win, yours or his? How will you raise the kids? Your family believes X and his Y.

What if one of you attends services and the other doesn't? How does that get compromised? What if your Sunday mornings are your sacred jazz and Bloody Mary time and his is sacred family at church time? How will you compromise?

In which church will you get married? Who will officiate? Lots of mixed religion couples have both ministers do a joint service.

Do you think there's any way of you changing his beliefs or him changing yours? Both of your beliefs and expectations have to be understood and compromise and agreements simply have to be made. Both of your families have to be told "no" and no matter the fallout you have to stick to your guns because your relationship with your man is about you and him and not about anyone else and their beliefs and expectations.

Money:

Money is another one of those extremely complex beliefs that's almost as difficult to manage as religion. Both people come to the relationship with different beliefs, different expectations and different needs. One person may be extremely security conscious while the other may go through money like it was water. These mixed relationships can be a constant battle ground and is the reason that money is the leading cause of divorce.

What are your beliefs? Who earns the money? Are you a spend some, save some person? Is he? How much is some? I bet you both have a different understanding of how much "some" is. How much money is too much for a new pair of shoes? How much is too much for a new TV? For new tires? For new dishes? For a new coffee pot?

What if your career takes off and you earn more and he less? This one aspect of money creates a whole slew of problems because, unfortunately, most women (I said MOST not all) still group earnings in with the other variables they use to calculate respect and this obviously breaks when you have a high earning woman coupled with a low earning man (i.e. doctor with a school teacher). The respect vs. money formula might look like this: Respect = Integrity + loyalty + cleanliness + compassion + ability to provide. When one or more of those variables are missing, it doesn't add up to respect.

I met Marilyn and Dave in Chicago. He worked full time as an engineer and had done well for himself. Not a millionaire and certainly nowhere near the top 2% we hear so much about but he had done well. Marilyn tells this story:

Marilyn's Story:

"I got into real estate when the youngest of my kids started school. I never meant for it to be anything more than extra income and a way to "get out of the house" and I was attracted by the flexible hours. One day, while waiting on Dave for a rare weekday lunch I overheard a conversation at the next table wherein a developer was complaining about the unresponsiveness of the real estate agent on the last project and how he didn't want to use them again. I apologized for eavesdropping and handed him my card. Two weeks later he called and after a half dozen meetings I was contracted to lead all the sales efforts. My income went from about $40,000 per year to almost $600,000 in the blink of an eye. Since that first project I've handled 12 more for this same developer and 6 for a few others. I routinely earn well over a $1,000,000 a year in commissions."

And Dave's comments:

"At first this was all exciting and new but soon the reality set in. Marilyn was no longer at home making dinners, I found myself having to pick up sick kids and I was missing work. So many of our roles got upended. Within 6 months she went from a minivan to a Mercedes SUV and our insurance nearly doubled. Everything was in turmoil. Marilyn was constantly tired, I wasn't happy, the kids weren't happy. But, as an engineer I had to be practical. After all, her income in one year paid for our kids college tuition. Marilyn was always easy to talk to so we muscled through this first contract and before the 2nd we sat down and created some new rules that worked for us. We both had to give up on our stereotypical beliefs, reevaluate what was right for us as individuals and our family and we found our own solution. I'm very proud of Marilyn, she's created her own success and she's learned to balance her work and home life better and everyone is happy."

The couples who have navigated this minefield do it with communications because both partners have a lot of beliefs and expectations that must be addressed and for men this can include a sense of inadequacy and shame.

One of the best solutions I saw was Marilyn and Dave. She contributed a salary equal to Dave's and everything else went into a joint savings/investment account that required both signatures for a withdraw. Their lifestyle went up, no one felt superior or inferior and they worked towards a common goal.

What other money beliefs do men encounter? "Money is the root of all evil?" "If we make too much we might forget who we are and become snooty." "What will my family say if I drive that new expensive SUV?" All sorts of beliefs and expectations come up when money comes into the equation.

One thing is certain; arguments about money are never about money! Money can represent Power and Control or it can be tied to a man's ability to provide for his family or your need for financial security. Money conversations become extremely difficult because money discussions access some of our deepest levels of intimacy and vulnerability because real money talks also include talks about our core beliefs, dreams, goals and fears.

This is why it's so important to examine your beliefs. Who's the breadwinner? Do you think you'd be happier if you had more money? How much is "some" from the spend some save some mentioned earlier? What is a "rainy day" to you? Does your partner have the same definition of a rainy day? You might think a rainy day is unemployment and he might think it's a busted TV during football playoffs! What are your dreams? Your goals? Your financial fears?

If these things are not understood and resolved, you can expect lots of arguments along the way.

Child Rearing:

You were raised one way, your man another. You may have grown up in the same town, attended the same schools and even the same church but you were still raised differently. Because you were raised differently you both bring your own ideas, beliefs and expectations about how a child should be reared.

What is your belief about fighting in front of the kids? What's your belief about you and your man showing affection in front of the kids? What kind of affection? Deep, passionate kissing, or simple handholding? Where is your line? Where's his line? How about yelling at the kids? Is it allowed? If you think it's okay to yell but your man hates it, do you know why? How will you discipline the kids? Will it be physical discipline such as spankings or be emotional discipline like timeouts? Who takes off work when the kids are sick? Who travels? What if both of you have to be out of town at the same time? What if you promised the kids a puppy and your man is dead set against a dog? What if the child is born with a deformity or other special need and one parent is suddenly required to stay home? Who will that be?

If you already have kids, you know how difficult parenting can be and how some of these issues can be very difficult to navigate. More than one marriage has ended because the parents were on two completely different parenting pages. During the divorce one parent did everything they could to keep the kids away from the other simply because they disagreed so vehemently with the other parent's methods. In the end, the courts allow both parents equal access and the only looser in such battles are the children. If you're single, it's a really a good idea to understand both you and your partners beliefs and expectations because once you're married and have kids, it's a little too late to wake up and say "how could I have been so wrong!"

When the children are teenagers or grown, how will you handle boundaries? If one child turns into a drug addict, what will you do? If one is always borrowing money, how will you handle it?

Obviously, when it comes to parenting there are a lot of beliefs inside of the core belief of "parenting" and each of those beliefs have expectations. Can you define yours? Are your kids grown? How will your new husband interact with your grown children? How will you interact with his? Even when you think this issue is "off the table" it's still an issue.

Sex:

During sex in a relationship is when we become the most vulnerable. It's when all our dark little secrets start coming out, it's when we're afraid that what we think is "normal" might be considered "perverted" by our partner. It's when we're frightened that what we might think or say or how we look or a sound we make might be taken the wrong way or lead to some unknown area. Regardless of what fears or beliefs we bring to our relationships, sex expresses and deepens the love between a man and a woman.

The only person who doesn't have a hard held belief about sex is the person who has never had sex and even then, they think they have hard beliefs. If you were raised in a strict religious environment, the thought of sex before marriage may make you shudder in fear. After marriage, you may believe that only one position is allowed during sex and that sex, for any reason other than procreating, is wrong.

Lily, a 38 year old divorcee in Atlanta shared this story:

"I was raised with the belief that sex was bad and that even talking about sex would send you straight to hell. Obviously, this hindered my development, not just as a woman but as a wife. To call me sexually reserved was an understatement. In fact, even the word 'prude' was too generous. After I got married, our sex life was dismal and I could see that my husband was truly dissatisfied, and that, more than anything, hurt me to my core. I felt like such a failure. Finally, I spoke to my doctor who suggested I talk to a sex therapist and he recommended one within my same faith. Secretly, mostly out of shame, I started seeing this therapist. She was a wonderful woman and very understanding of how I was raised and my beliefs. She gave me a list of new things to try and suggested that I pick something new from the list each and every week, experiment and then she and I would discuss it the following week. I learned, through trial and error, not only what I liked but what my husband liked. I grew as a woman and as a wife. I was able to leave my old beliefs behind. I was not going to burn in hell for discussing sex with my husband nor was I going to hell for enjoying sex. That was utter nonsense and I have no idea why my family, or any family, would teach such a thing!

On the other hand, if you were raised in a commune by pot smoking hippies, you may believe that sex is a natural and open process that can be freely shared among any combination of men and women. Some couples are avid swingers participating in wife swapping while others bristle when their mate is even looked at.

How should you communicate your needs, desires to your man? How should he communicate them to you?

Stanley, a 55 year old man told this story:

"Sex was boring. It was predictable in ways you can't even imagine. I could tell she wanted sex just by what we had for dinner. Everything was scripted from the dinner to the wine to every aspect of the evening. It was so predictable that I used to mess with the script just to see what would happen. I would change where we sat, I would change the music, I would do things to disrupt the script just to see what would happen and try to get some variety. When we did finally head for the bedroom, that too was scripted. Everything between the sheets was always the same and what's worse, the minute she had her orgasm, she was done. It was, by far, the most unsatisfying sexual experience of my life and she complained that I was too adventurous. It got to be so boring that I once fell asleep right in the middle. I tried talking to her about our sex life but that went nowhere so we ended up in a sexless relationship and eventually parted company."

Obviously we had two people with two entirely different sets of beliefs and expectations about sex.

What are your beliefs about sex? Do you know what you want in a partner? Do you believe you should have sex as often as possible or just once a month or so? Does it have to be great sex that leaves you walking around mindless and muttering to yourself all day or is something less awesome satisfactory? Are you one for routine or exploration? How will you share fantasies? Will you role play and if so, which roles and which roles are off limits? What happens when work and life gets in the way and you're too tired? Does sex with your man suffer? How about when he's too tired? What happens when you've put on a few pounds and you're not feeling very attractive? What will you do when your man comes home with a pair of handcuffs? And wants you to cuff him to the bed? Do you believe in sex with the lights off or broad daylight with the windows and curtains open? (I would bet if you asked your man these questions you would find that he'd like a lot more experimentation!)

Politics:

What are your political beliefs? Are you a Republican? An extreme conservative? A Democrat? An extreme liberal? Do you follow politics or are you in the camp of "they're all crooks and it doesn't matter so why bother?" Does it bother you if your man gets all worked up over politics? Do you share his views or oppose them? Can you have a conversation about politics without it ending in yelling or screaming matches? How important is it to you that your man share your political beliefs? If you volunteer for political candidates and often show up at political rallies you may not want a man from a different political party or one who doesn't follow politics at all.

What are your beliefs about the death penalty? Is that a religious issue, moral issue or political issue? Do you have room for compromise in your political beliefs? What happens when an extreme conservative in your own party gets arrested with illegal drugs or child pornography? Does that change your views? What happens when an extreme liberal gets arrested for domestic violence or shooting someone with a gun? Does that change your views? What will change your views?

Health:

What are your beliefs about health and fitness? About smoking? Are you a health nut or a couch potato? Do you eat a strictly vegan diet or cram down whatever you can get your hands on? Are their limits to your alcohol intake? Do you smoke pot or take other drugs?

Changing A Man:

This one Subject area came up in almost every session with every group of men. It was the one thing above all others that men cited as making them feel the "least loved, respected, desired and wanted."

Do you believe you have a God given right to change a man? Too "fix" all his bad habits? Do you believe "no man is perfect" and "all men must be changed in order to live with them?" What are your beliefs about acceptance and where do you draw the line on changing someone? Will you try to change him because he squeezes the toothpaste tube differently or will you just buy a separate tube?

Most men accept that when it comes to living with a woman, some things have to change but they recognize that change has to come from both sides. He doesn't want his old holey t-shirts thrown out, and he wants his movie collection where he can get to it.

If you want a man to change, it will only happen if there is a direct and identifiable benefit to him and that benefit isn't getting you "off his back!" The more you try to change a man, the more distance you will put between you and him.

Darryl, an architect in Los Angeles told this story:

"I have one of the shortest marriages in the history of marriages. The dating was awesome, the engagement even better. The wedding was flawless and the honeymoon was storybook but the moment we returned from our honeymoon the problems started. Everything that was fine for 3 years suddenly became a problem that needed 'to be fixed.' After 3 months of not being able to do anything right from morning till night, I asked for a divorce. No one could stand to live with that much criticism and complaining! What's funny is that I later heard from a mutual friend that my ex said 'Those things always bothered me but I thought I could change him!' I was willing to compromise on some things but no one wants to be bullied into changing!"

Changing The Rules:

Every relationship has rules. In healthy relationships, most rules are discussed and agreed upon, but even in the best of relationships, there are also unspoken rules. Unspoken rules usually occur when the two of you are out and about and witness something and one of you detects the others dislike for what you saw. Nothing gets said but it's apparent that what happened was not liked. It doesn't even have to be anything that one of you did; it can come from something another person or couple did. Since it was never discussed, this becomes an unspoken rule.

An example might be sitting in a restaurant and watching a pregnant woman lick her ice cream bowl. While you may want to laugh hysterically and buy her more ice cream, your man may be repulsed by the lady's actions and you decide to let things go. "No licking of ice cream bowls" then becomes an unspoken rule.

The Man Puzzle

No matter what the rule is or whether it's spoken or unspoken, we're all entitled to change. The rule, for all of well meaning may no longer suit you or may even limit your growth. You have a right to speak with your man and request a rule change.

People don't like change and most people are incredibly resistant to change. This doesn't mean you're not allowed to change or grow but that the entire rule needs to be renegotiated. Just remember, the change may meet resistance.

What men don't like are rule changes without a conversation and a new understanding.

Barb in Memphis explains changing the Agreement:

"The agreement was on Wednesday nights I would work later and then go straight to yoga class and he would feed the kids, make sure their homework was done and get them ready for bed and I was usually home around 7:15. This worked fine for about 5 months then one night me and some of the ladies went for wine after yoga. I texted my husband and he said 'No prob! Enjoy!' The next thing you know, wine after yoga became a Wednesday evening ritual and I was coming in at 8:45, just barely in time to tuck the kids in. After a month or so of wine we started having dinner and then I'd be 10:00 p.m. getting home and after three of those I was met by a very angry husband. I had changed the rules and he felt very taken advantage of. It really was unfair because I had a real problem with him going out with the guys after work. We needed a new set of rules and after we talked through it, I would keep my wine nights and be home by 9:00 and after dinner on Monday he would get Monday Night Football with his buddies. In all we both got the same amount of 'time away' and got to do something we both enjoyed and what was even better was the kids ended up with new Monday and Wednesday night routines that were unique to each parent."

What are your beliefs about changing the rules? Do you think you should just be able to make a change or that you should come to new agreements with your man?

Compromise:

Compromise is reached by each side making concessions. When you're having a battle of beliefs and expectations where Incidents are triggering the same arguments time and again, it's time to find a way to compromise and the only way to do that is for each party to come to the table with an understanding of their beliefs and expectations, and to figure out where the conflict resides and where each party can give and the center can be reached.

In business there is a process called Gap Analysis. Gap Analysis can be used to compare expected performance against desired performance, but it can also be used to compare two similar products for differences. You might do this when you need to buy a new coffee maker or refrigerator. You look at all the products in your price range, compare features, make trade-offs perhaps sacrificing the insulated carafe for the timer so your coffee is made automatically. The same process is what you go through when it's time to compromise on a difficult belief/expectation Subject. You both write down your beliefs, cross out the areas where you're in agreement, put stars next to your top two deal breakers, and what's left is where you compromise.

If it sounds easy, it's only because the problem has a process, getting through the process is not easy, it doesn't happen in one conversation but the growth, teamwork, trust and end result is more than worth the effort.

Respect:

In relationships, you often hear people talk about respect. "That was disrespectful." or "He just didn't respect me!" and even "What she did on our date was so disrespectful that I never want to see her again!" Respect is "not knowingly and willingly violating your partner's expectations." When your partner has an expectation that you be on time for your dates and you know this but you're still constantly late, you are being disrespectful.

"My man absolutely respects me!" "My wife is very respectful of me." This is what you hear when people are partnered with someone who has not only taken the time to understand their own beliefs and expectations but also their partner's. It comes from hard work, a lot of pain and more than a little bit of frustration.

Chapter 6

GETTING READY TO DATE

D O YOU WANT TO BE in a relationship or spend your life with a really good man? That's an interesting question and, although the answer should be obvious, often it's not. The problem is, on the other half of the relationship is a human being. He's spent about the same time on this planet that you have, he has parents, family, friends, needs, goals and dreams. He wasn't put here to satisfy your every need, he's not a prop in some Broadway play to be displayed, showed off and used to make a point. He's not here to fulfill your or your family's idea of the perfect husband, father or son-in-law. If you want all those things, you will never find them. He doesn't exist anymore than unicorns do.

In order to be happy with a man, then your heart, body, mind and spirit have to naturally adapt to their happiness and theirs to yours. That level of adaptation doesn't come without sacrifice and if you or he isn't ready and/or able to make the kind of sacrifice needed for true happiness together, then one or both of you are simply not ready.

You can't control whether or not he's ready but you can control whether or not you're ready. This chapter contains some of the "reasons" I've heard from women all over the country as to why they're not dating. When I hear one of these reasons, it just tells me they're not ready and making excuses for themselves. Mind you, there's nothing wrong with being "not ready" but there is something wrong in not recognizing it and owning it and, instead, making excuses for it.

Curry's Paradox:

A "paradox" is a statement or proposition that, despite apparently sound reasoning from logical assumptions, leads to one or more conclusions that seem senseless, logically unacceptable, or self-contradictory. So, a paradox means that somewhere someone's ability for sound reasoning has gone off track and, to everyone other than that person, their conclusion seems to be completely silly. A simple form of Curry's Paradox says that if the first part of a statement is true then the last part must also be true.

Curry's paradox: *"If this part of the sentence is true, then Unicorns exists."*

Example: *"I'm a good man so J. Lo. will want to date me."*

Enter Curry's paradox in dating! Because "I'm a good man" (that part of the sentence is true) then logic dictates that "J. Lo. will want to date me!" Of course, any logical person would hear me say that and think I was insane (J. Lo., I promise I'm not!)!

Truthfully, I have nothing... and I mean ABSOLUTELY NOTHING to contribute to J. Lo. That doesn't mean I wouldn't love to go out with her and it certainly doesn't mean I'm not a great catch! What it means is that, realistically, I have nothing to contribute to her. I have no fame, no fortune, no understanding of the inner workings of her world and no astonishing good looks.

So, holding out for J. Lo or someone like her would be completely senseless.

My point? What I'm saying is that when you're looking for a date, are you being realistic about who you are and who you can attract? Do you understand the intellectual, emotional, spiritual and, yes, physical value you bring to the relationship? Can you survive in their world and share experiences in a meaningful way?

I'm certainly not suggesting that anyone settle for anything or anyone less than they deserve. What I'm saying is that having the wrong expectations will (as you'll learn later in this book) lead to disappointment, failure and lower self-esteem. Are your expectations setting you up for failure?

DATING MYTHS

All The Good Men Are Taken:

Really? First, let's discuss how insulting that belief is. There are lots of single men and they're single for the same reasons women are; They divorced because they grew apart from their wives or the wives cheated; their exes were involved in drugs or alcohol; their kids are grown and after being in a loveless and sexless marriage they decided to move on; they're widowers. Just like you and why you're single, there is a man who is single for the same reason. If your reason for being single is a good one, then there are men who also have a good reason.

Now, let's do the math: In 2012, the last year for which there were any kind of census data available, the United States had about 115 million households of which 76 million were families and of which 56 million of those were married couples. That means that 20 million of those families were unmarried singles with kids, and that breaks down as 15 million were single (custodial) moms and 5 million were single (custodial) dads.

About 1/3 of all U.S. households, or 39 million, were single households. Of these 39 million, approximately 32 million of these consisted of one person living alone and the other 7 million were roommates and boarders. The numbers were pretty evenly split between age groups with the exceptions of the 25-34 year olds in which case there are a much higher number of single males living alone than single females.

In the USA, roughly half of all people are single and roughly half of those are males, so you're saying that in that 25% of the population there are no good men left? Not one?

I Already Had My One Shot:

I heard this statement quite frequently from widows, and it was a sign they were not yet through the grieving process and not quite ready to be out there. The belief that there is only one person for you and no one else could ever fit you the way your former spouse did is just not true. No one will ever be like your former spouse. They will be different and in surprising ways, with some of those ways being worse and some better. Since you're wiser and have more experience, the odds are in your favor that you'll even find someone more suited to you!

I also heard this from women who had been married 30, 40 years and ended up divorced. When I dug a little deeper into the reason for the divorce, I would always hear some form of remorse and regret for not having done things differently.

From the male perspective (logical and problem solving), I say two things: 1) You already found true love once and that means you can do it again; 2) You already know the consequences of your mistakes, you won't repeat them (or shouldn't!) and that means you will also make better choices up front.

Dating Guys Is Too Much Trouble:

Dating is a skill. If it's too much trouble you probably haven't developed your skills, done enough work on yourself and are making poor choices or you're simply not ready.

The questions you need to ask yourself are these: Have you learned anything about men along the way or have you just met with heartache after disappointing heartache? Do you understand each choice you made and why you made it?

Finding the right guy for you is not easy and it's not easy for him to find you either (and trust me, he's looking!). For every bad story you have, he has one just like it. It won't be easy and you're supposed to experience heartache along the way. That's a part of the process and how we learn about what we want, don't want, will give and not tolerate and, in general, prepare ourselves for when we do meet the right one.

I Only Date Mr. Perfect:

Perfection is an illusion. It can't be found and it can't be given. Just like there are no unicorns, there is no Mr. Perfect! This falls into one of those unreasonable expectation categories.

"But 8 years ago I dated this guy and trust me when I tell you, he WAS perfect!" No he wasn't! If he were, someone would have snatched him up long before you met him or you'd still be with him. You're not, he wasn't.

My Girlfriends Give Me Everything I Need:

This was the one excuse that I struggled with most and I struggled because I know many really great men who don't date because they're extremely happy as they are so, on one level I get this. But let's dig a little deeper.

There are numerous studies which show that women with strong female friendships are happier, have better self-esteem and think of themselves as prettier than similar women who don't have good, supportive female friendships.

In other studies, it has been found that women under stress tend to surround themselves with their females friends and in doing so release oxytocin which is the "feel good hormone." It seems as though oxytocin combats the body's normal flight or fight response and the more time you spend nurturing and being nurtured by your female friends, the better you handle stress. The flip side is that women without solid, supportive female friendships also suffer the same health risks as women who're smokers or overweight.

Obviously, no man will ever be like your best girlfriend. Ever! And if you have this expectation, all men will fail this test. We're not designed nor intended to be just like you and we're not designed to be "one of the girls" and on some level you know this, which is why you're reading this book. What's missing? What's missing is understanding what your needs are and which needs are met by the different people in your life.

The kicker to all this occurred when I talked to women who used this "reason" for not dating and asked them about the men they did have in their lives and all had men in their lives that they depended on for various things. There was a male relative or neighbor who fixed things; there was a male relative, neighbor or friend they took to work events or weddings; their was the "friend with benefits" because "a girl has needs you know". All of these women had managed to piece together a boyfriend from different men instead of finding one man to build a partnership with, and none of them were aware that they had done so. They simply believed all their needs were being met by their female friends.

Men Are Liars, Cheats And Are Only After Sex:

This is another of those "offensive reasons" and it makes me ask "So you know of no men that are good, kind and upstanding members of the community? Not your father, brother, uncle, cousin, pastor, boss? Not one single man?" This type of defense mechanism stems from very, very bad experiences with men and you need to take the time to recalibrate yourself.

If you were so deeply hurt that you actually believe this, you probably should seek counseling and work through the healing process with a trained professional. You'd be amazed at what happens when you can look at why you chose him, what signs you missed, what lessons you should learn and acknowledge that you did your very best or, if you failed in some area, acknowledge your failure and work to not repeat it. Then, in the end, let it go.

When you're ready and it's time to recalibrate yourself, get involved in more male oriented charities such as Habit for Humanity or volunteering at a family shelter. Don't jump out and start dating, instead get to know the men involved. You will meet dozens of fine men that will open your eyes to what a good man looks like! Allow good men to change your perspective. If you choose to see them, they're all over the community doing everything from coaching little league to delivering food to the homeless or elderly.

I Want Someone Interesting:

This was one of those excuses that I heard repeated often and, more often than not, the person who said it was very uninteresting and was looking for an interesting man to liven up her own life. Here's a bit of a sad news: interesting men date interesting women, and interesting men get lots of opportunities to date those interesting women.

Are you interesting? Are you doing interesting things? What is the most interesting thing you have done? Have you lived abroad? Gone hang gliding? Skydiving? Climbed Machu Picchu? Walked the Great Wall? How about the Walk of Santiago de Compostela? (I have a single, retired guy friend who's done it three times!)

If you're doing interesting things, you will meet interesting men! The key is to not mistake unpredictability for excitement and interesting and do not ever mistake drama for passion.

I Live In A Small Town:

"There aren't any single men here." Which I always find funny because usually earlier in the day or the previous day I had met with a group men, many single, several always in the dating range of the lady saying this. In one particular case, I asked the lady if she could name the professions of the last 6 men she had gone out with and she did. Not one matched up with the professions of the single men I had just met with. In my group, one was a doctor, one an accountant, one a plumber... you get the picture. All were very nice men, very articulate, successful and available and this lady hadn't dated any of them!

This excuse comes with several variations: "Everyone knows me because of my work so my options are limited" is what I heard from one local judge. There are no single men outside of your profession? No business people? No medical professionals? No firemen? Are you using your advanced position to block someone without your level of success from your life?

And again, I say do the math. In every census tract which has roughly 4,000 people, about 1/2 are single and 1/2 of those are men. While it's true that the higher up the beanstalk you go, the thinner the air becomes (the more successful you are, the fewer dating options you have). Just because someone doesn't earn the bucks you do, it doesn't mean he's not a good man and not successful in what he does. If men took the attitude that women had to earn as much as they did before they would date them, the human race would have died off decades ago.

Kathy in New Orleans tells this story:

"I had long ago noticed Jason. He was good looking, well spoken and polite but he arrived at every event with a different woman so I wrote him off as just another player.

At one event I found myself in line behind Jason's "date du jour" so, in an attempt to make conversation, I asked her how long they'd been dating and his date laughed and said 'He's my brother-in-law, usually one of his sisters comes with him but they weren't available so I'm the stand-in. Jason hasn't gone on a date since his wife died 4 years ago! He did recently mention that he was thinking of getting back out there, would you like me to introduce you?' I was completely stunned! I told Jason's date/sister-in-law that Jason and I knew each other and I had always thought he was handsome and nice. She told me she'd pass on that "I was interested" and about 30 minutes later, yep! Jason asked me out!

Men Don't Want Relationships:

It's not fair to lump all men into one category. Yes, there are men who don't want relationships and they don't want a relationship for some of the same reasons I'm listing here. Plus, you have those who just got out of a bad relationship, their company is transferring them in 4-6 months and they don't want to start something and then get hurt or hurt someone when it's time to move. The key is to date and learn to listen or just flat out ask them what they're looking for. Besides, think of it this way, if you were sitting in the break room at work and a colleague asked you how "dating life" was and just as you spoke the words "I don't date. Men don't want relationships!" a magnificent hunk of man walked into the break room, what do you think his impression of you would be? If your colleague had a single guy friend, do you think your colleague would want to introduce you if that were your attitude about men? Yikes!

Nurse Or Purse:

During my interviews, I heard several successful women say "all men are just looking for a nurse or a purse." I can't even begin to describe how offensive and negative this attitude is and it certainly explains why these women are only finding wounded men. Good men run from these attitudes.

I Have No Time For Dating:

Lots of people lead busy lives and sometimes we hit a patch where work and other obligations simply leave no time for dating. The truth of the matter is, you will make time for your priorities and if other things are your priority (and I suspect they're not because you're reading this book) then you absolutely should focus on those things but not to the point where you can't date or can't participate in your marriage. If you're truly not ready, then, as

I have said before, it's okay to not be ready but take ownership of it because only by taking ownership can you recognize and take the steps necessary to get you ready.

Participation is Key!

There are plenty of dating sites so sign up on two and make it a point to go on at least ONE coffee date every week and attend one singles event either through the dating site or through Meetup. com or one of the other social networking sites. There are tons of singles activities happening all around you and you should be participating!

Chapter 7

MEN AND DATING

Let's face it, when it comes to men and dating, most women are perplexed. What's going on? What does he want? Is he serious or just playing around? It's complex, tricky, confusing and often times painful. Honestly though, it really it doesn't need to be. Dating can be enjoyable, easy and funnier than anything you could ever imagine. So, let's take the pressure off!

In this chapter, I'm going to try to help you understand what the dating process is about and what you can do to make sure you navigate these initial waters well. Mostly, it's all about perspective and, well, understanding some of the ways that men think and dispelling some of the awful and terrible myths that surround men and dating which can help bring joy to what used to be a rather painful process.

If you've done your work from the "Are You Ready To Date" chapter you should be beyond the "all the good men are taken" and other nonsensical beliefs about men so now lets look at some other myths.

172

He Owns A Dog And Other Myths About Men:

In my opinion, one of the greatest sources of bad information about men comes from articles in women's magazines written by women about men. I've read articles that said that men who own dogs are not afraid of commitment and men who wear white socks make good husbands and the list of nonsense goes on and on. The truth of the matter is that men who own dogs have made a commitment to <u>their dog</u> but that doesn't mean he will commit to you. And that nonsense about white socks… well, let's just say that dating or marrying a man based on what he does or doesn't wear is just plain crazy.

The reality is quite simple: every single man is a good man and every single man is willing to make a commitment and every single man will make a good husband. He may not be right for you; he may not commit to you; and he may not make a perfect husband for you, but for someone else, he will be the love of their life. For that reason alone, you should make it a personal policy to "do no harm" during the dating process. Someday, he will be someone's husband and the father to her kids (who may grow up to marry one of your kids). Don't leave her to deal with scars that you inflict. As we get through this chapter, you'll understand more about why this approach will serve you well.

Understanding Your Need:

Before any "mission" you need to have a battle plan and that plan must include a full inventory of your assets. I'm not saying that dating is war as it certainly shouldn't be, but without having an inventory of your assets, needs, values and beliefs, then you have no hope of meeting anyone remotely worth your time without blind dumb luck being a factor. If you're relying on some romantic notion that fate will intervene, fate may have intervened dozens of times and because you weren't equipped, you let that man walk right past you.

In a previous chapter, we examined our beliefs about money, religion, kids, family, sex, respect, dating, chores and all the other "Trouble spots" and those should have given you some ideas about your needs in these areas. Without knowing your needs, you really can't determine whether a man is or isn't a good fit. Beyond being compatible in the core areas, can you describe the type of man you are physically drawn to? Can you name your physical and emotional deal breakers? I would suggest making a list and determining what you like, don't like, must have and can't have. Start by looking at your past relationships and listing the qualities that you liked in each man, the qualities you didn't like and those that started off as amusing and ended up being annoying,

I interviewed a woman in Atlanta who told me that she could deal with almost any physical attribute from a pony tail to a bald head but could not tolerate a weak chin. While another lady said she could handle a heavy drinker but not total abstainer. We all have our give and takes, what we'll accept and our deal breakers. This is an incredibly important exercise because, after all, unless you know these things, you could meet Mr. Perfect tomorrow and not even know it.

The Perfect Man:

I have heard it countless times, "I want the perfect guy!" and each time I hear this I cringe. Not only is there no such thing as "the perfect guy!" but seeking perfection in ourselves or in others is, essentially, taking the express lane to damaged self esteem. Since we can never achieve nor find perfection, when we seek it we get caught in a never-ending cycle of disappointment which leads to unhappiness and each failure makes us feel more and more unworthy.

Men and Dating

This following story has been told to me countless times, in dozens of cities by amazingly wonderful women. I met Maria in San Francisco as a member of a group of "successful single women" that had agreed to meet with me. Maria is a beautiful, 34 year old doctor who, by all appearances is the total package of beauty, brains, heart, compassion and class. Someone who should certainly be able to take her pick of most any man she wants.

Maria

"I first met James at a medical seminar here in San Francisco. He was my age, ruggedly handsome and we shared a lot of interest. We dated for two months and it became clear that our religious differences would eventually get in the way (I'm Catholic, he's Jewish).

A few months after I broke up with James, I met Luis when he came to my house to remodel my bathroom. Luis was very smart and had a very successful home remodeling business. We seemed to fit like a hand in a glove but he just didn't like getting dressed up and attending some of the classier things I liked to do. Eventually this became a problem for me.

About a year later I was on a singles cruise and met Mark, an attorney from Silicon Valley. Mark was not only good looking but also the funniest man I had ever met. For 3 months he kept me laughing and we had so much fun together but, in the end, he was looking for the perfect woman and for him that was a stay-at-home mom."

I don't advocate settling at all but certainly there are plenty of couples who manage to raise their children in both faiths, plenty of couples who manage to compromise on activities and plenty of couples who manage their work and parenting responsibilities. However strongly Maria felt about these things, had she been aware of her needs she could have asked good questions early in the dating process and saved herself months and months of dating men who didn't fit her needs or, whose needs she didn't fit.

I tell you this because it's extremely important to truly understand that perfection doesn't exist in ANY man OR woman and if you don't know your absolute deal breakers, you can spend untold hours chasing "unicorns jumping over rainbows." Besides, perfection would be boring. We need some flaws and imperfections to make life interesting and to allow us to grow and mature.

Are You Attractive Enough?

One of the most frequent comments I hear from women is that men only want models and young skinny girls. While I find this notion amusing I can tell you nothing is further from the truth. In fact, some of the loneliest women I know are extremely beautiful. The truth of the matter is that a man just wants to be proud to have you by his side and model quality beauty is not a requirement for that pride. However, what is important is that you take pride in your own appearance.

One of the greatest insights I've ever heard came from my Grandmother, who, after hearing a teenaged female relative complaining (yet again) that her hair was too thin, her boobs were too small, she was too short and every other flaw she imagined she had. My grandmothers words were softly spoken with this great southern drawl: "Every pot has a lid!" and what she meant was that for every flaw you can find in yourself, somewhere there is a man who thinks those very flaws are the greatest thing he has ever seen. Instead of beating yourself up, celebrate who you are and recognize that you are 1000 times more beautiful when you like yourself than when you are critical of yourself.

Having said that, I'm going to seemingly contradict myself a little in this next statement, one of the most frustrating things about men is this: Generally speaking, if a man is not attracted to you, he could care less how great and wonderful you are as a person. However, once a man is in love with you, he could care less about what you look like.

Back when I was married, my ex-wife and I had 4 children together and, as some women do, she packed on some extra weight. One day, while at the soccer fields watching one of our young kids play, a friend that I'd not seen since early in my marriage and I were standing on the opposite side of the field when he looked across and saw my wife and commented that she'd really "packed on a few pounds." I had no clue what he was talking about and when I looked up I was surprised that my wife had gotten big but then I saw the years of our marriage, the love, the four wonderful children she'd given me and those extra pounds just disappeared and, instead, what I saw was the woman I loved and who loved me. Believe it or not, most men are this way.

Now, this doesn't mean you should let yourself go, it means that you shouldn't sweat the small stuff and you shouldn't obsess over your flaws. (And just as a note, about a year later my ex-wife decided to lose that weight and less than 12 months into her journey she competed in a body building and fitness competition where she finished in fourth place!)

Putting your best foot forward, doing your nails, going the extra mile with your hair tells men that you value yourself, and if you value yourself then, we'll look closer. A woman who doesn't value herself will most likely not get a second glance and if she does, it won't be the kind of glance that any woman really wants.

WHAT HE'S LOOKING FOR

A Man's Outer Needs:

The bottom line is that every man's outer needs are different and just because you see a man with one type, doesn't mean you're not his type. I once had a friend named David, and he was never seen with a woman who was less than a DD cup. Not once, not ever. That was, right up until he met the woman who became his wife and she would have been lucky to fill an A cup. All of his friends were surprised! The lesson here is, even a man with a pattern of picking one certain type of woman will deviate when the right one comes along.

I remember David telling me that his wife had met a couple of his former girl friends and had commented on how inadequate she felt by comparison. And this leads me to my final comment on the subject of looks: If he's with you he must find you attractive. So relax and stop fretting over what you think your flaws are and how you compare with other women. Instead of focusing on your flaws and insecurities, accept and embrace them as something that makes you unique and desirable to him and then focus on the important part of the relationship which is getting to know your man.

A Man's Inner Needs:

When it comes to the inner needs, this is when things get really interesting. In the 1000's of men that I've interviewed about wives or potential wives, the qualities most often listed as "required" are: Kindness, loyalty, fidelity, dependability, intelligence, good health and attractiveness (that 'extra mile" of good grooming we talked about earlier increases your appearance of good health and attractiveness).

Think about that list for a moment. What was first? Kindness! Second? Loyalty and Fidelity! And third? Dependability! Look at the male priorities and how these might differ from what you were expecting! No man wants to date or marry a mean woman. No man wants to date or marry a woman who is not loyal to him. No man wants to date or marry a woman he can't depend on. You can continue to work your way right down that list and conclude with this: No man wants to date or marry a woman HE doesn't find attractive (which is very different from what you may think about yourself!).

Meeting Men:

Of course one of the fundamental problems in dating men is that you first have to meet men and although this seems daunting at first, it's really quite simple once you recognize this one truth: **There are no eligible bachelors hiding under your bed!** You have to get out, go places and do things in order to meet men!

Of course the best question is where do you go to meet single men? It's simple, you go where your interest are! With the exception of shoe shopping, which I hear is both a sport and a hobby, you can find men doing and enjoying almost anything you would care to do. Want to learn a foreign language? I bet there will be at least one single man in the class if not five. Want to learn to SCUBA dive? I bet there will be more than a few single men in the class and certainly several on the boats. Want to learn to paint? I'd bet better than even odds there will be more than one single man in the class. So what IF there are no single men in the class? You're still doing something that makes you happy and something that makes you more interesting to men. You can't lose!

It's always best to meet a man who has an interest similar to yours. You immediately have a common interest which can be used to start conversations, generate laughter and bond over. Even if the guys you meet are not matches for you, they have single friends and you have single friends. Expand your network, have social or cocktail hours and invite people from both of your social circles and see what happens. I've personally been to several mixers where you must bring either a same sex single person or an opposite sex single person. These mixers are always a complete blast!

There are studies which show that 60% of married couples met through a married friend or through a dinner or cocktail party at a married friend's house. When you ask married people about which singles they invite the answers are pretty consistent: "I invite people who fit in with my married friends." What does this mean? It's people who have more of a home life, who don't hang out in bars, aren't seen with a different date at every turn and who have left the party life behind them. Most married couples will tell you they're very careful about who they invite but that they also want to spread "the happiness." Married people typically like being married, and they want to share that happiness with their friends. If you're being invited to a lot of couple's parties, be thankful; you're being viewed quite highly. If you're not getting those invitations, you have work to do!

Bars And The Witching Hour:

Bars, for whatever reason, are an extremely popular place to meet people. Yes, it's fun to go dance and fun to be out with other people who're also out to have a good time but, by and large, bars are an extremely bad place when it comes to meeting someone for a serious relationship.

In theory, bars place you in a similar socio-economic place as the men you want to meet along with being with people who want to have fun and enjoy similar music. But the reality is often far worse. To begin with, alcohol clouds your judgment and lowers your inhibitions thereby enabling you to make bad decisions while providing him with liquid courage to say and do things that might not be a part of his normal personality. For instance, after a few drinks a man that might normally never speak to you will approach and start a conversation. While you may think he's confident and capable, it's really just the alcohol, and since your inhibitions are lowered, you'll participate in a conversation with a person you'd normally never converse with. Yet, somehow or another, you end up dancing a few dances, exchanging numbers, and depending on how much either of you have had to drink, you may or may not remember him when he calls, and that's if he remembers who you are when he finds your number in his pocket along with the 4 or 5 others he got that night.

Having said all that, there will still be the vast majority of single women who will still go to bars to meet guys and, knowing that, then at least allow me to give you some simple guidelines:

1.   Never go it alone. Going out to bars alone is simply asking for trouble. From the dangers of date rape drugs to just dealing with obnoxious drunks, you're far safer with a partner.

2.   If you go with a small group of women, sit at the bar, not at tables. A group of three or more women at a table is essentially off limits to any guy who knows the first thing about "picking up" women in bars. If you must sit at a table, sit near the dance floor as that will reduce the "barrier" and men will feel more comfortable asking you to dance.

3.   If you want upscale men, go to upscale bars and if you want a cowboy, go to a cowboy bar. Even though the reality is that the man you meet may be wearing his only suit, and they do have urban cowboys who've never seen a live horse, the odds are still in your favor that you'll be fishing in the right pond.

4. You need to leave the bar before Midnight or minimally two hours before the bar closes. Unbeknownst to you, there are men who have been watching you all night and drinking one beverage after another while trying to work up the courage to talk to you. Once last call happens, this guy figures "it's now or never" and will come over and make his drunken attempt to "win you" and when you reject him, you can expect him to get belligerent. The last thing you want or need is to have some drunk jerk acting like a fool and ruining your happy evening out.

Obviously, I don't think highly of bars. I owned one and I can tell you from years of watching tourists drink and party, that the bar experience boils down to physical attraction. Although the physical attraction must be present in order to proceed further, nothing good comes from mixing alcohol, dark rooms, loud music and an opportunity to ignore your instincts.

Online Dating:

Of course no discussion on meeting men would be complete without discussing the online option. While I personally believe online dating is a tool that can allow you to meet men that you'd normally never meet, I also think it can be fraught with dangers because it's too easy to miss vital clues until you've stepped into a mess that is difficult to deal with.

Besides the mess aspect, current studies have shown that most marriages occur among couples who met through traditional means with only about 1/3 of marriages resulting from online meetings.

With that in mind, the big question becomes "how do you make online dating work for you?" Although tons of books have been written on the subject, the vast majority of those are by single women. In fact, 8 of the top 10 books on Internet dating have been written by women and while I'm sure they gained some valuable experience and learned some great lessons, the reality is, no matter how smart she may be, a woman is simply not capable of telling you what guys are thinking. If you want to learn what guys are thinking, ask your guy friends to give an honest review of your profile or go find a book on Internet dating written by a guy for guys as those resources will give you more insight and get you up to speed quicker than months of online experience.

In the mean time, I'll give you a few pointers to get you started. First, you need to post some pictures so find a friend and take some current photos. You don't need more than two or three so take one to show a good face shot with you smiling, one good full length body shot and one showing some personality, preferably of you laughing. Leave off the pictures of sunsets, your dogs and cats unless you're the focal point of the shot. I've interviewed tons of guys that tell me photos of "Fluffy and Muffy in a doggy stroller is a complete turn-off." Leave off the photos showing cleavage, you in a bikini (no matter how good you look in it) because one simple thing is true: If you use your boobs for bait, all you're gonna catch is a boob!

Be honest and post an accurate age/body type. Remember, you're trying to find a keeper so don't blow it by lying! Keep your words true, honest and preferably brief because the less you tell the more room there is for him to ask questions and learn about you. I would strongly suggest that you avoid clichés because as Bob, a single attorney in Atlanta said "If I read one more Eat, Pray, Love quote I think I'm going to throw up! Why can't women be original? Why do they think men would be interested in another 'me too' profile?" Do something to get the conversation started, a great trick is to ask a question at the bottom of your profile that will engage the reader and prompt him to answer your question.

Ask any woman who has been online for more than a week and she'll tell you that if you don't answer an email, you get a nasty email accusing you of being stuck-up. If you do answer the email and tell someone no, you get a nasty email accusing you of being shallow! Who needs that, right? Yes, there are problems but there are also a lot of great guys online who don't misbehave. The simple fact is that when one of these bozos responds to your "no thanks" email in an inappropriate way, they have simply saved you time by validating your reason for rejecting them and although you don't want that guy, you certainly shouldn't allow one guy's action to dissuade you from answering all emails politely!

Women have told me they don't feel comfortable telling guys "no" as they don't like hurting the guys feelings. Wanna know a secret? Not answering is more painful to a man than an honest answer. By not answering, you are telling him he is so bad that he doesn't deserve an answer. Personally, I believe that one should answer all respectful emails, even if only to say "Thanks for your interest but I'm looking for someone else." However, you need to do what works for you just as long as what works is polite and kind.

One word of warning, if you think single guys (especially those under 40) don't email profile links to their friends or ask for each other's opinions, you'd be sorely mistaken. All it takes is one great guy emailing a buddy with "It says she went to the same singles event you did, did you meet her?" and the reply "No, but I emailed her twice and she doesn't answer." That great guy won't waste his time on you.

Once you've exchanged a few emails, it's best to talk on the phone. This may seem hurried but it's better to determine compatibility and chemistry before you invest a lot of time in someone. I know some women (and men) who will email for weeks before speaking and then talk every day for a week before meeting only to be greatly disappointed because the other person was older, shorter, heavier, balder, or anything else that was an illusion. Make sure you don't fall into that painful and disappointing trap!

When talking, you want to look for a conversation that was easy, relaxed and fun but remember that people respond differently when under pressure and this includes men. If he thinks you might be the one, he will feel very pressured and be nervous.

If you've done everything right up to this point, you should be heading towards the first meeting.

The Coffee Date:

Regardless of whether you met in a bar, at a cocktail party, a friend's house, online or anywhere else, I strongly suggest meeting in a place without alcohol where you can sit and chat and although it's rather cliché, the value of the coffee date simply cannot be underestimated. It's short, simple, casual, inexpensive and you have the opportunity to walk away at the first sign of discomfort. Call the coffee date your first "reality check."

Again, look for a casual and light experience and especially one where you could laugh. What you want to avoid is the "Interview" where you are asked questions like you were being interviewed for the position of girlfriend or wife. I think what you'll find is the men who do that are probably not in a good place from either too many coffee dates or overly anxious to be in a relationship. Either way it's not what you want and certainly not what you want to do to someone else.

Remember, the entire reason for getting to this point is to determine if the two of you have enough basis to continue dating. Can you talk to each other? Make plans together? Share enough similar interests or experiences to be able to build from? In other words, do you have enough in common that makes investing more time worth your time?

Turning A Man Down:

Because not everyone you meet is a match and you simply can't date everyone who asks, so the fine art of turning a man down is a priceless skill that must be mastered. Done right, the man will keep his ego intact, you will appear charming and he won't hesitate to be nice to you, come to your aid or introduce you to his friends. Done wrong, and all sorts of things can happen, the least of which is that you will be on his mortal enemy list and that means he could care less what happens to you and there's no way you'd ever see a date with one of his friends.

The first rule on the list of DO NOTS is DO NOT make excuses as excuses give hope. Saying "I'm sorry, I'm getting ready to leave" just leaves the door open to him coming up to you the next time he see's you or, if you don't leave, he'll wander back over and confront you with "I thought you were leaving but since you're not, can I have that dance now?"

The second rule on the list of DO NOTS is DO NOT lie. Not only is lying incredibly invalidating, lying can lead to angry outbursts and, sometimes, violence. Lying marks you as a woman lacking in quality. It's far better to be direct, honest and kind.

The third rule on the list of DO NOTS is DO NOT give insults as insults escalate and lead to very bad situations. No man, no matter how inept, deserves less than your very best. If he's rude, obnoxious or out of line, there are far better and safer ways to handle him than insulting him and while you may think you're more than capable of handling obnoxious guys, trust me when I tell you that A) you're not; B) it's only a matter of time before it blows up on you in a bad, bad way; C) there are far, far better ways to handle a man than being mean and; D) when you take the highroad good men will step in and when you take the low road, those same good men will leave you to cook in your own pot.

Besides, and I can't stress this enough, his best friend may be your perfect match and you lose that opportunity by lying to or insulting him. I can't emphasize this enough as I have seen it time and time again where a new guy comes out with his friends and sees a woman he's attracted to but his buddies warn him off by telling him "she's a liar and a waste of time" and the woman, feeling the same attraction as the new guy, spends eons trying to break through a wall that's never going to be torn down. Being honest and kind works just the opposite as his buddies will tell him "she's really nice and a straight shooter, go talk to her or better yet, let me introduce you!"

Experienced women have the best methods for turning down a man's advances and, by and large, quality women will tell you the best approach is always the direct, honest and kind approach.

The best lines I have heard have all been honest ones. One friend of mine, a very lovely and kind lady named Susan said that she found the very best method was simple and direct "That's very kind of you to ask but I have to say no." I asked her if a man had ever asked her "Why not?" and she replied, "Of course!" and I simply touch them on the arm tell them "It's not polite to put a lady in such an awkward position" and I smile to let them know the conversation is over and either turn away or walk away. Maria added, after turning someone down, it's always a good time to hit the ladies room or dance floor because it gives him time to focus on someone else while he licks his wounds. Strong, kind and classy and I promise you, unless he has a deeply wounded soul, he would not be insulted by her method.

Collette McLafferty, a singer and musician in New York and someone who spends a great deal of time in bars and touring with her band said her favorite way to turn a man down were the words "Thank you, but I am not interested." She goes on to say "You would be surprised on how often men have told me they really appreciate that forward, direct, honest approach, and how rarely women use it and saying 'Sorry, I have a boyfriend,' does not cut it. Guys simply don't care. Whenever I use the honest approach it's case closed." Colette goes on to say that it's "all in the delivery and you need to be kind and pleasant but firm."

Some of the other great "lines" women have shared with me are these:

- *"You seem very nice but I'm looking for someone else."* The lady who shared this gem said she has actually had guys ask her what she was looking for and then try to help her find him! Incredible! Of course I could also imagine a guy trying to convince her that he was it but she said that wasn't a problem for her.

- *"I really enjoy hanging out with you but just as friends. I'm not interested in dating you."* This is honest, direct and leaves no room for discussion but leaves the door open for continued friendship.

- *"I appreciate you buying me the drink but I am not interested in anything more than being friends. Perhaps if we run into each other again, I'll get the opportunity to return the favor by buying you a drink like friends do."*

- *"I'm not playing hard to get, I'm simply not interested."* Which several ladies have told me is useful if the guy comes back a second or third time.

Saying Yes:

Having covered how to say no, we now have to have a conversation about how to say yes and it can be summed up in one word. Don't! That's right. You don't say yes right away. If you've just met or you're on your coffee date then you absolutely do not say yes to an invitation to go out. What you do say is "I'm not sure but if you'd like to call me, we can talk about it" and of course when he calls that means accepting and returning his calls. Asking a man to call you and then not returning his call makes you appear weak, a liar and just not a nice person.

A lot of women have asked me why you don't say yes. There are two reasons: 1) It leaves you the option of changing your mind and, after reflection you may change your mind; 2) It keeps the man in the pursuer role and makes him chase you just a bit further.

Not under any circumstances should you accept text message invitations for a date. Make him call you. It's a respect issue. Just tell him to call you and you'll talk about it. Don't respond further. He'll either call and show respect or not call in which case you didn't really matter to him anyway.

Asking A Man Out:

The big myth is that most men prefer to be the aggressor. The truth is, just like you, it's extremely flattering when a woman asks us out. Being the simple creatures that we are, more often than not we're also genuinely surprised when a woman takes the aggressor role. And, yes, on reflection we can usually say that we saw all the flirtatious signs you were giving off but let's face it, sometimes we men can be completely daft and really be more focused on the comment you made about football and really think you're brushing your hair back because it's windy and that you really do want to keep talking about football!

I also know women who say they would never ask a man out because they don't want to appear desperate nor do they want the man to think "I'm easy." No man of quality will ever think you're easy or desperate, especially if you do it right but when I hear women say these things I often think of the quote by Ray Kroc, the founder of McDonalds who said "The two most important requirements for major success are: first, being in the right place at the right time, and second, doing something about it." With men, the same rule applies. When you have a great guy in front of you and you're interested in him, don't let him walk away and certainly don't stand there and think he didn't ask you out because he wasn't interested.

When it comes to asking a man out, it doesn't really matter where you are as much as what's going on around you. Crowded, noisy places are the hardest while quiet places like coffee shops are the easiest. Regardless of the location, you still want to make sure you have the man all to yourself. This will ease any potential discomfort he may have while making it easier on you. So how do you get a man all to yourself? Ask him! Just say to him, "Can I speak to you in private?" More often than not he will gladly accommodate you but if he doesn't (or can't) then be prepared to give him your number so that he can call you "to work out a time when you can chat."

Once you get your man to walk away with you, one of the most important things is to position yourself so that his back is to his friends. This gives you the benefit of having his undivided attention and he won't be feeling any pressure from his pals.

Whether by phone or in person, once you get your conversation the rest is pretty easy, and is really just about asking the question as simply and honestly as you can: "I really enjoyed meeting you and you seem like a really nice/smart/interesting man and I would like to spend some time and get to know you better. Would you be open to that?" After asking the question, SHUT UP and wait for the answer. If he's involved with someone else he will tell you and any other excuse means that he's not interested. If he's not interested, be gracious, thank him for being so nice about it and again, SHUT UP. Let him close out the conversation and lead you back to his friends.

On the other hand, if he's interested, and he should be, he will be surprised and more than open so make sure you have your next step planned out which should be asking him to call you and plan a date. This too is easy, "That's great. Let me give you my number and you can call me and we'll plan something we both like." Notice what you've done here? You not only made a polite and respectful request, you have also put the ball in his court and turned him into the pursuer while still positioning yourself for a full partnership within the relationship.

Handling Rejection:

Okay, so you emailed a guy on a dating site or you walked up and asked him out and horror of horrors, he said "No." This feeling of being rejected can feel devastating. So devastating in fact, that guys have a saying for it: "20 feet over and 20 miles back" which is used to describe the short walk over to you and how long that same walk feels coming back with rejection written on your forehead (I bet you didn't know that did you!). I hear women all the time saying "Oh My God! I could never do that! How embarrassing!" Well, welcome to a man's world! So, how do you handle this rejection without spending two hours watching a romantic comedy while eating a quart of Rocky Road ice cream? What you have to do is learn to put the process in perspective and for this I use the cookie theory which goes like this:

The Cookie Theory:

You're in the grocery store and you're walking down the cookie isle looking for a snack. Do you buy each and every kind of cookie on the shelf? Of course not! First off, it would make you sick but realistically, 75% of the brands you simply don't like and would never buy. Another 20% you would eat but only if that's all there was. The last 5% are the brands that you'd pay good money for... it's all you want; it's what makes you happy!

When someone is rejecting you, it's the same thing. They are shopping for the cookie that will make them happy and you're not their favorite brand! Don't believe me? Just stand in the cookie isle and watch all the people who buy the perfectly good cookies that you walked right by! You didn't want those cookies as they had no appeal to you, but other people are diving right in and looking forward to getting them home!

Just like there was nothing wrong with the cookies you didn't buy, there's nothing wrong with you. It's just the other person wants a different cookie and, just like all those people who buy the cookies you didn't want, there's a guy who is looking for you! You will be what he's looking for!

Pressures On:

Finally, it's time for the big date. Imagine yourself in his position. He had to have the courage to ask you out, he has to plan the evening, pick the venue and attempt to keep you, a total stranger, entertained for 3-4 hours! This is no easy feat!

The most important thing is for you to be gracious. He may have planned sushi and you don't like sushi. It's no problem. Order a salad and comment on the nice ambiance. After all, the important part is not about putting up barriers or being a pain in the butt as that will NOT get you a second date. It's about being gracious and kind and learning about this man sitting across from you. Some of my most memorable dates were with people who were gracious and kind, and one of those has since gone on and married someone else but is still a great friend of mine and someone I admire and respect immensely.

> **David in Dallas told this story:**
>
> "I had met someone online and we'd exchanged emails at a pace you wouldn't believe. Our first phone conversation lasted FOUR hours! Needless to say I was excited and nervous about meeting this lady.
>
> I was in my closet getting ready and picking out a tie when my teenage daughter walked in and asked what I was doing and I told her about my date. My daughter looked at my shirt and suggested a tie she had bought for me several years earlier. Now, this wasn't my favorite tie but I did wear it for certain occasions (a few years later at her high school graduation).
>
> As I met my date at the agreed upon restaurant and we were seated she looked over at my tie and said "That's not a very attractive tie. It doesn't look good on you and you shouldn't wear it!" and I knew at that moment that this would never work. My date, despite her great qualities, simply lacked some basic relationship skills. A wise woman would have asked where I got the tie and when I said it was a gift from my daughter that would have been the end of the conversation."

That doesn't mean that, when making plans for the evening, you can't say "I'm not a fan of sushi, do you know if they have other things on the menu?" Or "That's a place I've never been before, what's it like?" and you certainly can call the restaurant and find out what the menu options are and what the dress code might be.

Best Foot Forward:

This really shouldn't need saying but it does, you are dating so you need to put your best foot forward at all times. This means being on time, dressing appropriately and, just in general being on your best behavior.

If you are attending an event that is important to your man such as weddings, business events, holiday parties at a friend's house or any other type of event where the invitation came from his friend, family or work, then you especially need to be on your best behavior and this means not creating a stir, embarrassing him by drinking too much, flirting with another man or disappearing and leaving him to answer the awkward question of "Where's your date?" with a shrug of the shoulders and the old "I don't have a clue." Your role is to be his companion, to be supportive, to make him look good and to learn all about him, his friends and his work.

I know this concept is viewed by many women as a throwback to the 1960's, but the fact of the matter is this: If you're not on your man's team and you're not helping him move his cause forward, then you are a detriment to him and you shouldn't be going out with him. Put yourself in his shoes, you invite a new guy to accompany you to a friend's wedding and at the reception he drinks too much and is hitting on one of your married friends. Is this the kind of man you would want your friends, family or co-workers to see you with? Of course not, and he's no different than you. If you can't give your date your very best, then he's simply not the man you need to be with.

Things That Make A Guy Go Hmmmm:

Friends First:

"Friends First!" I have had some great and long debates over this phrase with some of my best female friends. I love to hear a women tell me "I want to be friends first!" because my first response is "So you're paying your own way when we go out?" Oddly enough, many women get offended by that comment and all of a sudden they don't want to go out with you. But wait! Isn't that what happens when you go out with friends? You drive yourself and you pay your own tab?

Of course, my comment is silly because I realize she is saying "I want to get to know you before I sleep with you." And to that, I agree 1000%, but what a man hears is something completely different. We hear "complicated" and we hear "she's confused and doesn't know what she wants." The fact of the matter is that dating is a process wherein people get to know one another with the hopes of building a future together. "Dating" does not define when two people have sex, it does not define who pays, it does not define anything other than what the two people involved want and need it to be.

The Independent Woman:

The "independent woman" is another term that will send men running for the hills. Men, and I mean ALL men, want to feel needed. An independent woman implies "I don't need you" and the argument is "I don't need a man, I want a man" and while that may be true, men want to be in relationships where they will feel needed. The level of need that a man wants is dependent on the man: Some men like to be REALLY needed and make sure their wives never put gas in the car, never take out the trash, etc. While other men only want a phone call when you have a flat tire on the side of the road and the mechanic can't get there for 3 hours.

To illustrate how men react to the "I'm an independent woman" statement, let me tell you a quick story: A few years ago I was at a dating seminar where a group of women panelists were speaking to a group of single men. One of the women went on and on saying "I have a job, I buy my own clothes, I pay my own mortgage, I make my own car payments, I pay for my own vacations..." and when she finished one of the men stood up and started applauding and after a moment he stopped and looked at the panelist and said "Congratulations! You're an adult!" The entire room full of men all busted out laughing. This rather harsh example again underscores the difference in what women are saying vs. what men hear.

Again, we men, in general, get that when most women say they're independent what they mean is they are capable of taking care of themselves and, therefore, are not looking to enter a relationship out of need but somewhere inside of us there's still a niggling feeling that you're not going to be easy to get along with.

So, how does an independent woman let a man know that she's capable of taking care of herself? If you must say something, and I really believe this is one of those things that doesn't need saying, try saying "I'm self sufficient" because being self sufficient means you are 100% capable of taking care of yourself but that you would like to have a man around to take care of some of the things where your skills aren't so strong. Most men would walk right past an independent woman to get to a self sufficient woman.

Another really important piece of information about being independent is this: Men who do not feel needed will feel less secure in the relationship. My advice is to find something that you don't like doing and that he is good at and tell him directly that you "need" him to take care of that and remind him how much you need him… even if you don't.

These last two points, "Friends first" and "Independent woman" illustrate how men are more literal and there are phrases you just want to avoid. Although we are both looking for the same thing, the way it's said means everything. My caution to you is to think through what you say and look at the literal meaning.

Things that Make A Man Say Yipee!!!:

Be Yourself:

Absolutely *the* most important thing that any person can do is to learn to like themselves and to be themselves. This is extremely important for men. We want to know that you are real, genuine and that when we get further down the road there will be no big surprises. Women who're happy and comfortable with themselves are fun and easy to be around.

Be The Honey:

What men appreciate about women most is the softness you bring into our lives. Men are physically and emotionally built and designed to battle and protect the village and for killing large beasts for food. Although society has somewhat evolved away from this, there are many holdovers in that we still have wars and men still have an emotional need to be the provider. So why do we need you to be soft, gentle and kind? It provides balance in our lives. Your softness knocks the hard edge off of life as we experience it and allows us to experience the joyful moments. This has nothing to do with gender roles or stereotypes, it's simply that we're built differently and have evolved differently and have different facilities for handling different tasks and different situations.

Date List To Lay List:

Most men start off with the best of intentions. They've invested time in asking you out, planning a date and showing up. No decent man is going to go through all that trouble just to get laid, and most men honestly do want to get to know you. The problem is, somewhere in the early dating process, something happens that moves a woman from the Date List to the Lay List. When that happens you're no longer a viable candidate as a lifelong partner and internally the man says "Okay, well, I'm here, let's see if I can just manage to get laid." Horrible? Absolutely! Unusual? Not as much as you would like to think. This also explains why he can be so charming during the first part of a date and then go straight for sex. When the date is over, you never hear from him again... you were moved to the Lay List, and he didn't get what he wanted so he doesn't want to invest any effort beyond that last date just to get laid. (And good for you, you dodged a bullet!)

Dating Do's And Don'ts:

It goes without saying, or it should, but everyone should follow some basic rules when dating. Although we can't control what others do, we can control what we do. Being a good date goes a long way in keeping you on the Date List and off the Lay List. Toys are meant to play with, treasures are meant to keep!

Cell Phone:

Cell phones can be absolute life savers, but they can also be incredibly intrusive, nagging devices that distract us from some of life's greatest moments. When you're dating, you need to keep the cell phone put away. If you have to answer it, be clear about the call you're expecting (the babysitter) and why you'll take it (my youngest hasn't been feeling well). Whatever you do, don't lie about the bailout call unless you need bailing out. If things are going well, just tell him "that's my bailout call but I'm not going to take it" (and yes, guys know about bailout calls and sometimes use them too).

Being Late:

Men, by and large, are pretty punctual people. We also know most women run a little bit late and we're generally fine with that.

198

However, you being 5 minutes late when we pick you up is one thing while your being 20-30 minutes late is a completely different thing. When you're 20-30 or 60 minutes late, most men not only feel disrespected but figure you're really not all that interested because, after all, if you were interested, you'd be on time. Besides, if you're getting ready to go spend a few hours with someone, do you really want to put your date in a bad mood? If you're going to be late, call, tell them why and how late you're going to be. Be respectful!

Being Rude:

I've said this before but I'll say it again, there is simply no reason to be rude. Not only is it unnecessary but in these times, it can be dangerous. Not only is being rude to your date unnecessary but remember, men rank kindness at the top of their list and that kindness extends to other people. The wait staff, the service station attendant, your date is watching how you treat everyone. We're all human, everyone gets upset on occasion but being rude early on is bad and being rude consistently is a sign of who you are. Good guys won't be interested in a rude woman.

Eating Like A Fly:

Personally, I've never understood this one but it's one that guys consistently complain about. I think you should eat what you want. If you feel like eating a leaf and a twig, then eat a leaf and a twig. If you want to put down a 2 pound burger, then chow down. But, again, most men want to know that you're genuine and authentic. If you eat a leaf and twig on every date and he later finds out you go home and have a real meal, you'll lose his trust and fracture the relationship before it even gets started.

Not Listening:

There is nothing worse than spending an evening with someone and them asking you where you were born and you spend 10 minutes describing the place and all the great memories just to have her ask you on the drive home, where you were born. It lets you know the entire evening was a complete waste of time.

Constantly Looking Or Facing Elsewhere:

There's always that one date where you sit in the booth across from each other and they automatically turn in the seat facing outward and spend the entire meal looking at everyone but you. Unless their leg is in a cast, it comes off as indifference and disinterest.

Checking Out Other Men:

Nothing, and I mean nothing, is as rude as checking out other men while on a date with a guy, and nothing will move you from the Date List to the Lay List faster. Most women think "My God! What kind of woman would do that?" and a lot of men will tell you "Yep, I've been on that date and it was the last date with that woman!" If the guy you're with doesn't hold your complete attention then you shouldn't be with him.

What Men Don't Want In A Women:

Most men really, really like women. Not just for the sex but because we really like how you smell, the softness of your skin, the way you have different perspectives and somehow just because the way you view things is foreign to us, it makes us laugh. So what do men not like about women? I think it's a pretty short list but all worth a little discussion.

The Meany:

You may think I'm beating a dead horse into glue but at the top of the list of don't likes is meanness. There is a time and place for everything, and there is rarely ever a time or place for meanness. Men look to you to soften them and we want kindness, so when you're mean, you're not just missing the kindness boat but you're actually killing your hopes of anything long term with your guy. If you're being mean to another man, you're probably escalating a situation that puts you, your man and other companions at risk, and no one appreciates that woman.

The Ball Buster:

Again, men need you to soften them so your being hard isn't contributing to his core needs. As Mike, an attorney in Phoenix observed: "Our culture has shifted and women are obtaining more equality in the work place and demanding more participation from men in maintaining the house and raising the children. Because of this shift, many women, while striving for success and balance, end up trying so very hard to emulate men that, in the process, they exhibit the very qualities they dislike most about men, becoming the very thing that men don't want and then wonder why they are alone." Does this mean you need to be a pushover? Absolutely not! It means you need to learn a better way of communicating. You don't have to be a "ball buster" to get what you want.

The Nag:

If you've not read the chapter on communications, go back and do so. There is simply no reason to ever nag a man about anything. If you find yourself having to nag then you're either not expressing your need appropriately, he doesn't view your need as meaningful or he simply doesn't care about you. Either way, nagging will not improve on these things and will increase whatever damage has previously been done to your communications.

The Daddy Hunter And The Gold Digger:

Most men have a built-in radar that detects certain types of women. The daddy hunter and the gold digger are chief among those that are easy to spot and at the slightest hint most men will run for the hills. Having said this, you should also know there are some males who recognize these women as vulnerable and will suck these women in using their vulnerability as bait, use them, and then cast them aside. This is why you need to really evaluate your needs and understand your value and what you need from your partner. You don't want to be road kill to a predatory jerk. And just so you know, quality men also recognize your daddy hunting or gold digging efforts but will walk away instead of taking advantage.

Talking About Exes:

Don't make him feel worthless by ranting on and on about your exes. If you say what you dislike in your exes, he might be put off and if you say what you like about your exes, he may not feel as though he can live up to those standards.

Friendship With Exes:

Everyone has feelings about whether you should be friends with an ex or not, and if you are, what that friendship entails. It was one of the most discussed topics among the men I interviewed. So, I did an online survey via a popular singles site and the survey had just over 2900 respondents who completed all questions and the respondents were 53% women and 47% men.

The first question: *"Do you believe your date/mate should maintain an active friendship with members of the opposite sex who are ex lovers?"*

Michael in Tampa tells this story:

"I had been dating this lady for a few months and had been invited to her house for dinner where I would be meeting her two grown children and her best friend of 25 years. During that dinner, the ladies were talking about jewelry and my date said "No one ever got me like [insert name of ex]." As soon as the words were out of her mouth, I looked at her and then around the table and everyone but my date was staring at me waiting on a reaction, and although I never said anything, I felt humiliated and I had a sense of "well then, why bother trying? Who can measure up to THAT?" and no matter how hard I tried, I never could."

Female:
No, not ever: 19%
As long as I trusted my partner: 69%
Case by case: 12%

Male:
No, not ever: 36%
As long as I trusted my partner: 54%
Case by case: 10%

When asked to agree/disagree with the following statements, the percentages shown indicate the number of respondents who agreed with the statement:

- Any violation of trust such as lies or infidelity with opposite sex friends ends the relationship - 100%

- Hanging out should be done at appropriate hours and appropriate, public places. - 100%

- I expect my partner to fully inform me of the date/

time/location of when they are meeting one of their
opposite sex friends - 92%

- If my partner is going to their opposite sex friend's
house for dinner, I'm not confused- it's a date - 79%

- If the male friend is picking up the female, taking her
to dinner and paying, I'm not confused, it's a date - 96%

- If, after some reasonable amount of time (6 months?)
you haven't met your partners opposite sex friends
(assuming they live locally), your partner is not being
honest about those friendships - 89%

- It's not worth risking my current relationship by
maintaining a relationship with an ex lover - 59%

- Your partner should not hang around with their
opposite sex friends unless/until you have met them
and you are comfortable with them - 84%

- My partner is responsible for maintaining their
opposite sex friendships in a manner that protects my
feelings of being respected, safe and secure - 100%

When you look at the results, it pretty clear that both sexes have
pretty strong opinions about friendships with exes and both sexes
are very consistent on relationships with opposite sex friends.
If you go back to the section in this chapter called "What He's
Looking For," you find loyalty and fidelity listed right near the top
of the list.

Many people argue that only insecure people worry about such
things but Evolutionary Psychologist Dr. David Buss says that
nearly 60% of all people have participated in "mate poaching" and
that jealousy is an emotion that we developed to protect us from
straying partners by giving us "early warning" alerts.

How Men Will Test You:

Men are pretty smart about relationships, often times much smarter than we're given credit for. We're also far more observant than the opposite sex might think. I'm going to give you some of the most common ways that guys will test you during the dating phase and I bet, as you read through these, you'll spot at least one that's been pulled on you.

The Withdrawing Test:

By not calling or being available for longer than usual, men will test to see how you respond. Will you call and check in or will you fret and get all anxious and withdraw? Will you send nasty text messages or will you send funny jokes? Are you insecure? Are you interested enough to pursue him? One thing is certain, men need distance to fall in love… or fall out of love!

The Humor Test:

Men need to know that you get their humor. You've ridden in his car for hours and all the time he's had Nickleback playing and all of a sudden he says "I prefer listening to country" and he's waiting to see if you can pick up on his sarcastic sense of humor. If, after a few shots you still haven't gotten his humor, he'll break it off and move on to the next woman.

The Sports Test:

It's no secret, most guys like sports and for most guys, they really don't care if you do or don't or if you root for their team or another. The question is, will you sit and watch a game with him on a regular basis. If yes, you pass, if not, it may not be a deal breaker, but it doesn't bode well for you. Remember, for men, your company is both comforting and intimate.

The Man Puzzle

The Makeup Test:

Guys want to know what you look like without makeup. Yeah, this is important because if we marry you we're gonna see you without makeup a whole lot! Some women wear so much makeup that somewhere in the night their entire face slides off and when you wake up in the morning you can't even recognize them as the person you went to bed with the night before. For most men, women who can go au natural or with minimal makeup are far more desirable.

The Music Test:

Music tells a lot about a person. Not just which bands you like but which songs are your absolute favorites can tell you where a person is emotionally. For instance, a woman who is constantly playing sad breakup songs is probably still pining for her ex.

The Adventure Test:

Are you adventurous? A guy will take a girly-girl to the gun range or a tom boy to a formal ball. By putting a woman in a situation that she'd rather not be in, you will see some of her real personality traits come through. After all, life is full of unpleasant situations.

The Teasing Test:

Can you take a joke? Can you dish it right back out? Most men will give a good natured tease just to see if you can laugh at yourself or whether you get all pensive and defensive. For most men, if you get defensive over the little things, you will be really difficult when it's time to work on a big problem.

The Judgmental Test:

In this test the guy will take you to a restaurant that's pretty grungy (think dive), and where the waitress may be pretty rough around the edges. We want to see how you respond. Are you nice? Judgmental? Accepting? Talk down at everyone? If you can treat everyone as an equal and be nice, for most guys that puts you in the keeper category. BTW, this also works with high-end establishments to see if you're comfortable in upper circles.

The Uptight Test:

In the uptight test, the guy will casually make a comment like "we should go _____." (fill in the blank with some insane activity like rob a bank, sky diving, cliff diving, diving with sharks, etc.) next weekend. He wants to see how you're going to respond. "Yeah, we'll go diving with the sharks, but you can't wear fins so I can get away faster!"

The Temper Test:

In the temper test, the guy will purposefully make you late for something (play, movie, dinner), and then ask you to drive. He wants to see how you respond. Will you stay angry all evening or shrug it off? When you drive will you be reckless or let everyone imaginable cut you off? How will you react?

As I said at the start of this section, I bet you recognize at least one of those tests, if not several of them. So why do men play these games? Because they're simple to construct and the guy gets immediate feedback. He knows by the end of the evening a lot more about who you are than he would dare let on.

How Men Bond:

If everything has gone right, you're dating and having fun. But do you know what else is happening? You're bonding! If you watch men with their guy friends, they're doing one of two things: Activities or sitting quietly together.

Men use activities, adventure, fun and laughter as bonding time. This is why it's massively important to make sure you're involved and doing things together and that you keep doing things together and that you make your time together enjoyable and uncomplicated.

The more you bond, another odd thing happens, he wants to spend more quiet time with you. By quiet time, I don't mean sitting and talking. What I mean is that men find it incredibly intimate to have your company. Your just being present is an amazing thing!

While women bond over words, and quiet time is meant for talking, men need time with you with no talking. Just you, him, and a good book or movie. You'd be amazed at how important and intimate men find this time.

On the other hand, when you never laugh, you make the experiences bad and the activities a pain in the butt, his bonding memories become bad memories. When you turn that quiet time into "let's clean the closet" or you never stop talking, then you rob him of his much needed intimate time.

It's All About Negotiating:

There is no absolute right way and no absolute wrong way to do anything. You are an individual and so is he, and you both have to negotiate AND compromise with each other. If you can't negotiate and compromise, then the relationship will either fail or be a very, very, long and miserable experience. Both of those options are undesirable.

How you treat each other during the initial dating period sets the tone for the remainder of your relationship. Kindness, honesty, respect, loyalty and open communications are the foundation for a lasting and healthy relationship with any man.

Chapter 8

FROM DATING TO RELATIONSHIP

WHAT IS A RELATIONSHIP? A relationship is the way in which two people are connected. So your relationship status defines how you are connected. When asked to define your relationship to others, what do you say? We've been steadily dating for 2 years; we're engaged; we're married. Each of these statements defines a set of roles and expectations about the relationship, within the relationship and with others towards you and your man.

When society looks at relationships, a man or woman who is dating someone is, technically, still on the market but investigating a future with someone. A woman who is engaged is taken and soon to be off the market. A woman who is married is definitely off the market.

Somewhere between dating and engaged lives a land called "relationship" that should lead to a promising future together but still includes dating each other. I want to help you get to this land and to be able to answer the question "are you seeing someone?" with "Yes, I'm in relationship."

Dating:

Dating is like window shopping. You haven't bought anything yet but the longer you spend looking at that one pair of shoes, the more emotionally invested you become and the more likely you are to make a purchase. So, you've been dating and now you want to move to the register and get in the checkout line. How do you make that transition?

The first question is of course, "What are we doing?" Are we just hanging out and having a good time or are we building something? If one of you (i.e. him) thinks you're just hanging out and having fun, then you can wait in the checkout line for 20 years and never get that purchase. It's a horrible place to be and it's terrible if you or he has invested a lot of time just to find out the other isn't ready to move forward.

For instance, if you're looking to get married then you only want to date men who're in the same boat. From our research, we found that most men would not even consider marriage for at least 2-3 years after completing school. For high school educated guys it was early 20's, college educated, it was mid to late 20's and for advanced degrees such as MBA's, doctors and lawyers it was their late 20's to early 30's. Most of the men we talked to considered marriage after they got tired of the bar scene and especially after a friend or two or even an older brother had recently married. For older guys, they wanted to wait 2-3 years after their divorce and they had regained some semblance of financial stability.

For some people, dating is a relationship. They date one person at a time and expect exclusivity while dating and for others dating means we're both free to see other people while we get to know each other. Make sure you're both on the same page and have the same expectations.

How do you know where you are without asking? During the

dating process you initiated your relationship by meeting each other, experimented by engaging in small talk and testing topics for compatibility. All of this is to determine if you have a basis for continuing forward and if you do, things begin to intensify and this is where you build on your common interests, find new things to do together, give each other pet names, your trust level increases and a deep friendship starts to bloom. It's during this phase that you assess your romantic future together, it's when you learn about each other's hobbies, friends, families, past relationships and personal habits. This is also when you overlook things that may annoy you.

This is dating and this process can take months or years, depending on the people and the time, energy and effort invested by both parties. Towards the end of this phase of dating is when we want to move into the next part, The Committed Relationship, or break things off.

What? Did I just say break things off? Why, yes, yes I did. During or at the end of the dating phase is when one or both of you are forced to decide whether there's a reason to stay or go. This has to be an individual choice based on your own inner voice, not the voice of your friends or family echoing in your ears. It has to be your own inner voice because you must live with the consequences of your choice for the rest of your life.

Regardless of who brings up the topic of moving to the next stage, there are plenty of things to consider:

- Actions DO speak louder than words. Do his actions match his words? What about just his actions, do those actions speak love, understanding, compassion or indifference, intolerance, negativity or even abuse? What about your actions? Do yours measure up? Sometimes our own actions tell us more about our own feelings than our heart does. How do your actions measure up?

- Have you had an argument yet? How did he behave? Was there anger? Rage? Were his actions "over-the-top?" Where you able to resolve the issue with no regrets or were things left unresolved?

- Are your life goals the same? What about your expectations? If you think forward 1, 5, 10 years, will his life goals mesh with yours and will the compromises either of you have to make to support the other be worth it? If your goal is to move to L.A. and be a movie star and his is to open an automotive repair shop, how will you reconcile these differences? Will he be willing to wear a tux to important events? Will you be willing to walk across a greasy garage floor in expensive heels?

- What if you're later in life and you have kids at home. If this goes the distance, will you live in your home or his? Or perhaps buy one together? Which kids will have to change schools? How will you step-parent?

These are serious things to consider and you should have the answers you can live with long before you think of moving into a committed relationship.

The Committed Relationship:

During the committed relationship phase your lives slowly start to become integrated and your relationship finds structure. It's when you know you have an automatic date on Friday night and you don't have to ask or be asked. It's when you know, in August, he will go to your office Christmas party and nothing other than the details of date, time and dress need to be discussed. It's when you have a key to each other's homes and nothing other than courtesy text needs to be sent before dropping by. You've long since met each other's families and friends and know each other's hopes, dreams and plans for the future. During this phase is when you try to figure out how to make it all come together and when he's figured it out or at least figured out that you're the one he wants to figure it all out with is when he proposes.

How To Make The Transition:

How should you move from dating to a relationship? There is no right or wrong answer, sometimes it just eases in and you don't even realize it until you're in it and sometimes it requires work and more than one hard conversation.

If you were one of those who had to have the tough conversations, then congratulations because, unless you used threats or blackmail (if you don't do this, I'm leaving you) you're actually on very solid ground.

However, if you're one of the women where things just eased in, then you need to take some steps to get on solid ground. Sometimes, things are just comfortable and flow and that's incredibly wonderful when that happens and if you're one of the lucky women who are in that relationship then you still need to put a stake in the ground. Look at it like a mountain climber; every time you reach a new height, you have to hammer a piton, or metal spike, into the rock wall as an anchor to protect against falls and to aide in climbing further up the mountain. More often than not though, things "ease in" because people are afraid to have the tough conversations. If this is the case, you're almost certainly headed for doom, disaster and heartache.

How would you have or approach this conversation? How about something like this: "Honey, I've noticed that we seemed to have eased into a committed relationship, have you noticed the same thing?" There really aren't many answers to that question, it's yes or no and if yes, then you can proceed on with other questions like "Are you comfortable with that?" and "What expectations do you have for me? For us?" I think that's pretty straight forward and leaves the door open for some in-depth conversations.

On the other hand, if you hear "No, I hadn't realized that at all." Then you REALLY need to back up and have the in-depth conversations. Start by asking "Where do you think we are?"

Soul Mates:

"You don't understand, it was easy because he's my soul mate!" There have been some recent studies published which show that couples who believe they've married their soul mates tend to have higher divorce rates. "How could this possibly be?" you ask. The reason is really quite simple, people who believe they've married their soul mates also believe there is a level of understanding that isn't really there and since they are depending on that level of understanding they tend to not work as hard and to take more for granted. On the other hand, people who don't believe in soul mates tend to work harder and be more willing to resolve conflict and their marriages last the longest.

What Does Being In A Relationship Mean?:

In order for a committed relationship to work and grow towards something permanent, you both need the same definition.

- I want to do this and see where it goes

- I want to do this until I get my promotion and have to move

- I want to do this until I finish _____ and then reevaluate.

If one of you is working from one expectation, and the other something entirely different, then you're working against each other. You have competing agendas and, if you can't resolve those to one agenda, then you're headed towards heartbreak.

You Both Need The Same Goals:

One way to make sure you have the same expectations is to make sure you're working toward the same goals. "While we're in this relationship we will work towards _____ and we will do this by doing _____." I promise you, having a commitment to work towards the same goal is incredibly difficult to get from someone who says they're committed just to get you off their backs.

A relationship is two people pushing a wheelbarrow up a steep hill. It's best when each person takes a handle and carries their load and you're pushing together. Sometimes, one may have to push the whole thing while their partner sits in the barrow but that's love. It will never work if only one person does all the pushing or if one is pulling the wheelbarrow back down the hill. Sometimes you have to take a rest; do that together. Sometimes one may feel like they're doing all the pushing, sit and talk about it. If your partner slows down, just remember that while you may be on even footing, they may be on rocky ground. Adjust your pushing to lighten their load and things will even out.

If you don't have the same goal to push the wheelbarrow to the top of the hill, you will never, ever make it.

Love That Last Forever:

We all have dreams of finding someone who will love us forever and whom we will love forever, but I think this comes without the understanding that forever love is built one moment at a time. It's loving someone in each moment and those moments become hours which become days which become years and those years add up to lifetimes. You won't go from dating one or two nights a week to marriage. You go from dating, to committed relationship, to engaged, to marriage and each step along the way takes work, dedication, patience, compassion and empathy.

No love starts off as a lifetime love, maybe it's a goal but even then, goals need steps to achieve and, to me, it doesn't seem like the dreamers understand the steps (remember, we guys are systematic thinkers. We need to apply a system to everything in order to understand it!).

I'm a romantic by nature, but even as a romantic, I know that romantic relationships are built. Romance rarely falls from the sky and when it does, it doesn't last long.

Understanding Social Proofing:

Social Proofing is a way for your man to gauge whether or not you're as good a choice as he thinks you are and whether you will fit in to his social circle. When he takes you to his favorite place and introduces you to his friends, he's wanting his friends to validate you by accepting you. You will, of course, be uncomfortable, a bit unsure of the social setting, rules for interaction, who he's very close to and who is on the outer edge of his circle. You have to both be yourself and take your cues from the other members of the social circle as to the correct behavior. If all he hears is "what a great lady" then you know you're on the right track. On the flip side, if all he hears is negative comments then you probably didn't meld well with his group of friends and all is not well in your world.

Men have a couple of different ways of bringing their women into their friends. You have "gradual" and "sink or swim" and, it depends on his feel for you and the situation on which method the guy will use.

In "The Gradual Method" your man is going to introduce you to one or two close friends in a controlled environment (dinner out) before you meet the entire group. In this method he wants their opinion of you AND he wants to see how you get along with his best friends. He may also use his friends to "prep" you for other people in his main group.

In the "Sink or Swim" method he brings you to an outing where all of his friends are present. This may or may not come with warning and it's not at all uncommon to think you're going out for a "drink and shoot some pool" only to get there and find his entire circle of friends are there.

When your man does this, more than likely he's given it careful thought and has good reasons for his choice. It may just be that he's absolutely so excited by having you in his life that he wants everyone to know or it may be he attends a lot of work functions and wants to see how you handle yourself.

Regardless of his motive, he wants to see how you do when you meet everyone at once; who you'll migrate to; who you spend the most time conversing with; who you avoid; if you'll stick close to his side or meet everyone and just circle back around to reconnect on occasion. If your guy cares anything at all about you he'll notice absolutely everything. Some guys will guide you around and introduce you to everyone while others will throw you in to the "den of wolves" and let you survive on your own. In each case, he's learning about you and whether and how you will "fit in." The only way to survive this is to just be yourself, do what you're comfortable doing. If you try to be something you're not, you're ultimately going to create problems down the road.

Never even consider entering into a committed relationship until after you've been through the social proofing exercise with his friends. If you've been dating for months and never met anyone, that's a really bad sign because he either doesn't have friends or he has a reason for not introducing you.

Meeting the parents is a special form of social proofing and may or may not be a big deal. Some guys have introduced 20 women to their folks and it means nothing other than he's comfortable with his folks. Other guys would not even consider bringing anyone around their parents unless it was VERY serious! Don't overreact. Let the situation unfold and just be normal.

Evan from Pittsburgh tells this story:

I had met a really great lady who was great looking, she was a doctor as am I, her kids were grown as were mine, we had a blast together and the sex was awesome.

I decided it was time to introduce her to my friends and because I organized a lot of very large social events I opted to introduce her at a party I was having at my house with about 60 friends in attendance.

About an hour into the party one of the regular guys who was known as a "ladies man" approached her and asked who she was with and she very politely told him she was with me. This guy then asked her if we were dating and she paused and looked at me for an answer. To me, the answer was clear. We had been dating, we'd made love, taken a weekend away together and here she was in my house meeting all my friends. I didn't answer the question because I wanted her to take ownership. She didn't. About an hour later she asked me to walk her to her car and as we stood beside it she told me it would never work out between us and she left.

It was a shame too because I really liked her but she couldn't hang and if she was uncomfortable answering awkward questions at a party at my house with my friends, how would she handle a party at work with 500 people?

Understanding the two forms of social proofing explains why it may take awhile for you to meet his friends. He may be in a couple of "all-in" situations and think that you need to meet people gradually or he may be attending a series of intimate dinners and really want to take you to a "sink or swim" event.

Signs He Might Be Ready:

I hate talking about signs. I think looking for signs limits you and there can be plenty of reasons for each action. By and large though, the positive things happening over and over can be considered encouraging and that he's interested in going further with you while the negative things occurring over and over can be sure signs of doom.

Some Good Signs:

- **Communications:** Returning phone calls, emails and text within a reasonable amount of time i.e. not waiting days

- **Planning dates without asking:** He's feeling secure in the relationship and has the expectation that you're in. This isn't a negative thing because he's seeing you as a partner and as dependable.

- **Talking about the future:** He's imagining a future with you in it. Whether he realizes it or not, he's painting a picture that includes you. This means that he's either beginning to accommodate you into his plans or he already has.

- **We versus Me:** There is a huge difference between "On my next vacation" and "On our next vacation."

- **"Hey, it's me:"** – when he starts leaving messages without identifying himself, he's moved into a place where he knows you should recognize and be comfortable hearing his voice. It's a very subtle sign but certainly one you should pay attention to.

- **Leaving stuff at your place:** Men have often accused women of "marking their territory" by leaving things at the man's place. You find earrings, hair clips and all manner of "innocent" items left behind. Men are not prone to leaving jewelry or hairclips but they will bring and leave deodorant, body wash and other items and will make it clear they're leaving it "so they don't have to keep carrying it back and forth."

Some Bad Signs:

- **Communications slows:** He no longer calls or texts as often and takes longer to return your calls, texts and emails

- **Creating distance:** This is a subtle way of saying "we're not a couple" and includes things such as dropping your hand when other women are around or even standing adjacent to you instead of next to you

- **Reducing date time:** When he starts reducing the time he spends with you and planning nights out with friends or "the guys" especially on a night you have traditionally gone out (i.e. Friday night) or even cancelling dates at the last minute

- **Bootie call:** He only wants to see you after a night out with the guys. He's been drinking; he's feeling amorous and wants to see you on his way home

- **More bickering.** Every little thing gets turned into an issue. Things that never seemed to matter before now, all of a sudden, seem like big deals

- **Pulls away:** If he suddenly pulls away he may be feeling rushed or not be ready to make the same level of commitment that you are. This is something that requires an honest and heartfelt conversation.

When considering the above "bad signs" a onetime event should not be considered a bad omen. Instead, when these things start happening consistently, then you need to have a conversation.

Some Obstacles:

Flowers, Cards And Letters:

All men want their women to feel special. Flowers, cards, letters, and token gifts are just one way of our trying to do this. It's important to recognize and acknowledge the thoughtfulness behind the gesture, failure to do so will result in these small tokens stopping.

There are also a fair number of men who don't give these small tokens and it's not something to get upset over. Some men have simply never been taught how to give gifts, they may never have seen their Dad bring flowers home to their mother or they may believe that giving flowers is just for getting out of trouble. There's probably not a man in the world who hasn't bought a dozen roses on a Tuesday night and not had another man (or woman) ask him what he did to get into trouble. That means there's a certain amount of embarrassment that comes with buying these small tokens so we have to make sure that the reward is far greater than the pain.

A Danger Zone:

There are also a lot of men who have spoiled a previous partner rotten only to learn that, in the end, it made no difference. These men describe 4 stages they experience when spoiling a woman:

1. **Adoration** - This is the "Oh My God! I can't believe you did that!" phase.

2. **Expectation** - This is the "Do you realize that today is the first Friday since we met that you didn't buy me flowers?" phase.

3. **Taken for granted** - This is the "It doesn't matter, he will buy me flowers when I tell him too!"

4. **The boot** - This is when the woman has lost respect for her man and considers him a doormat. If you ask most guys who have been there, they will tell you that their exes typically end up dating "some jerk who treats her like crap."

Many men go through these stages one or more times and suffer so much personal pain that they simply will not go there again so, either consciously or subconsciously they decide they "don't do" flowers, cards, letters and those small meaningful tokens.

Meeting The Ex:

When you go to an old favorite restaurant, a church or just about any place else, it's inevitable that you will, at some point or another, run into one of your exes. When this happens, there are some rules that tend to work really well with men.

If it's a known encounter, give your new man the option of making the encounter. He may not be ready to go so deeply into your life. If it's only a probable encounter, give your new man a heads up by saying "I really want to go to this restaurant, but before we do, I want you to know that I've bumped into my ex there a few times before." Your guy may, again, prefer to delay the encounter until he feels like he's on more secure footing with you. Regardless of when it happens, you have to make sure your ex knows where your loyalty lies, and you do this by making a clear distinction of who you're with.

Above all, don't engineer any meetings or try to make anyone jealous. Men are pretty adept at recognizing this for what it is and you'll just end up looking needy, and fracturing your current relationship. Plus, look needy and crazy to your ex.

In The Relationship:

Never Stop Dating:

Don't. Dating is far more than a courtship ritual. As relationships mature, dating is how we show our partners that we're still attracted to them. Sure, money can get tight, you can have young kids or there can be illness, but none of those reasons should stop a date. There is nothing that says a date requires going out. A date can be a nice movie, a fire in the fireplace and a bottle of wine, a long walk holding hands. A date can be a lot of things and no matter what form a date takes, the important part is to make sure you have at least one a week!

Never Stop Climbing The Mountain:

At every significant milestone, it's important to remember the mountain climber metaphor I used earlier because you want to keep putting new anchors in the mountain so that you're both sure of where you are and that your goals are the same. If things start unraveling, it helps to know where and when the problems started entering the relationship so you can back up and have conversations about what has happened from that point forward.

What you don't want to do is put an anchor in the mountain after every date or two. You do this after significant milestones.

Keep Your Appreciation Alive & Well:

It's important to be appreciative. Always. It's easy to get comfortable in a relationship and start expecting certain things or taking certain things for granted and when that happens you're slipping into a very dangerous phase of the relationship and in that phase, things start going wrong and two people start withdrawing from each other.

Ask Questions:

The biggest relationship mistake I see made with men is when a woman jumps to conclusions about something. A man can purposefully do or not do something because he has the best of intentions and his woman will assume his actions were because he was thoughtless or doesn't care. He ends up feeling hurt, unappreciated and not understood. This pattern of misconstruing actions and assigning negative meaning is a fast way to end a relationship. Before you accuse your man of doing something wrong, of being forgetful or unappreciative, ask questions and listen to his answer!

Chapter 9

MEN AND SEX

MEN AND SEX. NOW WOULDN'T you think this would be a one page chapter? The truth of the matter is that there are tons of myths and misconceptions about men and sex. What I'm going to do in this chapter is work to dispel some of those misunderstandings and give you the information you need to move your sex life towards a healthy, happy and fulfilling place.

Since there are so many myths to dispel and misunderstandings to clear up, I've divided this chapter into five sections:

- Things Men Want In The Bedroom
- What Men Want Women To Know About Sex
- Things Men Don't Like
- When He Thinks You're Not Interested
- Men's Dirty Secrets

Things Men Want In The Bedroom:

Pick up any advice book written by women or any women's magazine, and there is just guaranteed to be some advice instructing you on how to spice up your sex life, telling you what really turns men on or some other tidbit that, if men bothered to read, would either leave them shaking their heads at the nonsense or laughing hysterically (I've done both!). Because of that, most of what I'm about to tell you will seem completely foreign but I promise you it's all completely true. Remember, we want to make you happy!

Figure Out What You Like:

If you can't drive your own car, you can't teach someone else how to drive it. Learn what you like. Experiment on yourself and figure out how and why something drives you crazy and then teach us!

Men Need Foreplay Too:

As teenagers it seems like boys are "instant on" devices. Just hint about sex or let a strong breeze blow and they're ready! Although it may seem that teenage boys are perpetually aroused for no reason, it's not really like that. Teenage boys are stimulated by things they see, smell and feel and these stimuli create moments that, to an outsider (female) may seem like one perpetual state of arousal. The little cutie in the short skirt or tight jeans who walked by his desk smelling like fresh strawberries and who brushed his shoulder with a light touch would be seared into his memory for later recall.

As we men get older, thoughts of that cute girl from high school fade and it takes more to send us in to a state of arousal than the cutie at work walking by our desk. Things change even more once a special woman enters our life and our sexual focus turns to her. As a special woman becomes our romantic focus, we men look to her for our sexual arousal and we need her to make "what we think about" sexually interesting and when she does, she keeps our focus on her. So, just like for women, with men, foreplay is both mental and physical and we need both. We both want AND need you to tease and arouse us.

This may come as a complete shock to most women but in a New Brunswick Study women thought men wanted about 13 minutes of foreplay while men think 18 minutes is ideal - that's about 5 minutes more that what women think.

The truth is, foreplay starts when you wake up in the morning and continues all day long, through dinner, through putting the kids to bed and well in to your alone time. Don't believe me? Try it!

Learn New Tricks:

That old saying "you can't teach an old dog new tricks" was meant for dogs, not humans. As humans, we have complex minds capable of learning at almost any age. Explore the world of sex and if you don't want to do something because you don't know how or because it may seem gross, do some research. Go online and read up on it, read a book about it. Learn! The old excuse "good girls don't do that" simply isn't true. Good girls DO do that and many good girls do it very well and your man knows this!

We Like Variety:

Doing it the same way on the same day with the same sets of rituals gets boring! Not just boring but so boring that after awhile it loses its ability to arouse us and we start thinking "why bother?" So, mix it up, learn new ways, examine some of the rituals and the beliefs that guide you and see if there's a reason for those beliefs. I once had a girlfriend who was so ritualized that I could tell she wanted sex by what was cooked for dinner. Some rituals are comforting but when it comes to sex and men, variety is a requirement!

Sex IS Emotional For Men:

I know, I know. This simple statement flies into an entire lifetime of beliefs, jokes and ridicule but the truth of the matter is that when we are in a relationship, sex IS emotional for men. Especially soft, slow, love making where we have to become tender. It's when we become the most vulnerable and you have to make these experiences safe and secure for your man. While it's well known that women need emotional intimacy in order to have sex, what's not so well known is that men build emotional intimacy through sex.

Your Flaws Are All In Your Mind:

Men are really odd about this. When we first see you we probably notice that one boob is bigger or that your third toe sticks out an inch longer than all the rest and every other little flaw. We see them all and we do it mere seconds. It's during this time that we decide whether or not we're attracted to you and if we are, then those flaws simply don't matter. Once our decision has been made, we don't care. As we grow in love for you we no longer think about, remember or actually even see any flaws you have. In fact, you could put on 20 or 30 lbs and odds are we'd never notice. When you focus on your flaws you force us to focus on them as well and not only do we not like focusing on your flaws, it's really not where you want our attention!

We Want You To Tell Us:

If you're not satisfied and you need something more, different or better then speak up! Remember what I've said repeatedly throughout this book including at the beginning of this chapter, your man wants nothing more than to please you and despite what you may want or think, we're not mind readers.

What Men Want Women To Know About Sex:

Just like in "Things Men Want In The Bedroom" listed above, which are things many of you are probably still shaking your heads over, there are more things we want you to know about sex in general and, understanding these things, will move your relationship to a much higher level of satisfaction.

Sometimes A Quickie Is Just Fine:

Nothing makes a man feel desired faster than a woman initiating a quickie. It lets us know you desire us and that we can bring out those animal desires in you and it lets us unleash our animal desires on you. When you make a big production every time you want sex you feed into most men's #1 complaint about women and sex. I'll talk about this more below.

We Don't Always Need To Take Care Of Each Other:

Sometimes it's okay for you to make yourself happy while we make ourselves happy. In other words it's okay to not depend on us for your big finish and it's okay for us to not depend on you! If a little self play along the way gets you there quicker we are okay with that and, in fact, the vast majority of us find it quite sexy! Likewise, we don't always need to "finish" - yes, it's nice and yes, not finishing can be uncomfortable but if we only have 5 minutes before work, that 5 minutes will leave us thinking about what we're gonna get when we get home that night!

Never Say No To Your Man:

Okay, this isn't really a rule but there's a lot tied to this that you need to be aware of. Saying no creates a sense of rejection and undesirability while a quickie will make your man happy. Would you rather have a 15 minute quickie or 3-4 hours of grumpy, moodiness? I'm not advocating that you forgo your own needs or that you always be submissive to your man, quite the contrary. I'm advocating that you be aware of what happens when you say no. A little later in this chapter, I'll help you understand how to turn no into a major teasing opportunity.

We Always Want You To Get To Your Big Finish:

Believe it or not, we really do want you to have a big finish each and every time and even better if you can have your big finish multiple times. We do understand that with some women they simply will not get there every time but that doesn't mean we don't feel bad because you didn't. What we want you to know is that we want you to help us get you there and especially if that means you have to slow down our big finish so that you can have your big finish. For instance, changing positions is a great technique for slowing him down and saving his favorite position for last is a great way to make sure you get satisfied. When sex is good for you, that's when we want to thump our chest and give our best Tarzan yell! It's important to us!

Don't Make It So Complicated:

As I've stated before, men like things simple. Sex doesn't have to be complicated. The lights don't have to be out, the vacuum doesn't need to be run, the bed doesn't have to be turned down and the pillows don't have to be stacked just so. The more simple you make having sex, the more of it you are going to have and the more your man is going to want to make sure you are fulfilled because we want to keep this train running at full steam!!!

We Are Not Mind Readers:

Have I said this before? We like it when you give directions and it's far more satisfying for you when you give directions and get what you need than to live with an unfulfilling and unsatisfying sex life. There are lots of ways of giving directions from moving his hands to where you want them, using your hands to slow him down or speed him up, moaning or just outright telling us what you need. Help us make you happy and if you're happy then we're happy and when we're happy we feel more secure in the relationship. Some women express fear that telling a man what you want will take him out of the assertive role and make you seem pushy. As I've stated before and will say countless times again. There is a time and place for everything and pillow talk is a great time to tell him what he's doing right and how it turns you on and how "you think it would be really hot if he took that one move a little further."

What Is Kinky?

Comedian Chris Rock once said in a comedy bit "Just because a man had an orgasm doesn't mean you made him orgasm!" What Chris was saying is that in the absence of meaningful foreplay, appropriate stimulation and engaging activity a man will turn to his fantasies or the memory of an experience with a previous sex partner.

Ouch!

Now, before you go running off to question your man about what he's thinking about during sex (He's just gonna lie and say he's thinking about you and to stop reading these crazy books!) the simple fact is, if he didn't want to be having sex with you he wouldn't. Does that mean the sex you're having is over the moon for him? No, not at all. It simply means in the overall balance of things, your sex life is good enough and when taken into account along with the other aspects of your relationship he can live with what he's getting. That doesn't mean he wouldn't like for your sex life to be more, different or better.

I often hear women say "I'm not a bad girl and I'm not into all that kinky stuff!" to which I reply there is no such thing as kinky and if there were, your idea of kinky would probably bore your best friend out of her mind and your own mother would wonder how you turned out to be such a prude. The real truth of the matter is that your man knows this as well.

DeeDee, a 34 year old from Green Bay tells this story:

As a divorced mother of two, I enjoyed sex but I had never had an orgasm "because orgasms were what bad girls and whores did." Several years after my divorce I met a man and after several months of dating we had sex. As was my usual pattern, as I neared orgasm I would invoke any number of other methods, such as asking for a change in position, so I wouldn't climax. With this new lover, this worked the first time... and the second... but then all of a sudden it was too late and I had the first orgasm of my life and I immediately burst into tears. I was ashamed. My lover, not having a clue what was happening could only sit back in stunned silence until I stopped sobbing and he could make out what I was trying to tell him. After learning what my problem was he gently held me and after awhile asked her 'How have you changed? What part of you has suddenly turned bad? Are you going to run out and start charging men for sex?' Of course I was the same person and I had no inclination to turn to a life of prostitution. His point was made. My orgasm didn't make me a bad person. I'm not even sure where I picked up that belief but it was wrong. Enjoying sex, having orgasms, being a good lover and partner changes your life and I would advise any woman to examine her beliefs about sex!"

Of course this is a rather extreme point, but the point is the same. Sometimes our beliefs about something are misguided and falsely held. It's only by experimenting and experiencing new things do we get to grow as human beings.

Does this mean you should run out and do something crazy? Absolutely not. I don't need to make a porn film nor do I need to be beaten with a rod to learn those are not things that would bring me pleasure. On the other hand, there are things that do bring me pleasure that I wouldn't know about if I hadn't experimented.

Why We Sleep After Sex:

There are several reasons men get sleepy after sex. First, the physical exertion of sex depletes the muscles of the energy-producing glycogen, which leads to tiredness. Also, sex therapists tell us that our male body chemistry changes after orgasm and a biochemical called Prolactin is released which physically alters our body and makes us very drowsy. This combination of tired and drowsy can almost guarantee we fall asleep.

Beyond the over 300 bodily functions that Prolactin is associated with, it also provides the body with what we sense as sexual gratification after sexual acts and effectively counteracts the effect of Dopamine, which rises during sexual arousal. This Dopamine/Prolactin cycle is thought to cause the sexual refractory period which is how long it takes for a man to achieve another erection. The amount of Prolactin released indicates the amount of sexual satisfaction and determines the subsequent level of relaxation; the higher the level of Prolactin released, the greater the level of sexual satisfaction. In fact, after orgasm from masturbation, the measured Prolactin levels are 4X lower than what is measured after orgasm from sexual intercourse and this shows that men typically find masturbation to be far less satisfying than actual intercourse. Moreover, when left with masturbation as the primary outlet for sexual release, men will become less satisfied in their relationship.

Another major hormone, Oxytocin, which is sometimes referred to as the "love hormone" because it's associated with bonding between partners, is released during orgasm. In general, Oxytocin increases social interaction and promotes love and trust of people who are intimate with each other. The fact that your man can feel more relaxed around you also means that fear and anxiety (both stimulants) are reduced or gone, which makes this is the perfect time to snuggle in and build that closeness.

One specific sleep hormone released is serotonin. Serotonin, which can be purchased over-the-counter as a sleep aide, is known to have a calming effect on the brain and help induce sleep.

As for the penis, there is also a chemical process that occurs during ejaculation. Nitric oxide is released by the prostate gland and basically promotes relaxation throughout the entire penis.

From an evolutionary standpoint, many scientists believe the 'sleepy response' is there to keep men from running off with another partner, or jumping to another woman's bed and this sleepy response is chemically built for pair bonding.

With the combination of the stress hormones being removed, the relaxation, the increased "love hormone" and trust, this makes the time after sex an incredibly important time to snuggle up with your man, even after a quickie taking an extra 5 minutes to snuggle can increase closeness and intimacy.

Timing Is Everything:

Male testosterone levels peak around 7:00 a.m. daily which accounts for those early morning erections and is the lowest around 11:00 p.m. at night which is why, after that great evening with your man, spending 20 minutes taking off your makeup before getting into bed can leave you with a man sound asleep. While you may take his lack of interest personally, it's not. With lower testosterone levels, he does have less interest and, unless he's a night owl, his body may drive him towards sleep instead of sex. This is especially true after men have passed through their "mid-life crisis" phase when testosterone levels are already declining.

Researchers have also discovered that a man's sex drive goes up and down over the course of a month. Dr. Marcus Laux, a naturopathic physician, discovered in his research that men have more energy, a greater sense of well being, lower body weight and less need for sleep during the peak of our testosterone cycles with our valleys bringing apathy, indifference and a general crabbiness which you experience as our tendency to magnify small problems into big ones.

So you can think of this like a PMS cycle but I would STRONGLY advise you to not make jokes about this as you'll build more resentment and do more harm to your relationship than you would ever care to imagine. Even making the joke about a male boss could lead to serious trouble and would be just as inappropriate as a male employee making comments about you being on your period. Just keep track and realize, just like we men have learned about women, certain times of the month can lead to some moodiness.

Why Men Stop Having Sex:

Of course we're all familiar with the jokes about the fragile male ego but the fact of the matter is male sexuality is complex, delicate and fragile because so much of a man's self worth is linked to sexual intimacy.

But there is a time and place for joking about our delicate male egos and a time to understand some facts, symptoms and to roll up our sleeves and get a little dirty.

Numerous studies tell us that 40 million Americans live in sexless relationships. In previous studies conducted in 1960's, 70's, and 80's, the vast majority (70%) of the time, it was women who chose to remove sex from the relationship. During the 90's researchers started noticing more and more men withhold sex. In current studies we find that men are equal participants in sexless relationships choosing to withhold sex in nearly 50% of all sexless relationships.

Sexless relationships are sad, lonely and destructive places to be. A sexless relationship doesn't mean the relationship is over, it means that some corrective action needs to be taken and taken rather quickly. Notice I said quickly, not harshly or critically.

When either of you are withholding sex, the lack of sex kills intimacy on all levels from basic physical touch to intimate conversations. Remember what I said earlier, when it comes to love, men need sex as a way to connect emotionally. No sex and that emotional connection starts withering and will eventually be severed.

Since men often express emotions through sex and use sex to connect emotionally, when we shut down emotionally, we also shut down physically. That means physical withdrawal should be a clear sign that something is seriously wrong.

Numerous sex therapists cite the # 1 reason men stop having sex as boredom, but in my own research, the vast majority of men who had stopped having sex named several reasons why they did so. Let's look at some of the survey results, which, for the record, don't add up to 100% because most men in sexless relationships chose more than one reason:

She isn't sexually adventurous enough (68%):

"She isn't sexually adventurous enough for me" is another way of saying "this is boring!" And what did men say about needing variety?!?! Variety isn't even about changing positions but also about the routine leading up to sex. There are some women who orchestrate the sexual encounter so closely that the men can tell simply based on what's for dinner, the music played or the wine poured.

She doesn't enjoy sex with me (61%):

"She doesn't seem to enjoy sex" is saying "I'm not getting any positive feedback so I don't feel good about myself so I won't do this." What would be worse is if the woman was making it seem like she was doing her man a favor and that she really disliked sex as that would be an incredibly emotionally abusive position to take.

I no longer feel close to her (58%):

In ways, this is the classic "we've grown apart" and most of these men felt like there were still reasons to stay together such as finances, kids or even hope that things will change, they also recognized that the relationship was or could be over with little emotional damage.

I'm angry with her (41%):

"I'm angry with her." **Most every** sex therapist will tell you that when men feel criticized, controlled, undervalued and insignificant they feel angry towards their partners and stop having sex. When there is no room for his opinions or feelings, men shut down emotionally and when they shut down emotionally, they shut down physically.

I'm no longer attracted to her (33%):

Since some of the questions in the study asked about how emotionally fulfilled the men felt in their relationships, how happy they felt, how much drama they felt the relationship had and how active their sex lives were (frequency): In the responses, where men felt emotionally fulfilled, they still had very active sex lives and felt extremely attracted to their partners even when those partners had gained 20, 30 or 40 extra lbs. However, there was a direct and distinct correlation between a man being no longer attracted when he was emotionally unfulfilled, were unhappy and they thought the relationship contained too much drama. Essentially, the reason the men had stopped having sex was because the relationship had become unfulfilling on levels other than physical attraction.

If you are in a sexless relationship, you have your work cut out for you. There are a lot of reasons why your man may have chosen to stop having sex and you should consult a qualified marital therapist for help. If your man won't go, and if he doesn't feel heard and understood there's a really good chance he won't, you will have to fix this yourself but you still need to see a therapist during the process. Remember, you need to remove the barriers to communications, start listening and work to restore your man's trust and emotional fulfillment. Try not to let it go too long before you reengage in sex because of how it helps rebuild those emotional bonds but you can't force this and trying to do so will just drive a bigger wedge into your already wounded relationship.

Things Men Don't Like:

There are very definite "mood killers" and women are just as guilty of them as men are but men typically won't say anything to their partners. What you want to do is remove as many barriers as is possible in order to make your love life as fulfilling as possible. Here are some of the things men have said they dislike most:

You're Not Into Oral Sex:

I've yet to meet or even hear about a man who's not into both giving and receiving oral sex. If you have problems with either side then you need to start having discussions with your man, reading books and talking to your physician. This is absolutely not something that only bad girls do and for most couples is an essential part of foreplay.

You Jump Out Of Bed:

Okay, we all know you want and need to clean up after sex but when you jump up and run off to clean up like you just did something disgusting it sends a loud and clear message that you're not into sex with your man. Really! It does! Is that how you feel and really the sign you want to send? If it's how you feel about your partner then you need to be kind and end the relationship. If that's not how you feel, then you need to be kind.

Instead of jumping up and running off, what you should be doing is taking that time to cuddle, try the lovers embrace as that's when most men feel the most content. Use that time to validate him by telling him how much you appreciate him. Tell him the one thing he did that pushed you over the edge or take this time to tell him what you liked and how it would turn you on even more if he would take that further.

Getting Ready For Sex Takes Too Long:

If your pre-sex routine takes more time than just slipping off your panties, you're going about this all wrong.

You've just spent the evening enjoying a nice romantic dinner, had a few glasses of wine, listened to some soft music, had a little make out session and you've got your guy all wound up and you head off to the bedroom. He turns towards the sheets and you veer erringly off to the bathroom where you're going to wash off your makeup, take out your contacts, brush your teeth, brush your hair, pee, clean up a little down there and then come into bed. By the time you've gotten to where he is, he's either engrossed in ESPN, reading his book or rolled over and gone to sleep. Men hate these delays and the signal you send is that you're not as turned on or as interested as he is.

Your Routine Is Routine:

Remember, the number one reason men stop having sex with their partner is because it's boring. As I mentioned earlier, I once dated a woman who was so regimented that I could tell if she wanted sex by what we had for dinner and every move after that was equally orchestrated. After the 30th time I had her moves down so pat that I started making a game out of not responding the way she expected me to just so I could add some excitement to the routine. We later had a conversation where I expressed to her that sex was extremely boring and predictable and that I needed some variety. She never made any effort to change and the relationship eventually ended. Every single day countless relationships end over this one thing. Variety IS the spice of life!

If you are stuck in a routine, get a copy of the Kama Sutra and start working your way through each of the positions. Make Tuesday "Try a new position Tuesday" and see how quick he gets home from work!

You Want Him To Always Be In The Lead:

While it might be nice to have a strong man leading the relationship or as a partner, men need to feel desired just as much as you do and if it's always up to him to start the process then he's not going to feel desired. You have to take the bull by the horn (so to speak) and make your desire for him known. When you do this, he'll not only feel appreciated but he will also feel more secure in the relationship.

You Act You're Doing Us A Favor To Have Sex:

Comments like "Okay, but you're gonna owe me!" are not exactly endearing and actually damages the security he feels in the relationship. Everyone understands too tired and even the horniest of men can understand that you've just had a horrible day. Instead of making it bad experience, tell him how you really feel and then after the lights are turned off and you've snuggled up together, tell him that tomorrow will be a better day and whisper a few of the naughty things you're going to do to him. Watch how he dotes on you and how smooth your morning goes! Again, don't promise what you can't or won't deliver as you will erode trust.

And don't forget to text him a few times during the day to let him know you haven't forgotten those naughty things and that you're looking forward to them.

You Get Your Big Finish And You're Done:

Things have gone well, very well in fact and then "fireworks" and then you're done. Most women can go over and over again but some women hit that one orgasm and they're finished. Well, in cases where your man is also finished that can be okay, but if he's not done when you lose interest it creates all kinds of problems. First, he can be left hanging which is emotionally frustrating and can lead to him feeling uncared for and undesired. Second, it can be physically painful for him.

Now, if you happen to be one who gets her big finish and, although you lose interest you're willing to hang in there and make sure your partner gets his, if you don't do this with enthusiasm, it sends a signal that you just don't care and you appear incredibly selfish and this too will change the tone of your relationship in negative ways. Be enthusiastic!

When He Thinks You're Not Interested:

As we grow in our relationships we become more knowledgeable of each other's habits, patterns and routines. We become comfortable and relax. You stop closing the door when you pee and he takes more liberties when he passes gas. Those types things are parts of intimacy that couples share. However, when it comes to sex, and remember, men build intimacy from sex, it's important to not send the wrong signals. As such, the men I have talked to listed the things that tell them "don't bother trying." The more of these things they encounter and the more frequently they encounter them, the more they feel sex is off the table.

Your Bedroom Looks Like An Office:

This sends the signal that you are probably distracted by all you have to do. What guy wants to look at stacks of papers, unpaid bills and then try to make love to you? Really! We want to know your focus is on us and not your unfinished work.

The bedroom should be about sleep, relaxing, snuggling, quality time and SEX! Not about office memos, the report due tomorrow morning or other mood killers. Most men would gladly give up the dining room table for a free and clear bedroom! (And the same goes for him too! Kick the office out of the bedroom!)

Your 'Lounge Around' Clothes Look Like They Came From A Homeless Person:

Honestly, we men are visual creatures. We like the way you look, and we like when you look nice. When you're parading around in your old, worn out, stretched out, gray cotton shorts day after day after day, we're really not turned on. I'm not saying that you need to hit Victoria's Secret to buy clothes to cook in but really, there is a very happy medium. Switch it up, keep it interesting. Go without a bra, wear the short denim skirt and give him little flashes. But find a way to spruce it up a little!

You Compare Him To Your Ex:

It doesn't matter if your ex was tiny and the worst lover ever and especially if your ex was an absolute stud that pushed every button you had, you never ever, ever, ever talk about your ex. You make no comparisons of any kind at all ever.

Steve in Hollywood tells this story:

"I once had a girlfriend tell me 'No one ever made love to me like Paul!'(her ex) 'He knows I like it soft and tender'. Do you think I ever slept with her again? Nope. If she wanted sex, she could go see Paul."

No man would subject himself to that level of criticism and thoughtlessness. Imagine how you would feel being compared to another woman your guy had slept with? Your goal is not to produce insecurity; it's to produce security in and out of the bedroom.

What works is to talk about what you want and what's good between you. Encourage what he does right and ask for what you want to try.

You Are Insecure About Your Body:

You don't like your legs, your boobs are too big, too small, droop too much, your belly is too big, your waist is too small, your this that or the other isn't perfect.

The first rule to remember is this: When you're the only naked woman in the room, you are absolutely the sexiest, hottest woman in the room.

The second rule to remember is this: Unless he has stopped having sex with you, then he still finds you a turn on and if he's still turned on, then you have nothing to worry about.

The third rule to remember is this: A man in love doesn't see flaws so stop pointing them out to him! Your man is with you for a reason and if he didn't find you attractive in the beginning, you wouldn't be with him.

Men are constantly dismayed by partners who buy lingerie they thought flattered certain aspects of their body and hid one or two flaws. Small breasted women buy push-up bras, large breasted women buy support bras, and the whole time they end up masking the attributes that made them so sexy to begin with!

The bottom line is this: put your insecurities aside and enjoy the experience and let him enjoy you. Once you do, you will grow in confidence by learning that he does accept you and your flaws are in your imagination.

Silence Is NOT Golden:

When making love, most men like sounds and although not every man likes a "screamer," men do like knowing what they are doing is turning you on. If you're not the vocal type, you need to learn to let loose with a few moans at the appropriate time. This will reinforce and encourage him to repeat or continue doing what he's doing.

As was covered earlier, men want and need feedback. We want to please you and if you're not telling us what you want, we get lost. Women who know what turns them on and can lead us there are sexy! We like it!

One woman friend of mine confided that her husband just couldn't get her off but with her Battery Operated Boyfriend (BOB) she could have an orgasm in 2-3 minutes. I asked her if she had ever taught her husband how to use BOB and she looked at me like I had two heads. Then she got a mischievous grin. A few months later, she told me she couldn't find room for all the new "toys" her husband kept buying. (That's a different problem and one I would not offer suggestions for!)

Trial and error is a long and tedious process to figuring out your partner's sexual needs, desires and fantasies. Too much valuable time gets spent trying to figure things out when, with proper communication, our sex lives could be so much better. Share, communicate, share and communicate some more!

Not Feelin' Groovy:

In the immortal words of Simon and Garfunkel in their 59th Street Bridge Song (Feelin' Groovy) **"Slow down, you move too fast,** you've got to make the morning last!" Every guy appreciates a quickie but not every time. Especially when the first thing you do is pick up that report that's due tomorrow morning. If your motto is "get it done quickly", your man is going to sense that sex with him is not an important priority. No one wants to feel that way.

Men's Dirty Secrets:

Sex Is 24 X 7 For Men:

Hopefully, I've been able to dispel this myth a bit. Sex is not all men think about and it's not our only thought. The good news is that even the men who have stopped having sex are still interested in having sex.

> **Myth:** Men think about sex every 7 seconds

Reality: If a man were to think about sex every 7 seconds that's all he'd be thinking about and he'd have no time to think about sports, driving, eating or anything else! Even subtracting 8 hours for sleep, thinking about sex once every 7 seconds would mean that a man would be thinking about sex 8,229 times per day.

According to the Kinsey Institute (FAQ, 2010), one of the world's foremost sexual and reproductive research facilities based at Indiana University, 54% of men think about sex everyday or several times a day, 43% a few times per month or a few times per week, and 4% less than once a month.

19% of women think about sex everyday or several times a day, 67% a few times per month or a few times per week, and 14% less than once a month.

In another study, conducted by the psychology department at Ohio State University (Fisher, ZT, & MJ, 2012), college aged men spend more of their day thinking about need based things which also include eating and resting than women did. But on the sexual front, according to this study, women averaged thinking about sex 18.6 times per day while men had an average of 34.2 sexual thoughts per day. As such, based on the findings from the study, young men spend substantially less time thinking about sex than originally believed.

So why do men not speak up when they hear this nonsense? Probably because the minute you said this we started thinking about sex! Well, that and you would think something was wrong with us and you wouldn't believe it anyway!

Teasing Your Man:

Teasing your man in an important part of foreplay and can take several forms. From what you say, how you say it, what you wear and what you reveal to him and all those slight touches at just the right place in just the right moment can drive us to a state of extreme anticipation.

Learning to tell your man that you're looking forward to getting him in bed; whispering naughty things in his ear or writing notes and leaving them where he can find them are all excellent strategies for building anticipation.

I will tell you that you also need to be careful. A colleague of mine was scheduled to give a departmental presentation that involved a lot of higher ups. As was his routine, he got to the office early and reviewed the slide presentation prior to the meeting. His wife, knowing this, stuck a very sexual slide in the presentation. As luck would have it, he got a flat tire on the way in and didn't have time to review the presentation. I'll spare you the details of absolute humiliation he experienced but he also told me it was some of the hottest sex he'd ever had! We are an odd lot!

When you tease a man, he feels desired, special and significant (important to you) and feeling special and significant increases his feeling of security within the relationship. When a man feels special, significant and secure within the relationship, that's when you get his best.

What Is Sexy Underwear?

In the survey on sex I conducted for this book, do you know what came out as the Number 1 sexiest thing that a woman could wear? I bet you think lingerie came out on top? Nope. By a very slim margin the number one sexiest thing a woman could wear was one of her man's button down, oxford style dress shirts and nothing else (42%).

Admittedly, lingerie was a close 2nd (35%) but I think this goes to show that men have very different views on what constitutes sexy than women do.

And for the record, nothing but a pair of heels came in 3rd (18%) while wearing nothing at all was 4th (15%). So, essentially 65% of men prefer something other than lingerie. Now that's a dirty secret!

Why doesn't your man tell you that lingerie is a waste of time and money? Because that would be a stupid thing to say and men are not stupid!

Did He Just Say That?:

It's important to understand that, as a guy gets increasingly aroused, his inhibitions will lower and he may say some surprising things in the heat of the moment. If something he says really bothers you, address it with him - post-intimacy but if it doesn't bother you, then take heed because he just gave you a key to something going on in his fantasy world.

My Man Watches Porn, Why Am I Not Enough

> **NOTE:** My job is not to pass judgment on whether porn is right, wrong, good or bad but simply to report the findings in my and others research studies. It's up to you to form your own opinions and to do what is right for you.

Studies have found that men who watch porn have the same pleasure centers stimulated that occur with drugs and alcohol. Now, before you go off screaming that your man is addicted to porn, those same pleasure centers get activated when a man sees a pretty lady at a restaurant, which is hardly an addicting activity (dangerous maybe, but not addicting!). In another study, men who were shown sexy pictures of women were far less stressed than the group who were shown non-sexual images meaning that men find images of sexy women to be relaxing.

What men say is that that porn allows for a quick and easy masturbation session while maintaining fidelity within the relationship and that more often, during orgasm, the men are not thinking about the actresses on screen but about the person they're in a relationship with. The porn short circuits the male fantasy system and by focusing on the images on the screen, all those work issues and other life stresses get pushed to the background with no effort.

Women's attitudes towards porn are shifting and now over 75% of women don't believe that watching porn is cheating; over 50% of women have watched porn with a partner and over 40% report having made a homemade movie or allowed pictures to be taken of themselves or have taken naked pictures of themselves to text to a partner.

But isn't porn unhealthy? It depends on who you ask. Any minister in any organized religion will tell you that porn is a bad thing. Any sex researcher will tell you that porn is like anything else: in moderation and with agreement between both partners it can be healthy. In fact, one study reported that couples that watched porn together at least once per week reported being more committed in their relationships and the women felt the porn helped them feel more comfortable in asking for what they wanted. Some women even admitted using porn to lead or show their partners things the women wanted to explore and to gain insight into how to explore those things with their men.

Chapter 10

THE UGLY SIDE OF MEN

L̲ET'S FACE IT - SOME men are known to have a number of less than desirable traits. Most of these, such as leaving their socks on the floor, are just annoying, some can put a relationship under extreme stress and others can be just downright dangerous.

Sometimes, we find ourselves in a relationship and we simply can't figure out what's going on but we know, deep down inside, that things just are not quite right. There are some behaviors such as insecurity, jealousy, etc. that can be dangerous OR those things can just be a sign of a dysfunctional or broken relationship. The key is determining the root of these problems. That's what this chapter is about: talking about the ugly side of men and to give you some insight as to when these behaviors indicate a relationship problem or when they're the sign of something more harmful.

In the next chapter which is on Domestic Violence, we'll see how some of these same behaviors can turn to violence. Let's start with something easy!

Socks In The Floor:

Why is he so messy? He throws his socks on the floor, leaves his wet towel in the bathroom floor and God only knows where is underwear will turn up! He couldn't hit the dishwasher with a dirty dish, constantly leaves the toilette seat up, and if he changed a role of toilet paper his fingers would fall off!

As I traveled around speaking to women's groups this was a common complaint and the theories expressed were varied. I heard women say "he was never taught right at home" but you could go into the house where he was raised and find his mother was neat and clean and will tell you that he was never allowed to behave that way when he was growing up. Another common theory is "he thinks I'm his maid" and while I highly doubt this is his reason, I can certainly understand how a woman could feel this way. Another common theory you hear is "he's just marking his territory" and that is really just as implausible but is certainly getting warmer.

A Different Perspective:

A few years ago I was sitting outside at a coffee shop with a bunch of friends. One was a German friend in town for a visit. This lady was known to be outspoken, and she generally made conversations quite lively. With her and I were 4 couples and a few other single people so we had quite a little crowd. At one point, one of the women asked how my book was coming. I told her what part I was working on, and her eyes lit up and she asked "Well then, maybe you can tell me why my husband leaves his socks all over the floor!" I sat there thinking about her question for a moment and not because I didn't know the answer but because I didn't know how to answer her question tactfully. While I was thinking, my German friend spoke up and said "The problem with American women is that you like the idea of a man, but you don't actually like men!" The table went to stunned silence and my friend continued "I hear American women complain about their man leaving socks on the floor or the Sunday paper all over the living room and I think, you're complaining because you've made a home where he feels comfortable and then you spend all your time trying to make him feel uncomfortable in that very home." She continued "Personally, when I see my man's dirty socks on the floor, I know he's happy and that he's MY man! It's when his socks start going in the hamper or the paper gets neatly stacked that I worry because when he starts doing that, he's found another place where he's more comfortable." After a very long and uncomfortable silence, the lady asked me, "Is she right?"

While my German friend was exactly right, he's doing this because he feels really comfortable and feels like he can let his hair down. He's not marking his territory because it already IS his territory. He's won it and that's all there is about it.

That explanation certainly doesn't mean you need to put up with behavior that bothers you but it does allow you to recognize it for what it is and to find ways to make allowances for some things and figure out how to compromise on the others. Certainly though, you don't want to take away what you've created and although you may not feel comfortable with it, you're not the only one in the relationship. If you behave as if you were, then one day you will be and some other woman will be over the moon with the socks in the floor!

Insecure Men:

There are two types of insecurity. There is developmental and situational. Developmental insecurity stems from how a boy was raised and his past life experiences. With developmental insecurity, he probably grew up with a great deal of criticism and shame and over time he's failed to develop a full sense of authentic pride and as a result, he is an insecure man.

Situational insecurity is about the uncertainty or anxiety a man feels about the situation he's in. This can be anything from suddenly being thrust in to public speaking role to his relationship with you. Some forms of situational insecurity can be overcome by the man. For instance, he can learn the art of public speaking. Other forms of situational insecurity he may try to work through, but only for a short while and if the situation doesn't change, he'll leave the situation.

Situational Insecurity:

If you're not honest with your man and he catches you lying or cheating, you don't keep your word, you don't talk to him about things, you criticize him and/or you stop listening to and encouraging him then your man will judge himself as someone who has a very low value to you and when a man feels he has very low value to you, he becomes insecure in the situation which is your relationship.

"But if I'm not cheating on him or lying to him, isn't this just his trust issue?" Just remember, when a man doesn't feel like he's significant to you, he becomes insecure. A minor onetime thing will probably be ignored but as these things stack up they start chipping away at his feeling of significance and safety in the relationship until he hits a point of feeling insecure.

"But we live together, shouldn't he know?" or "We've been dating for two years, isn't that enough?" Being in a long term relationship or living together doesn't mean anything more than you have history and some bonds that connect you. The fact that you are connected is the thread that he hangs on to and he will hang on to that thread until it breaks in which case you or he will walk away and until that time, you will both be miserable unless the situation is fixed.

Developmental Insecurity:

Developmental insecurity starts in childhood, some even argue from birth. These types of insecure men are insecure about everything. They may seem strong and secure but sometimes that's just to mask the real issue.

Some of the things you need to recognize so that you know if you're dealing with an insecure man are:

- He will resort to name calling when things get too emotionally intense
- He can be a sore loser and an ungracious winner
- He will speak badly of other people
- He will make fun of or have an extreme dislike of the super rich or the very poor
- When you're frustrated he may encourage you to quit
- Everything has an ulterior motive or hidden meaning
- He is very selfish
- He becomes very defensive over everything
- He is extremely competitive
- He is extremely bossy

When you're dealing with an insecure man there are a series of steps to take and the first thing to do is to determine whether or not your man is insecure because of how he was raised and his past experiences or whether he's experiencing a situational insecurity or both. This takes a great deal of self evaluation and honesty on your part because it's very, very easy to believe that you're doing nothing wrong and that he's simply an insecure man. After all, no one wants to believe or admit that we are neglecting or mistreating our partner and/or our own behavior is causing the problems.

If you determine that your behavior is causing all or part of his situational insecurity then you need to stop! Your behavior will destroy your relationship. From there you need to go into damage control and work on rebuilding trust and communications.

If your man is developmentally insecure, what part, if any, of his insecurity is tolerable and what part does he needs to fix before the relationship gets destroyed? Once you've figured that out, then it's time for a conversation, and as a part of that conversation, you need to express your support for him during the process including joint counseling. You must also be open to hearing his perspective. After you've had the conversation, then you need to assess whether or not he is actually capable of making that change, and if he's not, then you will either have to chose living with the insecurity or leaving the relationship. From insecurity stems many other problems.

Jealousy:

Jealousy is about showing suspicion of someone's unfaithfulness or potential unfaithfulness in a relationship. and there are good, evolutionary reasons for jealousy or, mate-guarding. Typically, men are far more concerned with sexual infidelity which evolved from a need to protect resources and make sure the dinosaur leg went to feeding their own offspring. Women, however, evolved to be far more concerned with emotional infidelity because they needed to make sure the man didn't become attached to another woman and abandon her and the offspring leaving them vulnerable. Emotional infidelity is detected 9 times higher in women than in men, and women experiencing emotional jealousy are typically more prone to violence such hitting, slapping, kicking and hair pulling than men. In modern society, men not only guard against sexual infidelity but consider any "threats" as a direct attack on his masculinity.

Jealousy consists of a combination of emotions such as anger, resentment, inadequacy, helplessness and disgust. Why would emotions such as disgust enter into jealousy? Cultural exposure influences the way we perceive situations, and that perception can lead to anything from disgust to rage. Some psychologists suggest that jealousy is actually a secondary reaction stemming from one's needs not being met. Those needs may be for secure attachment, undivided attention, reassurance or some additional form of care which the jealous partner expects from a romantic relationship.

Jealousy, then, is any negative or protective reaction to a perceived threat to a valued relationship. When a negative or protective reaction comes from a situation where one partner's involvement with another person or activity conflicts with the jealous person's personal or cultural definition of their relationship and violates the jealous persons understanding of how both parties should behave in a relationship, then both partners have to decide where the relationship will go from that point on.

Jealous men tend to act in an accusatory manner in order to protect themselves from any possibility of being hurt. When a man feels vulnerable and powerless in the outcome of your actions, jealousy drives him to confront you with unfounded accusations. His jealousy is an outward demonstration of his own apprehension in trusting you in the relationship. Men who exhibit jealous behavior accuse women with often (but not always) unsubstantiated allegations of flirting, putting other men before him and cheating. Jealous men want constant reassurance that their partners' interests rests solely in them.

There are two types of jealousy, founded and unfounded.

Founded Jealousy:

Founded jealousy is jealousy based on an actual cause. Comparing him to your ex, lying to him about a relationship with another man, keeping your contact with another man a secret or having him catch you flirting with another man are actual reasons for a man to feel insecure within the relationship and is the basis for legitimate jealousy. What's happened is that you have violated the trust of the relationship, reduced his significance in the relationship and taken away a part of his masculinity. Depending on the man, the other things going on in his life (i.e. unemployment), together with your violations, can stack on top of one another and be as damaging as actually cheating.

Dave in Arizona tells this story:

"My roommate had real issues with his girlfriend and accused her of always flirting with other men. One night, she called while he was eating so he put her on speaker and I heard him tell her that he 'was completely over her constant flirting with other men' to which she replied 'You're insane! I never flirt with anyone and you can ask all my friends who have known me for 20 years that I don't even know how to flirt.' Without acknowledging her, he changed the subject, chatted about a few other things and then invited her over for dinner on Friday night, two evenings away. I had never met his girlfriend and had no desire to infringe on their evening but I had to admit to being curious. Friday rolls around and I had just finished dressing to go out with friends when the door bell rang and I answered it and I can tell you that from the moment she walked in the door she was the biggest flirt I had ever seen. About 10 minutes later one of my buddies showed up and we all chatted for about 5 minutes and when we left my buddy said 'was it me or was she flirting with me?' My roommate broke up with her not long after that."

Unfounded:

Unfounded jealousy is a result of the man having low self esteem and his beliefs, behavior and actions are completely the result of what goes on in his own mind. While he may believe his needs are not being met and he may believe his reasons for feeling jealous are founded, they're actually not.

Here are signs that you're dealing with a jealous man:

Possessiveness: Treating you as if you are one of his possessions reveals that your man's jealousy may be a deep rooted psychological issue and a warning sign for abusive behavior.

Isolation: Men who are motivated by jealous behavior want women all to themselves; this means that they don't want to share their partners with anyone, including family and friends. A controlling man often believes that your association with others may lead you to turn against him, so he places stipulations on your contact with others, especially those who pose the most threat - other men.

Control: Controlling behaviors include monitoring your movements, refusing to allow you time by yourself or with your friends and asking invasive questions about your interactions with co-workers, acquaintances and even strangers.

Intimidation:

Insanely jealous partners rely on threats and intimidation for control. Intimidation tactics include "threatening looks or gestures, smashing things in front of you, destroying property, hurting your pets, or putting weapons on display," warns the Help Guide website. It is important to note that even if your partner doesn't put his hands on you, he is still attempting to bully you through implied threats of violence.

Extreme behavior is a strong sign there is something significantly wrong with your man. If you are experiencing threats, bullying, intimidation, isolation or other forms of control, you need to evaluate your own safety and seek the counsel of professionals. I will go into further detail about all this in the chapter on Domestic Violence.

Grumpy Or Moody Men:

There is a huge difference between moodiness and bi-polar disorder. Bi-polar disorder is generally accompanied by extreme highs and lows that seem to come on for no apparent reason. When people hit the highs that come with bi-polar disorder, it's not uncommon to see them throw caution to the wind. When they hit the lows, there is no possible solution to their problems and the world will surely end or, minimally, be better off without them. If you suspect a man in your life is suffering from bi-polar disorder, you need to seek professional help immediately!

By contrast, moodiness, comes and goes rather quickly and can be caused by stress, being tired, hungry or undergoing some emotional problems such as fighting with the woman in their lives. Some other causes of moodiness can be drugs, alcohol, food allergies or even a medical condition.

When you're dealing with a man who's moody, it's important to understand the cause and to watch what's going on in his environment. Is he only moody when he's coming home from work but not on the weekends? Only after eating certain foods? Has his alcohol intake increased? Is there someone he's in conflict with? It's perfectly fine to say "Honey, I've noticed that lately you're distressed when you come home from work and that you're drinking more than usual. What's going on?"

If your man doesn't want to talk about it, it's perfectly Okay to accept his answer and still provide comfort. Ask him what he needs, and then give him that. If he needs to be left alone, give him that… for awhile… and then join him in his space but don't talk to him, just sit quietly nearby and let him start talking first and follow his lead. He may or may not bring up the topic, but he will understand that you are there to support him.

I also think it's perfectly acceptable to tolerate this grumpy/moody behavior for a while and then to draw a line in the sand by saying "Look, you've been grumpy for a week now and you're taking it out on me. If it's something I did, then we need to talk about that. If it's something else, then I need you to clue me in because I want to be supportive, but I also need you to stop being grumpy with me."

Stubborn Behavior:

When you hear men described as stubborn, you typically hear phrases like "he keeps his heels dug in" or "with that man it's always 'my way or the highway'" and the man is essentially saying "No I won't and you can't make me!" This leads to the belief that stubborn men are particularly difficult to deal with because they resist everything. This is not only frustrating but can prohibit stubborn men from achieving their dreams or from showing the love they need to show.

The question we need to ask is this: "Where is this resistance coming from?" With men, resistance is rooted in three primary areas: Fear, Threat and/or Invalidation:

Fear:

Fear is a broad feeling and encompasses a lot of areas: fear of change; fear of being out of control; fear of the unknown; and these fears are generally deeply rooted and stem from a lot of childhood instability such as frequently moving for a new job, frequent family turmoil due to changing parental situations (divorce, new parents, another divorce). Regardless of the situation, the young boy experiences all of this as change forced upon him and this change has created a sense of uncertainty that the boy was never able to recover from. The more of these the boy endures, the more entrenched he becomes as an adult male.

Threat:

Men are designed to avoid threats. It's a huge part of our nature so change is often seen as a threat. Men are very prone to guarding themselves, their families, their standing in the community and their masculinity so any change that is a threat to these is to be avoided at all costs.

Invalidation:

Invalidation occurs when the other person is suggesting a course of action or pushing for a behavior without understanding all the logical facts, issues and concerns the man may be weighing OR without understanding his feelings; Men describe this in a number of ways such as "I feel like I'm being treated like I'm stupid" or "No one cares how I feel about this!" A good example would be changing a diet. You may be pushing for your man to stop eating fast food, to give up the potato chips or sweets and to eat more vegetables, and he may be complaining the whole way that he doesn't have time during lunch for anything other than a quick burger, that he likes chips or cookies, that he doesn't like vegetables and the biggie "there's nothing wrong with how I eat!" I'm sure most women have heard all of these "excuses." Solutions exist. There are healthier alternatives, but nothing will happen until you take the right steps.

Stubborn men need to believe in your course of action which means they typically need lots of information, and they need to have their concerns heard and addressed. They need to be assured that no matter the outcome, you will still respect them, respect their masculinity and that you will still accept them.

ADD/ADHD:

Many, many people believe that Attention Deficit Disorder or Attention Deficit Hyperactivity Disorder are things that you outgrow. The truth is, you never outgrow it and it doesn't go away. What happens is that by the time most men reach adulthood, they have developed a set of coping strategies that allow them to adapt to their wandering and disorganized minds. ADD affects more males than females, and people with ADD tend to have higher IQ's than the average person (by some estimates 10-20 points higher). According to some reports many famous people such as Albert Einstein are ADD/ADHD, and ADD has been linked to creative geniuses such as Picasso. But, more often than not, ADD/ADHD is considered a disadvantage because of the inability to focus on things that aren't interesting.

What signs can you look for in your man? There are many and most of these can be found in some of the other issues mentioned above, and some of those issues mentioned above can be driven by ADD/ADHD. The most common signs of ADD/ADHD are:

- Chronic boredom
- Chronic lateness and forgetfulness, difficulty concentrating when reading, working puzzles or playing board games
- Difficulty controlling anger and prone to frequent eruptions
- Employment problems which includes frequent job

changes or having to work long hours in order to accomplish ordinary tasks

- Impulsiveness
- Easily frustrated by normal, everyday problems such as appointment changes, waiting in line, slow cashiers etc.
- Low self-esteem
- Mood swings
- Procrastination
- Relationship problems

The following are some outward and obvious signs you can look for:

Self Medicating:

Stimulants such as caffeine have the opposite effect on someone with ADD. While it jacks most people up, a stimulant works to calm the ADD mind and allow it to focus. For that reason it's not uncommon to find an adult male with ADD/ADHD to constantly be drinking coffee, cola's or other caffeinated drinks.

Coping Strategies

One of the biggest coping strategies is extreme organization. Everything has a place and everything MUST be in that place. His car keys always go in the same place. The coffee is always stored in the same place. His favorite mug is always kept in the same place. The cream in the refrigerator is always in the same place and when something gets moved, all hell breaks loose. The reason for this is that organization allows the man to turn off that part of the brain and to relax and when things get moved, it creates a massive amount of frustration and anxiety bordering on helplessness and that all combines to create anger.

Cheating:

In a survey I conducted on male "Attitudes on Sex and Relationships" as part of my research for this book, I was able to document some findings that women will find surprising but men will instinctively know as right.

How often do you hear women say "all men cheat" or "if you make it easy enough, a man will take it, I don't care who he is." Although these statements aren't very flattering, they do reflect a societal belief about how men view sex.

The BIG surprise is that among married or coupled men, cheating is widely considered as "always wrong" and this belief is actually trending upward. According to research conducted by W. Bradford Wilcox, an associate professor of sociology who directs the National Marriage Project (Wilcox, 2012) at the University of Virginia, in the 1970s, only 63% of men said adultery was wrong, but as of 2008 (the last year for which data was available), the number had increased 23% to a whopping 78% of men believing that cheating was wrong. That's a huge shift in cultural beliefs!

Ok, but what does that break down to in terms of real numbers? Again, using the General Social Survey, a large social science survey of trends between the 1990s through 2000 and from 2000 to 2008, Wilcox reviewed data and found that 21% of men and 14% of women who were currently married or who had been married said they had sex at least once with someone other than their spouse. So, 21 out of 100 men and 14 out of 100 women who are married or coupled (living together) have cheated.

While many people believe that cheating is really a problem of the poor and uneducated, the numbers don't actually support that belief. In fact, while cheating is found at all levels of the socio-economic scale, it's actually more prevalent among people at the top of the economic ladder. So the smarter and richer you are, the more likely you are to cheat or be cheated on.

So, of those men who do cheat, why do they do it? The answers are far more complex than "she was hot" but essentially fall into three categories:

Emotional Dissatisfaction:

Of the men in my study who cheated, 59% said they did so because they were emotionally unhappy in their marriage. On the outset, that seems kind of whiny but the responses actually showed they described that dissatisfaction as:

- **Grown apart** - essentially living separate lives and attending only the most necessary family functions together
- **Rarely speak to each other** - conversations have been reduced to a minimum and only include the core essentials for cohabitation
- **Share no intimate aspects of their lives** - there are no secrets, joys, trials, tribulations, worries or fears shared
- **Constantly fighting** - every conversation is an argument
- **Enduring constant criticism** - every action is viewed critically and condemned

Sexual Dissatisfaction:

Another 29% of the men claimed the reason they cheated was because their dissatisfaction was with the actual sex itself. Like other answers, this topic has sub-categories which helps explain much of what we discussed in the chapter on Men and Sex. The primary reasons for sexual dissatisfaction were:

- **No or infrequent intercourse** - men reported having sex less than once per month

- **She doesn't like sex** - she just lays there or I have to beg, plead and cajole

- **She's selfish** - "once she gets hers, she's done" or "it's always about pleasing her and just forget anything I want or need"

- **It's boring** - "it's always the same way" or "every Thursday night at 7:00 p.m." or "it's so orchestrated I know what she wants just by what's for dinner"

The Dogs:

This group was 8% of the respondents and is the group that people often refer to when they say "all men cheat." According to my survey these men said they had no compunction against sleeping with someone other than their spouses. What was interesting was that most of these men didn't feel they had that much to lose in their existing relationship. In other words, they viewed their spouses as easily replaceable. My view is that these men don't value women and I suspect they battle with a high degree of insecurity. Remember though, this was only 8% of all the men who cheat.

Those In Denial:

The smallest group of respondents was the 4% of men who reported being in moderately happy marriages with minimal conflict but reported feeling a need for something "more" - many of these men said they had no intentions of leaving their spouses (at least not while the kids were still at home) and a small minority of the group reported their wives as being "good women" but the men were struggling in other areas of their lives such as with drugs or alcohol.

Chapter 11

MEN AND EMOTIONS

EMOTIONS ARE FEELINGS AND, AS humans, we all have them. Some people seem to feel more and express more while some people appear to have no feelings what-so-ever and therefore express very little. Men are often accused of feeling little and sharing even less. The truth is that men feel everything a woman does but these emotions can be experienced and expressed differently. It's not uncommon for a man to internalize his fears, sadness, and anxieties (we can't appear weak!) so it's important to understand these emotions and how your man processes them.

It's important to understand that how we process, or work through, our emotions is unique to each individual and is based on his (or her) lifetime's experience. Just like the 5 stages of grief (denial, anger, bargaining, depression, and acceptance), where each person, man or woman, moves through each of the 5 steps differently and at different speeds, each man will process his own emotions differently and at a different pace.

Remember, our mothers teach us how to understand our feelings, our fathers teach us how to share our feelings and because we incorporate all these things into our own definition of masculinity, every man will be different. Some men may internalize everything, stay away from everyone and work through a process alone. Some men may surround themselves with lots of people and activity and appear to not even process the emotion while what they're doing is processing it in small, bite sized pieces. Yet still other men may process more along the lines of what a woman can relate to. There isn't a right way or a wrong way and just as long as the feelings get processed in a constructive way without anyone being physically or emotionally hurt then all will be good.

CORE EMOTIONS

Researchers have identified four core emotions that are present in all human beings and these are: Sadness, Anger, Joy and Fear.

Sadness:

Sadness helps us to reflect on the significance of something we have lost or something that has disappointed us; when you feel sad, it's natural to need to be alone. Solitude helps to work out the significance of the loss and to learn from the experience. Withdrawing when you are sad protects you from further hurt until you feel strong enough for further exposure. Often times you will find men need alone time after an argument to process through their sadness.

After a breakup or divorce, men typically go through a two chemical processes: 1) as the relationship ends, testosterone levels increase. This gives men the boost they need to start competing in a single world; 2) Dopamine, a hormone and neurotransmitter in the brain which controls the pleasure and reward centers drops substantially and while these levels are low, men become far more likely to "mope around." As men process through the sadness we become more active, start "getting out and about" and as we do, we start feeding the reward centers of the brain and our dopamine levels rise.

Anger:

Anger has its roots in either hurt, fear and/or frustration (and it's not uncommon to have two of these present) and it (anger) provides us with motivation to fix or change something that is not working. If the causes of anger are not addressed, unresolved anger may lead to long-term moods of resentment, hostility, even depression.

Interestingly, men have been encouraged to express anger more overtly "knock him on his ass!" while women have been encouraged to keep their anger toned down. While males acting out anger can be seen as manly when women try to keep it "toned down" this can lead to passive/aggressive behavior such as pouting, sulking, giving the silent treatment and other unhealthy behaviors that are very destructive to relationships.

An example would be Mike who has a fear of public speaking and his boss has asked him to give the big presentation at the annual employee meeting. His wife Mary, while trying to be supportive can find herself in a war zone.

Mike: *"I hate the idea of doing this, I hate speaking in front of large groups."*

Mary: *"You'll do fine. I know you hate it but you have to step up to the plate and deliver for your boss!"*

While Mary's comments are meant as encouraging, Mike has all 3 feelings going on. He has the fear of public speaking (and probably failing in front of the entire company); hurt of having not really been heard by Mary; the frustration of having no way out of the predicament and the further frustration of Mary pushing him further in to the mess.

Triggers:

The primary triggers for anger are also very different between men and women. Women are far more likely to get angry over a feeling of powerlessness, injustice, a perceived lack of relationship reciprocity or the irresponsibility of others. Men, on the other hand, will more often get angry over personal attacks (which is why you should be very careful in how you argue with a man), perceived slights connected to his personal view of right and wrong (truth, fairness, loyalty, sportsmanship, professionalism); being controlled by someone or something; being unable to control a circumstance that is hurting his standing, family or definition of masculinity such as losing a job or promotion; or when they can't fix things such as car, computer; or when you have a problem they can't fix.

Target:

Women are much more likely to get angry at and take their anger out on those closest to them while men are far more likely to get angry at strangers or things. While women will name names (your mother!) men tend to generalize with phrases like "some guy at work" or "the stupid car".

Control:

As men age and gain more experience with anger most of us tend to learn that we're better served taking a different approach, to not escalate or make the matter worse or to just let it go and not worry about it. Younger men will react more strongly to perceived wrongs.

Because men have direct and overt releases of anger, we tend to get over things much quicker and move on while studies have shown that women tend to stay angry longer. Once a man has had his angry outburst he's generally ready to move on while women are more prone to ending relationships during fits of anger.

Although men view some anger as acceptable, by and large we don't like anger and believe it's an emotion that we should try and avoid. Most men tend to regret their anger and consider it a heavy burden and something they would be far better doing without. This is why you see a lot of men who will simply walk off instead of getting into an argument.

WARNING!!!

NEVER, EVER, EVER chase after a man who has walked away in anger! Let him walk away and cool off. When he's ready, he'll come back.

Studies have shown that men, when angry, release very high levels of cortisone which is a hormone released during periods of stress and it can take almost twice as long for a man's cortisone levels to drop as compared to a woman's. Among other things, cortisone effects the immune system by suppressing your body's ability to fight diseases so fighting in a relationship is literally, physically killing your man!

Joy:

Joy is what we feel when everything is going right. When your man is happy, pay attention to what brought him to that point and work to re-create the circumstances as often as you can. Men are very grateful to women who can bring peace, joy, happiness, and contentment to their worlds and a man's level of satisfaction escalates when he experiences these feelings.

When men experience joy, the cause of the joy has activated

the pleasure center in our brains and released dopamine which encourages us to keep seeking that joy.

During times of joy, another hormone released is oxytocin which is the "bonding hormone" and it's important to understand how this works with men. Take a group of men who play softball or go hunting together; when one of them scores a run or takes down a champion buck, his dopamine levels goes up (joy) and his oxytocin levels rise creating a bonding experience between him and his pals. Those close friendships come from sharing the experience.

For women, it's vitally important that you be nearby and participating in the joyous moments and also why, after an argument, it's important to embrace and let the "bonding hormone" get released and increase that sense of happiness and "completeness" that men need.

Fear:

Fear is an emotional response to a set of stimuli that we believe threatens our physical or emotional survival. We are born with two natural fears: the fear of falling and the fear of a loud sound; those two fears are hardwired into each infant and remain with us from birth through death. Along the way we develop many, many other fears, some rational and some completely irrational. Most of these fears are taught to us by our parents and other societal influences. For instance, as a small child, you witness your mother screaming in a fit of horror over a spider in the bath tub, she runs grabs a broom, a fly swatter, 5 gallons of insecticide and proceeds to destroy half the bathroom in order to eliminate the threat. You learn spiders should be feared.

Regardless of how we acquire our fears, they're rooted and tied to a deep, deep evolutionary process that's designed to protect us from unsafe situations. For instance, if we get to near the edge of a cliff we feel a sudden urge to back up or if we hear a sudden loud sound we jump and move away from the sound. These fear situations invoke our well known flight or fight instincts.

Not only does fear tell humans when to be cautious, it also tells us when to prepare for an emergency. For instance, when we're at the park and hear a sudden clap of thunder, fear tells us to take cover indoors. We men feel an especially strong need to make sure all family members are accounted for, the windows and doors are closed and we have enough food to survive the storm.

Fear is also a normal response when we encounter the unknown. Whether it be an unfamiliar social or business situation or dealing with an unknown emotional issue. Being afraid doesn't mean we can't or shouldn't do something, but with men what you find is a hesitancy to agree to something where the outcome is unknown.

Mary: *"I want you to promise me you will never again work on a Sunday."*

Mike: *"Stutter. Stammer. Pause. Stall."*

Mike obviously understands your request, but he also knows he can't predict the future. While you may think he's non-committal about working Sundays because he "doesn't care about your needs," he fears making a commitment to you because his boss may make demands he can't control. Mike doesn't want to make a commitment he can't keep. (From the anger perspective, Mike is being pushed into something he can't control so you have two components: fear and frustration.)

Remember, also, that men go into flight or fight response when you start yelling during an argument. Cortisone gets released, dopamine drops and the entire male system is primed for action, and that action can be fighting or fleeing. Neither of which is what you want.

With men, it's amazing what can invoke the fear response and what doesn't. For most men, emptying a mouse trap is a complete non-issue while for women it represents total disgust! (Did you know that disgust is one of the clusters of emotions tied to fear?) On the flip side, having to go home to a screaming wife can be terrifying!

Now that we've discussed core emotions, I want to introduce you to a new set of emotions called Social Emotions. These emotions drive many of the behaviors that you see and deal with on a daily basis with most every man.

SOCIAL EMOTIONS

Unlike "core emotions" which are inherent in all human beings, "social emotions" require you to be emotionally and self aware in order to experience these feelings. Unlike a sociopath, psychopath or narcissist who puts themselves first and views others as "tools" to be used to their own end, emotionally aware men are very capable of understanding how others feel and of forming behaviors based on those feelings. These self-conscious emotions are called "Social Emotions" and consist of shame, guilt, pride and embarrassment.

Why Do We Have Social Emotions?

As we evolved into societies we constructed some sure-fire ways to regulate behavior and we did this by establishing peer group norms. When a person's behavior falls outside their peer group norms, they get kicked out of that group. If they behave inappropriately at work, they get fired. If one goes too far outside the norms, such as a robber or killer, they fall under laws created by society to protect us against criminal behavior.

So where do social emotions fit into all this? Social emotions govern our behavior and allow us to get along with our partners, with peer groups and to avoid being rejected. These emotions are required for survival in social groups. For instance, some evolutionist believe that women developed a higher capacity for empathy because, in tribal times, women were often married off to men in other tribes (to prevent inbreeding) and her survival depended on her ability to understand, adapt and get along with her new tribe.

Researchers have defined the social emotions we use to govern our behaviors as Pride, Embarrassment, Guilt and Shame.

Pride:

Pride is what makes us feel good about ourselves. Men often take pride in our appearance, in our work, in our homes, in our vehicles, in how we treat others, in how nice our lawn looks, in our accomplishments at work. All of these things (and more) dictate how good we feel about ourselves, and how good we feel about ourselves is directly linked to our Joy.

However, there are two kinds of pride, authentic and hubristic, and only one of them contributes to our happiness. Authentic pride comes from real accomplishments and motivates us to further achievement, to reach out to others and, in general, caring more about our experiences and the people around us. Men with authentic pride are far more likely to have good self-esteem, a higher tolerance of others and an ability to care more deeply about others.

Hubristic pride is a false pride and is far more common among men than women. Hubristic pride is not based on real accomplishments and is linked to low self-esteem and also closely tied to Shame, which we'll discuss shortly. Men with hubristic pride are typically more arrogant, more willing to express prejudice against others, are far more likely to be intolerant of other races, religions, politics, etc. and are less likely to show caring towards strangers.

Men with a lot of hubristic pride also don't seek to replace their hubristic pride with authentic pride but instead prefer to "puff" themselves by using tactics such as affiliating themselves with very strong religious, political or racial organizations. For instance, many people associated with the KKK could be thought to have predominately hubristic pride and this same thing could be attached to gang members, religious fanatics or political extremists.

In relationships, extreme hubristic pride can lead a man to narcissistic behavior where everything becomes "about him" and hubristic pride has been associated with aggression. Think of it like this, hubristic pride is a disagreement with the truth so when that disagreement is pointed out or that truth challenged, you end up with anger based eruptions. Hubristic pride does not allow a man to be wrong, and he'll perceive any questioning as a challenge to that truth he's desperately trying to mask.

Embarrassment:

As humans, we use embarrassment to regulate our social behavior and control our transgressions against others. Embarrassment is simple, short lived and happens only in social situations. We never experience embarrassment when we're alone. Think of it like walking out of the restroom all through the dining room at the restaurant with a 2 foot long trail of toilette paper stuck to your heels. This is embarrassing but it only lasts for a short time and then you'd get over it and move on. If you were home alone, it wouldn't phase you at all and at most you'd just tsk tsk yourself, pick up the toilet paper and forget the entire incident ever occurred.

Men tend to experience embarrassment over things that have to do with their masculinity such as their friends teasing them about being wrapped around your little finger or competence at being or doing manly things. Most men would not be the slightest bit embarrassed to be seen with your lipstick on their cheek, but they would be mortified to be teased about not being able to change a tire. A man could walk out of an outdoor toilet with a 2 foot long trail of toilette paper attached to his shoes and walk across a two acre parking lot and never think twice about it. But arrive at his car to find a flat tire and either not have a spare (ill prepared man) or not know how to change the flat (inadequate man) and he would be very embarrassed.

There is a huge difference between embarrassment and humiliation. Humiliation is embarrassment combined with shame. If you were at a backyard BBQ with a bunch of friends and neighbors and said "My husband is less than useless with a hammer" even if the statement were 100% true, your husband would feel a deep sense of humiliation. Oddly though, he could make the same comment about himself and not feel the slightest bit of embarrassment and may even make the admission with some sense of pride. However, when you say it, it's interpreted as a "put down" in the form of a challenge to his masculinity, and it becomes humiliating.

If you remember back to my balloon example of why men leave relationships, embarrassment and humiliation are things that make a man not feel good about himself. On the flip side, if one of his guy friends were embarrassing your man, one public comment showing your acceptance and support would tell your man and everyone else that you have his back and that would cause your man to feel good about himself.

Guilt:

We're all raised with a sense of right and wrong. When we've done something wrong to another person, guilt is the feeling we experience. Without guilt, we'd have nothing to help us regulate our behavior and treatment of others. Unlike the other social emotions, guilt is directly and easily fixable. You have to right the wrong you have committed. Most men are generally pretty good at buying a dozen roses and coming through the door with a sheepish look on their faces and most men are generally very good at apologizing to other men.

While most people associate guilt with some action (lying, an affair, overspending), guilt can also stem from inaction such as not doing or saying something when you could have and when doing so would have protected or helped your partner.

Dave, in D.C. told this story:

"I was engaged to a wonderful woman. She'd put a ton of work into the wedding plans and the invitations were late. She called around noon and asked if I would pick them up before 5:00 p.m., which generally would not have been a problem. This particular day I was over an hour away, I had a meeting that wouldn't end until 4:00 p.m. it was the start of rush hour and the store would have surely been closed by the time I got there and I told her this. She not only got angry but then the guilt started "After all the work I've done, I ask you to do one thing..." so I agreed. I drove like a maniac, it rained, I'm sure I ran over three people and I got to the store just as the owner was putting his key in the lock. I frantically begged him to let me pick up the invitations and he looked at me with this look that was a cross between "You don't know and you poor sap!" and then he politely told me that my fiancé had picked them up hours ago. Ultimately, we ended up calling the marriage off and I've always thought that I dodged a bullet."

Another form of guilt is the "guilt tripper" and this is the person, often women, who continually bring up past transgressions.

This form of guilt is highly manipulative, self-centered because it places the needs of the guilt-tripper above all else and drives a wedge between you. For men, this becomes another "I don't feel good about myself when I'm with you" moment. If your man is continually bringing up past transgressions, there has probably been a fracture in the trust that hasn't been heeled and it's time to go back to the Chapter 3 (Communications) and Chapter 4 (arguing).

Men can create their own guilt and can feel guilty over their weight, their health, not going to the doctor, not eating right, sneaking that snack you told him not to have, not getting that promotion, not earning enough, forgetting the gallon of milk you asked him to pick up. The list goes on and on. These feelings of guilt come from feeling stupid, inadequate and not manly and originate from self-criticisms. When you hear your man making guilt-ridden negative comments about himself, he's probably experiencing some form of guilt from a self-criticism. Look for comments like:

"How could I have been so stupid?!"

"I can't believe I did that!"

"You'd think I would learn my lesson!"

"If only I had worked harder, I would have gotten that promotion!"

And when you hear statements like these, it's important to recognize what's going on and that it's your opportunity to be reassuring. "Look Honey, I can tell you feel bad about that but you're a good man and I love you." will go a long way towards showing the unconditional acceptance that men need.

Not fixing guilt can have severe and long term effects on men. Unresolved guilt will lower a man's self-esteem, cause anxiety (fear), stress, emotional and physical health issues. Unresolved guilt can lead a man to drugs and alcohol as they try to numb the pain they're experiencing. This can either be a short term process while he realigns his definition of masculinity or a long term chronic problem.

Shame:

Shame is the most powerful of social emotions and stems from the fear that we're not good enough. Unlike guilt, where we feel bad about a behavior, with shame we feel bad about ourselves. Because of this, shame is not something anyone can make us feel, and although it's roots are probably back in our childhood, it's a wound that we continually inflict ourselves with a sense of worthlessness, powerlessness and by judging our own perceived shortcomings or feeling disgrace from bad or foolish behavior. Shame is a painful feeling of humiliation.

According to Jessica Tracy, an associate professor of psychology at the University of British Columbia in Vancouver, Canada, whose research focuses on emotions, the expression of emotions, and, in particular, on the self-conscious emotions of pride, shame, and guilt (and who graciously spent more than her fair share of time helping me with this section), our culture hates shame. Shame is neither an emotion we should have nor one we should express. On the other hand, in Asian cultures, to feel shame is not only allowed, it's expected, and if you don't feel shame you can't be trusted.

For men, shame comes from the fear of not being manly enough, tough enough, smart enough, wealthy enough or simply, good enough. The number one shame trigger for men is being perceived as weak. Men go through each day walking a path where any sign of weakness invokes this feeling of shame, and because of this men are afraid to become vulnerable because, as we discussed back in Chapter 2, vulnerability is weakness.

The problem with this position is that if a man can't be vulnerable, then he can't truly grow and be a better man, a better partner and a better lover. Women, have a choice and can either allow their men to be vulnerable by embracing those moments when they are, or, you can silence him by being unsupportive and/ or critical.

While some people are simply more genetically prone to certain behaviors such as being shy or boisterous, the primary cause of shame is in how we're raised. Unwittingly every parent pours some shame into their children. We do this by making the child feel blamed for how something turns out that was out of their control or for something about themselves that they can't change.

Shame is learned and families which have a deep sense of shame tend to raise boys with a deep sense of shame because when the boy does something that invokes the same shame feelings that already exist within the family, the family will echo that shame back onto the boy. An example would be a boy wanting to take a foreign language class during elementary school and hearing from family members "no one in this family has ever been able to learn a foreign language."

In another example the boy comes in from playing and a broken door slams and the child is yelled at for slamming the door. Because no on in the house has bothered to fix the broken door, the child is blamed for something beyond his control. His value is diminished because adults have not performed their duties in fixing the house.

Imagine:

A little boy has a friend over and the friend spills milk and your own son gets blamed for not paying attention to what his friend was doing.

The Man Puzzle

A little boy wanting to play dolls with his sister and being told that if his friends find out they will tease him.

A little boy forgetting to put fresh water out for the family pet and being told he'll never be a good father.

> **Casey, a 28 year old man in NY told this story:**
>
> "I hate my hair. When I let it grow out, it's a curly mess. Even my mother hated it. All through my childhood my mother would complain about my curly hair and how tangled it got and how hard it was to wash, and dry and brush and how it always looked unkempt."

Here we have Casey who, every day, faces such shame over his hair, a genetic gift he has absolutely no control over, that he keeps his hair buzzed. Imagine how different Casey would feel about himself had he grown up with a mother who loved and complimented his hair.

When you make these types of statements, you create a sense of shame in the boy by not allowing him to be who he is. Yes, responsibility needs to be taught, but teaching responsibility by attacking a boy's sense of masculinity is simply cruel. Likewise, if you feel something is inappropriate for your son, as the parent, you need to take responsibility by saying something like "I don't care if all your friends are watching it, I don't think it's appropriate."

In a boy's world, the same messages are delivered over and over all throughout his childhood and teen years. It occurs in football (you're too small), art class (you never could draw), dance class (you're too big), drama class (you're too shy). No matter what it is the boy wants to try, there will be an adult to tell him that, for some reason beyond his control, he can't because he's not good enough to do what he wants.

Men and Emotions

Even when the boy is perfectly fine and capable, shame messages get passed from adults.

The coach: *"This team should have won. You really let the team down!"*

The teacher: *"I can't believe you got another bad grade! You're smarter than that!"*

As a result, some boys become stubborn and angry and determined to prove everyone wrong. If the boy fails the failure only serves to reinforce that shame message. If they succeed, the shame message and anger stays with them well into adulthood. Other boys take the opposite route and become afraid of adults. They grow up to resist authority figures of all type. Both sets of men become afraid of failure and are driven by the underlying belief that they have no value. One will go to extremes to prove the belief wrong (think of someone like a Bernie Madoff who embezzled billions from innocent people), but no amount of success will ever be enough, while the other will never accomplish anything because it would be pointless to try.

As the adult male has defined his masculine identity (Chapter 2), when things in life don't pan out the way he expects, he feels shame. When he has to deal with something and doesn't know how, he feels an even deeper sense of shame. As men age, these experiences of shame and rejection continue to pile up like stones, and the bigger the pile of stones the more men withdraw from society, their neighbors and even their family to where they eventually only venture into areas which are completely safe.

Adult men also teach boys how to handle shame inflicted by others. You'll hear a father say "I don't care what the coach said, there are 12 men on a field and everyone has a job. You didn't cause the team to lose. It's a team effort, you ALL lost together."

The Man Puzzle

As we move in to adulthood and look at the men in our lives, it becomes important to understand the types of shame that a man experiences. Researchers have broken this into two types: Overt and Passive.

Overt shame consists of: accusations, yelling, demanding.

Passive shame consists of: Abandonment, neglect, lack of support, lack of recognition, lack of appreciation

When you look at overt versus passive shame, men are far more adept at detecting overt shame than passive shame. A woman who yells at her man for forgetting to pick up the milk she asked him to buy is shaming her husband. This is an overt shame and, for most men, easily recognizable. However, the woman who strokes her husbands cheek while softly telling him how disappointed she is that he forget the milk is also shaming her husband but doing it passively and he may not recognize what has happened and becomes less able to process the interaction. How a woman speaks her words have significant meaning to men, and when it comes to shame, soft spoken and passive can often be far more destructive.

Regardless of how you deliver your "shame message" men will receive the message as rejection and experience that as "I am not worthy"

Each and every day, your man, no matter who he is or how accomplished he is, experiences shame in one form or another. Showing Weakness is shameful. Not being manly is shameful. Not being a good father is shameful. Not being a good husband is shameful. Not being a good provider is shameful. Not being "adequate" (I don't know how to deal with this problem, I feel shame) is shameful.

For men, shame is felt whenever culture, family, bosses, kids or our lovers/wives oppose what we believe or have been taught is what a man does. That instance when we feel we're wrong or have done something wrong is when we feel shame.

Women often wonder what's going on when a man withdraws, silently distances himself or all of a sudden turns abusive by belittling, name calling or resorts to physical abuse and what's most likely going on is the man is experiencing extreme shame.

Regardless of the level of shame, when it's experienced, there is no doubt that your man wants to withdraw, run, escape, be anywhere but where he's experiencing that horrible feeling. He certainly doesn't want to be reminded of his failure, his inadequacy and this current rejection.

In some cases, a man can be so damaged by shame that he can't be present and fully available in a relationship. His needs will always be the last met. He never cares what's for breakfast, lunch or dinner because he never wants to speak out. He can seem absolutely normal and even "easygoing" because he never has an opinion, never expresses a want or a need.

When you look at men who have become alcoholics or addicts, the more these men demonstrate their shame, the more likely they are to relapse. Furthermore, deep rooted shame has been linked to extreme anger and some form of shame is present in almost every case of domestic violence.

In extreme cases, shame is such a deep emotion that it becomes a debilitating "chronic shame." According to John S. Guarnaschelli Ph.D. in his article "Turning Shame To Gold: Men Feeling Shame, Men Healing Shame" (Guarnaschelli, 2010) Chronic Shame is an incapacitating destruction of a man's sovereign authority to be himself - to stand in his own feelings, define his own truth, possess his own energy or power, confidently pursue his own needs and goals."

The Man Puzzle

The "Great Irony" is that for every instance of shame that a man feels, he wants to turn to and share his "crisis" with his woman. Of course, when your man does feel shame and thinks of sharing this with you, that universal message "that being vulnerable is weak and weakness is something to be ashamed of!" crops up. So, instead of sharing, the man becomes emotionally closed off and unavailable which is the expected response. However, for those women who do finally convince their man to open up and start revealing themselves, these women become shocked and repulsed by the absolute raw weakness and vulnerability that a man can show. This "revulsion" is a result of the total shock that women experience at the depth of emotion that their man is experiencing.

If it were a sister, a girlfriend or almost any other woman who was revealing such a depth of emotions, it would be completely normal but when a man does this it's a complete shock, and for many women it calls in to question her own beliefs about masculinity and causes her to question whether or not she wants "such a display" of emotions. Some women even become repulsed by her man sharing a deep rooted feeling.

The antidote to shame is gentleness, caring, kindness and empathy. For a man to be able to share his feelings and experiences with you without fear or regret and certainly without rejection of who he is requires safety. That safety, once established, must never be violated. If you want true happiness, you have to allow your man to unlock who he truly is, and when he does, you must be supportive of who he is.

Chapter 12

VIOLENCE AND ANGER ISSUES

B EFORE WE START THIS DISCUSSION, I think it's important to begin by saying this chapter makes no excuses for those men who would raise a hand to a woman. In my mind there is simply no reason, justification or excuse for domestic violence and I will make no excuses or rationalizations. Violence simply should not be tolerated in any form by any person for any reason. With that in mind remember this:

> Under no circumstances should you ever allow yourself to be abused

> Under no circumstances should you ever hit or provoke your partner for any reason

> If you are hit or think you may be hit, leave! Seek help!

> If a man walks away from you in anger, never, ever, ever follow him. Doing so makes you the aggressor!

My goal in this chapter is to help you identify the traits and behaviors of men who are more likely to be abusive, to understand the process of abuse and to understand how to leave an abusive relationship.

Why Hasn't This Been Stopped?:

Domestic violence is a very complex subject and it's only been in the last few years that researchers have begun making progress in understanding the true causes behind domestic violence and even so, much of the new research has not made its way out to therapists in the form of actionable treatment programs. In many of the groups I visited, the therapists were either unaware of the new research, very slow to adapt their thinking OR they were aware of the research but their hands were tied by a government or court mandated system. Regardless of the reasons why the system is slow to adapt, let's look at the old thinking versus what the new research tells us.

Some History:

Originally, domestic violence was viewed as a private matter, between a couple or between the couple and their families. A man who battered, would, if anything, face the wrath of either his own male family members or her male family members, and in most cases, domestic violence went largely unreported.

Police got called when the woman had no male family members who could or would protect her and the battering was so bad that an ambulance had to be called. Even then, the abuser was usually arrested and jailed to "cool off" and formal charges were rarely filed.

As this problem grew worse, those responsible for intervention which included the police, churches and shelters began grappling with the problem. As professionals tried to figure out the problem and how to fix it, two camps were formed:

The first camp was the Situational Violence camp which viewed most domestic violence as something that happened when drinking and arguing got out of hand, and this type of violence would remedy itself.

The second camp was the Power and Control camp which viewed all domestic violence as a form of power and control, and this camp has, by and large, won out because it's easy to categorize and a form of "treatment" could be put together.

Old Thinking:

For decades, people in every civilized country in the world have viewed domestic violence as one partner needing to control the other. Because the aspect of control is undeniable and so visible, it was easy to conclude that insecurity was the driving cause of abuse. Since that's the belief that we all grew up with and because most every male batterer can be thought to be "controlling" and "insecure," it's easy to see why this belief has persisted. What's worse is that treatment programs have been designed around these beliefs, and by the best estimates, they are only about 30% effective.

During my interviews for this book, I had the privilege... I say privilege because I spoke to men at their most vulnerable, and they were ready, willing and able to share some of their most intimate feelings... of speaking with 100's of men in dozens of court ordered domestic violence treatment programs. Some men I spoke with were new to the programs while others had been around long enough to have turned into volunteers. While addressing these groups, I would ask early in the interview process "why do you need to control a woman?" My question would be met with blank stares or polite chuckles. These men were acutely aware that power and control was rarely the root cause of their battering but recognized it as a symptom, and treating the symptom of power and control with anger management techniques is like treating a broken foot by fixing a hangnail.

New Thinking:

The truth is that power and control is rarely the root cause of domestic violence, but, is instead, a symptom of an emotional problem that runs deep and for which we can trace much of its roots back to Chapter 2 and the section on "Derailing The Male Maturity Process."

What men in these programs know and the current research shows is that battering occurs primarily in men with weak or broken definitions of masculinity and begins with real or perceived attacks on the man's masculinity and real or perceived instances of disrespect, both of which invoke very deep shame and humiliation responses.

We now know there are consistent personality traits among abusers; that there are definable behaviors among abusers; that there is a definable cycle of abuse, and there are even predictors for which cases of domestic violence will end in death.

Types Of Domestic Violence:

Professor Michael P. Johnson, Emeritus Professor of Sociology, Women's Studies, and African and African American Studies at Penn State and one of the top researchers says there are 4 types of domestic violence (Johnson, 2008) and his research has been confirmed by numerous independent studies. In an interview Professor Johnson described the types of domestic violence as:

Common Couple Violence:

Common Couple Violence is violence where both partners physically attack each other during a single argument. In this form of domestic violence an argument starts, escalates and both partners simply go at each other with a vengeance.

Intimate Terrorism:

Intimate Terrorism is what we traditionally define or call domestic violence. In Intimate Terrorism, one partner (typically the man) abuses the other with the abuse escalating over time and more than likely involving serious injury. Abusers in this category typically fall into two groups: Those men who are emotionally dependent on their partner and the relationship, and those men who are what we know as the true psychopath (estimates say the psychopath accounts for about 10% of all male abusers).

Violent Resistance:

Violent Resistance is often what we think of as "self-defense" and this violence is when the abused fights back or attacks their abusive partners.

Mutual Violent Control:

Mutual Violent Control is rare type of domestic violence which occurs when both partners are battling for control of the relationship. It's essentially two abusers going at each other, and neither person is safe.

In this chapter we're only going to talk about domestic violence in the traditional sense which Dr. Johnson refers to as Intimate Terrorism.

Stereotypes Aren't True:

Most people think the typical abuser is a tough guy - an obvious criminal, poor, uneducated, perhaps a big bruiser who has a history of drug or alcohol abuse and generally violent behavior. In reality men who batter are broadly representative of the general population of men; many are solid citizens with no criminal records, no substance abuse history or long term employment. They are construction workers, businessmen, lawyers, doctors, clergy, policemen and even judges. There are no professions, races, or religions without abusers. In fact, there are some studies which claim that law enforcement contains the highest percentage of abusers per profession.

Statistically, men are more likely than women to commit acts of domestic violence and the female instigator is a very, very small percentage of the cases in which men batter women. Mutual abusers may have a higher percentage of female instigators but even then, that instigation isn't usually physical assault on the man, but is generally a verbal attack or what we commonly refer to as "pushing his buttons."

According to various versions of the National Crime Victimization Survey, while higher rates of substance and alcohol abuse among men are linked to increased rates in violent crime, in domestic violence the absence of alcohol or drugs in no way makes you safe. An abuser can turn violent while perfectly sober.

Get To Know His Background:

So, if abuse is not related to profession, education or religion how's a woman to identify which men to avoid?

Get to know his background! Get to know how he was raised. Research shows that men who come from homes with physical violence between parents are more likely to use violence as a means to resolve conflict in their interpersonal relationships.

While a child raised with domestic violence is not a predictor that he/she will become an abuser, it does raise the probability. Research shows that when children are raised around domestic violence, the exposure creates emotional and intellectual numbing regarding acts of brutality. Remember from Chapter 2, boys pull their definition of masculinity from a lot of sources and the primary source is their father figure.

Get to know what he's experienced in his life. Besides childhood, there are other predictors and one that is constantly in the news these days is Post Traumatic Stress Disorder or PTSD. PTSD is not just something veterans have. It can be found in anyone who's suffered one or more traumatic events. PTSD is such a special case that I'll cover it later in this chapter.

Get to know his alcohol and drug habits. Besides, his childhood and life experiences, other predictors are substance abuse which includes alcohol and/or drugs (including prescription), long term unemployment and/or extreme levels of stress such as facing financial ruin or even divorce.

Common Personality Traits Of An Abuser:

Research has found some personality traits which are common to abusers, and while not all men who exhibit these personality traits are abusive, combining these personality traits with some of the other signs I'll cover will give you a pretty good idea of what you're facing. So what are these personality traits? Here are the ones you should be watching for. The more of these you find, the greater the danger!

Mr. Greedy:

He is characterized by a tendency or desire to acquire at any cost, especially during the courting phase and in relation to you.

These men will go to extreme lengths to "win you" and early in the dating process you'll hear statements such as "You're mine!", "You belong to me!" or "You'll do what I tell you."

Anger Man:

Not just any anger but an anger characterized by it's destructiveness to both sides. Of course, this begs the argument "isn't all anger destructive to both sides?" but the answer to that question is, no. This anger is characterized by an attitude that "I don't care how much it hurts me just as long as it hurts you."

Dr. Prejudiced:

Not just any prejudice but extreme prejudice bordering on or including hatred and discrimination towards a given race, color, religion or political party. Highly prejudicial men typically have weak and fragile egos, and men with weak and fragile egos can be quick to misinterpret your actions which will lead to conflict and escalations.

General Cruelty:

Cruelty comes in many forms and can range from highly embarrassing comments or actions that leave you humiliated to abuse, exploitation and killings. This can be experienced as the bully/man who constantly laughs/boasts about his picking on a guy at work to the man who throws rocks at cats in the yard for no reason other than he doesn't like cats. These types of actions are signs of cruelty and reflect inner personality traits that should be avoided.

Sergeant Sectarian:

This is the guy who's highly partisan and completely intolerant of anyone with different loyalties. This could be as simple as the football fan with an extreme loyalty to his team and thinks that anyone who follows another team is an idiot. This guy has probably been in a fight at a game, would taunt someone wearing an opposing team's jersey and has probably been banned from his team's stadium or other public venues. Although this example uses sports, his extreme views may be racial, political, religious etc., and anyone not of a like mind is wrong and stupid.

Captain Absolute:

You would recognize this as the "my way or the highway" stance on virtually every aspect of life. This guy is hard headed and no other point of view will penetrate his thick skull. He has problems with relative views and has a tendency to disregard the views of others and is non cooperative in communal life. Extremism, of any kind, distorts perspective and thwarts compromise, and when the extreme view gets fractured he lashes out. He has very distorted beliefs, especially rigid authoritarian or religious beliefs. He's the man of the house and what he says goes.

The Blamer:

He's selfish and blames others. Men who blame simply refuse to take responsibility for their own actions. A great example is the jaywalker (selfish act) when they get honked at, they blame the other driver for being stupid.

Common Behaviors Of An Abuser:

Over time, researchers have been able to assemble a list of behaviors present in abusive relationships. While the presence of one behavior doesn't mean that someone is abusive, it doesn't mean they're not. One thing is for certain, the more of these behaviors your man demonstrates, the more likely it is that you are in a relationship with a man who either is, or has the potential to be, abusive. In some cases, an abuser may have only a couple of behaviors which can be recognized, but generally these behaviors are very exaggerated (e.g., extreme jealousy over ridiculous things). The most common behaviors are:

Negative Attitude Toward Women:

These men display a "male supremacy" attitude. They are insecure, cannot handle strong women, and must be emotionally, physically and verbally in control. These men use pressure and intimidation in their relationships. They respect their mothers, but not other women. They join in on sexual jokes.

Current research shows there are two forms of sexist attitudes towards woman. There is an overt disrespect in which a man will talk negatively and disrespectfully about women in general and specifically, the women in their previous relationships. The other form is far more subtle but just as dangerous. This type starts off as nurturing like a father or older brother, but under the surface the message is still the same: because you are a woman, and you are incapable. These men brag about their conquests and live out cycles of one bad relationship after another.

Quick Involvement:

He will often claim "love at first sight" and tell you how you are "made for each other." You may hear how he has never loved anyone so much or how he has never felt so loved by anyone. He is desperate for someone and will pressure you to commit to him exclusively and to make love before you feel ready. If you don't commit, he will do everything he can to make you feel guilty.

Good men take their time. They want to know you on a real, personal level. They won't pressure you for sex. While a good man may feel "love at first sight" he will be patient in letting the relationship unfold. Real love doesn't feel a need to rush into something.

Jealousy:

The jealous man will question you about who you came in contact with during the day, whether or not they flirted with you or you with them, question why you're spending time with friends, family, children or hobbies and not that time with him or her. He may start showing up at work unexpectedly with flowers or coffee or surprise lunch invitation. While these may seem sweet, they're really just a masked way of checking up on you and, after awhile, he may even ask you to stop working.

Supportive men encourage your work, dreams and goals. Although a secure man may surprise you at your office, it's not a regular thing. A good man will ask about your day but trust you to handle unwanted advances. Secure men encourage you to spend time with your friends, family and children and they want you to pursue hobbies and other things that give you joy. If a good man needs more of your time, he will tell you so. Supportive men can feel jealous but, as we discussed in the previous chapter, this is situational and, as you can see, the two are very different.

Hypersensitivity:

Most abusive men have very low self-esteem and can take the most ordinary statement as an insult and become overly upset, or take unrelated comments as personal attacks. He may downplay his feelings by saying they "are hurt" when, in fact he is really angry. He may perceive everyday normal obstacles such as having to work late, getting a speeding ticket, etc. as personal attacks. He may view your preference for something different from his as a criticism or personal attack.

A good man will ask for an explanation of any statement he doesn't understand. He will take ownership for his actions and accept the consequences for the speeding ticket. Working late he handles in stride, and he appreciates your differences.

Controlling Behavior:

Controlling behavior starts with concern for your safety and grows to be concern for your mental health. He will get angry or "distraught" if you get home later than usual. He'll question you closely about where you were, who you were with and what you talked about. His goal is to make you feel inadequate about managing your own life, and he may even feel as though you are incapable. Eventually, he wants to control all your decisions about the home, meals, how you dress, where you worship, and even make you ask permission before spending money or venturing out.

Good men will be concerned for your physical and emotional safety, but they will express that concern openly and honestly and be able to tell you why they are concerned such as "It worries me when you walk the dog in that neighborhood so late at night. There have been a lot of people robbed over there." And many couples have agreements on spending limits or even about checking in if you're going to be more than 30 minutes late, but these agreements are far from someone demanding that you ask for permission before you do something that normal people do every day.

Isolation:

He will slowly try to limit your social interactions and may try to prevent you from spending time with your family and friends. He/she may accuse you of being "too involved with your family," or "not committed to the relationship," or view people who are your personal friends as "trying to cause trouble between the two of you." He/she may want to live in the country without a phone, not let you use the car, stop you from working or gaining further education or qualifications, not allow you to travel on business "because of the kids."

Isolation is not to be confused with expressing concern over toxic friends, or agreements that are made to stay away from certain non-family people who have proven to be disruptive to the relationship.

Unrealistic Expectations:

This is an extension of the control process and is designed to break you down further by making you feel inadequate. He will expect you to be the perfect wife, mother, friend, cook, house keeper, volunteer etc. He will depend on you for his every need and then criticize you for not being good enough.

Good men are willing to accept your faults. He will not criticize everything you do and, instead will be grateful, appreciative and complimentary. A good man will have discussions with you when he feels like agreements have been broken and/or the relationship may be at risk because of something you do.

Unrealistic Expectations For Children:

Just like his unrealistic expectations for you, he will have the same unrealistic expectations for your children. He views children as "small adults" and blames them for not being responsible or having common sense. He expects his children to be capable far beyond their ability. For instance, he will be incredibly angry with a child for wetting the bed, throwing up on the carpet, having nightmares, etc., He will punish the child for "naughtiness" that the child could not possibly be aware of and the punishment may exceed what would be considered appropriate. He will demand the perfect child as their imperfections will be a reflection on him. He may not want his children to eat at the table with him or he may expect them to stay quiet, or stay in their rooms while he is watching TV. He may demand all your attention and resent any time you spend with the children even so much as resenting normal childcare efforts.

Good men, obviously, support and encourage their children and enjoy spending time around them. It's important to differentiate between the above behavior and a man needing "couple time."

Blame-Shifting For Problems And Feelings:

Very rarely will an abusive personality accept responsibility for any negative situation or problem. If they are unemployed, can't hold down a job, or disowned by their family. They may feel that someone is always doing them wrong, or out to get them. He will make mistakes and blame you for upsetting him or preventing him from doing as they desired. No matter what it is, it is always someone else's fault, be it the boss, the government, or their mother/father. But generally it is your fault.

The abuser will deny feelings stem from within him but see them as reactions to your behavior or attitude toward him. What he does, thinks and feels will be "because you…" Feelings will be used to manipulate you, i.e., "I would be angry if you..." Oddly, positive emotions will also originate outside of him, but these are more difficult to detect. Feeling statements such that begin with "You make me _____" happy/feel good/sad/depressed are all signs the he feels you are responsible for how he feels. In his mind, you are responsible for his emotional well-being and happiness. This also puts you at fault when he is upset, angry, depressed or failed at something.

A good man accepts responsibility for his own actions and his own feelings.

Rigid Gender Roles:

He strongly believes in stereotypical gender roles. He will expect you to serve him, stay at home, obey him in all things. He views women as inferior to men, less intelligent, unable to be a whole person unless they're in a relationship. (An interesting note and one of my personal pet peeves is the use of the term "real man" by women as this is a phrase used by female abusers to shame men into behaving in a certain way, when he shows weakness or emotion, or is less than gallant.)

Forced Sex:

He will pressure you into forceful or violent sex acts. He will show little concern about whether you want sex and uses sulking or anger to manipulate you into compliance. He'll initiate sex while you are sleeping, demanding sex when you are ill or tired, or refusing any form of intimacy unless you are willing to go 'all the way' can all be signs that he could be a sexually abusive or sexually violent man.

While many couples share in forms of sex that others may find inappropriate or even abusive, the good man respects your boundaries and will not force anything on you or manipulate you in to anything. The difference between the abuse and enjoyment is willing consent. What's done between consenting adults is one thing while being forced to participate in violent or distasteful acts is abusive.

Verbal Abuse:

Verbal abuse comes in many forms. It can be an angry screaming rant or soft spoken words and can be in public, in front of family, friends or in complete privacy. Regardless of the delivery, the message is always degrading and includes putting down your accomplishments, telling you that you are stupid, incompetent or incapable and it's all designed to reduce your self worth and make you feel you could not manage without him. In some cases, the abuser may say nice things to your face but to your family, friends and coworkers talk about what a train wreck you are.

Good guys are not verbally abusive. They are kind, caring and supportive. They never want to detract from your self worth but, instead, want to build it up. They will value your differences and will only say kind things to those around you. This doesn't mean that a good guy won't say things that aren't hurtful but that's not the norm and is something you can discuss with him without you being attacked, blamed or criticized for your feelings.

Dr. Jekyll And Mr. Hyde:

Very rarely do abusers conform to the stereotypical image of a constantly harsh, nasty or violent person, either in public or in private. More frequently the abuser portrays a perfectly normal and pleasant picture to the outside world (often they have responsible jobs or are respected and important members of the local community or Church) and reserves the abuse for you in the privacy of your own home. Nor are abusers always overtly abusive or cruel, but can display apparent kindness and consideration. This Jekyll and Hyde tendency of the abuser serves to further confuse the victim, while protecting themselves from any form of suspicion from outsiders. Many victims describe "sudden" changes in mood - one minute nice and the next explosive or hysterical, or one minute happy and the next minute screaming at you and calling you names. This does not indicate some special "mental problem" but are typical of abusive personalities, and related to other characteristics such as hypersensitivity.

Good guys, like everyone, have good days and bad days. Good moods and bad moods. The difference is in how they treat you when they're in a bad mood.

Alcohol Or Drug Abuse:

While neither drinking or drug use are signs that a man will be abusive, heavy drinking or drug abuse do increase the risks of verbal abuse or violence taking place. The truth is, most men who are at risk of becoming violent while under the influence have most likely already been violent or in fights while drinking. These men are well aware of the risk and any man who knows there is a risk he could be violent when under the influence of alcohol or drugs is, in effect, choosing to put you at risk. Of course, it will always be the drink or drugs responsible for his abusive behavior and not his own actions.

Good men understand the affects of drugs and alcohol and certainly understand "moderation" and never put themselves or you in a situation where you will be at risk.

History Of Battering Or Sexual Violence:

Very rarely is abuse or violence a one-off event: a batterer will beat any woman he is with; a sexually abusive person will be abusive toward all his intimate partners. Situational circumstances do not make a person an abusive personality. Sometimes friends or family may try to warn you about the abuser. Sometimes the abuser may tell you himself/herself that he/she has hit or sexually assaulted someone in the past. However, they may further go on to explain that "she made me do it by ..." or in some other way not take responsibility and shift the blame on to the victim. They may tell you that it won't happen with you because "you love them enough to prevent it" or "you won't be stupid enough to wind me up that much". Not only is he denying his responsibility for the abuse, he's also shifting the responsibility for the abusive relationship from him to you. Past violence is one of the strongest predictors that future abuse will occur. If at all possible, try to speak to their previous partners.

Threatening Violence:

This would obviously include any threat of physical force such as "If you speak to him/her again, I'll kill you", or "If any wife of mine acted like John's did, I'd give her a right seeing to". Threats are designed to manipulate and control you, to keep you in your place and prevent you from making your own decisions. Most people do not threaten their mates, but an abuser will excuse this behavior by saying "everybody talks like that.", maintaining he/she is only saying this because the relationship or you are so important to him/her, tell you you're "over-sensitive" for being upset by such threats, or obviously want to hurt him/her. Threats can also be less overt, such as "If you leave me, I will kill myself", or "You are so wonderful, I will never let you go/couldn't live without you".

Breaking Things:

Breaking things can be used as a punishment for some perceived offense on your part and generally what gets broken are items you treasure, items the two of you have collected in the past or gifts you have given him. Breaking your things has the effect of de-personalizing you and denying you your individuality.

This behavior is not just restricted to breaking items but may also include pounding on items of furniture or throwing objects (i.e. a plate). Often times, he will justify his behavior by blaming you for making him so angry. This is simply blame shifting.

Everyone is human and even good men lose their temper but there's a difference in losing one's temper and using violence to intimidate someone.

Physical Force:

There is simply no room in a healthy relationship for unwanted physical touching which includes pushing, shoving, restraint and obviously hitting. If a man holds you, pins you to the wall to prevent you from walking away from an argument or keep you in front of him so he can yell at you, this is domestic violence. When a man crosses the boundary between acceptable touching and physical force, no matter how small the incident, you are headed down a bad path. If this occurs during an argument, then you're simply one step away from becoming a battered woman.

Good men have no need for physical violence, and they neither tolerate its use against them nor use it against another.

Cruelty To Animals:

He may neglect to care for pets to the point of cruelty, such as not feeding them all day, leaving them in areas he/she knows will cause them suffering or distress such as inside a hot house or outside in a thunderstorm. When he punishes a pet, he may do so brutally and be insensitive to their fear, pain and suffering. There is a strong connection between cruelty to animals and the psychopath.

How It Starts - Early Signs Of Abuse:

Abuse generally starts slow because if, on the first date, the man called you names and slapped you, the date would end with his butt in jail.

There are two primary early signs of abuse, Aggressive Verbal Behavior and Controlling Behavior. Often the abuser will initially try to explain these behaviors as how he shows his love and concern for you. While you may initially be flattered, as time goes on, the behaviors become more severe and serve to dominate, control and manipulate his victim.

Early Stage Predictors:

Aggressive Verbal Behavior - this can be anything from constantly criticizing you including how you look, your cooking, to name calling and profanity and attacks on your character and/or your identity. You can expect ranging from "that wasn't your best meal" to "you lying slut!" I can't stress how important it is for you to set boundaries early on. If he didn't cook it, he has no right to complain about it! A good man will correct his behavior, while an abuser will push back and try to control you.

Controlling behavior - this typically starts as something simple and relatively innocent and then it escalates. According to Dr. Jacquelyn Campbell, at Johns Hopkins University in Baltimore and a leading researcher of domestic violence, two common scenarios are:

1. He suggests installing apps on your smart phone to track movements for "safety" and "so that you know where each other are just in case something happens to one of us, the other can find us" because "I care for you." Then when you tell him you're going to the dentist on Tuesday, but you don't, he starts demanding to know where you were instead of at the dentist.

2. You exchange email or social media passwords and you get an email from someone he doesn't know, perhaps an ex or just someone random, and he gets mad and confronts you over the contact.

Regardless of how the behavior reveals itself, his behavior will escalate until you begin pushing back, at which time the first physical aggression will come in the form of a push or shove. It may even "appear" as though he's pushing you out of his way so he can leave. Unfortunately, once that physical aggression barrier is broken, it's a very short step to holding or restraining you, choking you and finally beating or battering you.

The Abuse Cycle:

Researchers have found that with domestic violence there is a clear and predictable cycle of abuse. The cycle is broken into phases or stages. While these stages are good predictors of abuse occurring, they are by no means what one should rely on because violent people can erupt over seemingly nothing, and it can appear to come out of the blue.

However, assaults that come out of the blue are rarely the case. More often, the aggression follows a clear and distinct cycle and that cycle is well documented so I want to break it down for you so that you can recognize each phase.

Normalcy Phase:

The Normalcy Phase is where we all want to live. It's our happy place. It's the place we all dream about. It's what we work for and getting here is why you're reading this book.

- Things are normal
- Everyone seems happy
- Life is going well

Tension Phase:

The Tension Phase can creep up on you. You get a sense that something's not right but you can't put your finger on it. You figure he's just had a bad day so you tend to let things go. What's important to know about this phase is that the tension builds. Depending on your circumstances, it can take weeks to reach a place where you feel like the strings are wound so tight they're going to break... or it can take days! Regardless of how long it takes for that tension to build, once you feel like the strings are going to break, they are! Some of the signs of the tension phase are:

- You will sense tension growing
- He's moody
- He criticizes small things
- He humiliates you (this is the beginning of asserting power over you)
- He becomes angry and agitated over nothing

Explosion Phase:

It's during the Explosion Phase that actual abuse and violence occurs. The tension has reached a breaking point and all that anger is going to go somewhere and you are likely where. The signs are:

- Threats and verbal abuse are in full force
- Humiliation escalates (he wants you to feel a sense of self-hate which renders you incapable of meeting your own needs or the needs of others)
- Hitting begins
- Use of weapons (the use of weapons vastly increases the chances you will be killed!)
- Rape may occur
- Choking or life ending gestures

Remorse Phase:

The Remorse Phase occurs after he has abused you. All of his rage has been emptied on you and he's starting to realize that he lost control. He wants to make up with you and your forgiveness is essential to his self acceptance. You will see him go through the following motions:

- He apologizes
- He begs for forgiveness
- He promises to change
- He cries
- He vows to get help
- He vows to go to church, quit drinking, stop doing drugs, etc.

In most cases of domestic violence, verbal abuse and standing uncomfortably close to the intended victim were the most common behaviors immediately prior to the assault. In the 3 days prior to the assault, there can be a marked increase in verbal abuse, threatening gestures and threatening or intimidating body posture.

He's Not Abusive, He's Just Mad!:

Are you sure? Do you understand communication and its core components and how these can reveal signs that you're in a potentially dangerous situation?

Communications is made of three components: Body language, tone, and words spoken. Your body language accounts for about 60% of the message you're communicating, your tone of voice is about 30%, while your actual spoken word is a mere 10%. What's important is that your posture, tone, and words are transmitting a message which must be in agreement otherwise, doubt arises and people don't believe your message.

An example of this would be a man clenching his fist, his face red from anger and spitting through his gritted teeth that he's going to beat you to a pulp. This message is being transmitted through his body language (clenching fist, face red in anger), by tone (spitting words through gritted teeth) and his words (I'm going to beat you to a pulp). This man means what he says. Now, take this exact same thing but let's change out the words so that now, we now have a man clenching his fist, his face red from anger and spitting through his gritted teeth that he'd never hit you. This message being transmitted physically (clenching fist, face red in anger) tells you that you're not safe, by tone (spitting words through gritted teeth), he's confirming the physical signs and his words (I would never hit you) are not in agreement. 90% of his communications tells you that you're in danger! So, in this second example, would you really believe you're safe? No!

When He's Going To Hit You:

As we discussed previously in the section "The Abuse Cycle", in most cases, the violence has a progression or pattern and there are signs you can observe and each of these signs is an escalation to the next stage of aggression. Sometimes it can take days or weeks to progress through these stages; while other times, it can seem like seconds. Either way, it's important for you to recognize the stages so that you can protect yourself.

When we break down the Explosion Phase of the Abuse Cycle, we find that it, too, generally has stages or steps. It's important to understand and recognize these stages so that you can escape or seek immediate help. It's also important to understand that these stages may not be present or may occur so quickly that you have no time to recognize and respond to them.

Stage One, The Stare:

At this stage, the abuser is evaluating you. He's trying to determine if you are going to take the abuse or if this is the right time and place where he can get away with the abuse without getting caught. He's also waiting on you to provoke him or give him the slightest reason.

To Do: No one wants to fight or argue. You need to stay in control and when things heat up, leave. Consider all the factors: Has he been drinking? Was he a victim of childhood domestic violence? Does he have a history of physical abuse? There are no heroes in domestic violence. Get your keys, your phone and leave NOW!

Stage Two, The Question:

This is an escalation. It's a question with no right answer. "What did you do around here all day?" "Why didn't you get my clothes from the cleaner?" "What the hell were you doing talking to that man?" "Do you think I'm stupid or something?" Beware! At this stage he has already planned to attack you... depending on the circumstances at least verbally, probably physically.

To Do: Put your hands in front of your chest, palms facing towards the abuser and tell them you don't want to fight. Keep your chest to them and back away. Your posture and tone should be soft and you should appear to cave in to them. By complying with their rules you are giving them the sense of control that they need. You are buying yourself time to get away.

The Body Language:

His body language will change, his chest will puff out, his hand gestures will be more animated (look for pointing and stabbing at the air), his face will redden, jaw will tighten and teeth will show more and maybe stomping his feet, and he will constantly be looking around.

To Do: Appear non-confrontational, keep your hands in front of you with your palms facing outward. This sends a clear physical message that you don't want to fight. Give them what they want to hear even if you have to keep saying "I'm sorry, I'm sorry." Give them power and by doing so it's really you that's in control because you're managing the crisis. **Many women who have been abused often report that it's better to say very little. Only you can decide what's best for you.**

Stage Three, The Provocation:

At this stage the abuser becomes unreasonable. He can't be talked to or reasoned with. No matter what you say he'll respond with things like "Yeah, yeah, so what." He'll spend more time looking at your body trying to figure out where he's going to attack you. A truly violent man can build up to this point in a matter of seconds.

To Do: Stay away from them. You have options: You can run, you can call 9-1-1, you can hit a panic alarm if you want. If you're in a public place you can keep loudly repeating "I don't want to fight, I don't want to fight" over and over. The attention will generally either drive the attacker away OR bring help to you. This extra attention will also help you legally. Whatever you do, if you're in public, do NOT get in the car with or go home to a man in this agitated state because things will only get worse when you get home because he will not only carry the issue that set him off but now it will be compounded by the public humiliation.

Stage Four, The Attack:

The distance between you and the abuser will close. He will be looking for a sign, an opportunity to attack. Sometimes, your body language and position can diffuse or even dissuade those who are not so determined. **The important thing to note here is that if someone is intent on physically attacking you, there is absolutely nothing you can do to prevent the attack from happening.**

To Do: If you are attacked, try to stay away from him. Keep your head and face covered and scream for help at the top of your lungs.

Most people are right handed and because of that, they usually strike with their right hand first. By staying to their left, you make it inconvenient and awkward for them to strike you. If he's right handed, you need to make sure your left side is blocked. If you're sitting, a good strategy might be to sit on the left side of the couch with an end table and lamp blocking your left side, but escape is always the best strategy.

Perpetrators of domestic violence frequently report symptoms of autonomic arousal (flight or fight) and a sense of overwhelming fear and/or loss of control at the time of the violence. These abusers literally lose control through rage. These are exaggerated fear-related behavioral responses, and nothing will stop them from attacking. They won't stop until their rage is vented.

When Abuse Turns Deadly:

The news is filled with stories of wives or even entire families being murdered by the husband and father. Each story is met with cries of "How can we stop this?" The truth is, awareness is the first step to stopping this. Getting out of abusive relationships with the help of trained professionals is the second step.

The Deadly Dance:

According to researchers, domestic violence that ends in death has a very distinct pattern. He becomes violent and blames the woman for his violence. The woman attempts to resist, and he becomes more abusive and more violent. She attempts to escape and end the relationship, and he punishes her for her defiance.

A landmark 2003 study by a team of international researchers, led by Jacquelyn Campbell (referenced earlier) and published in the National Institute of Justice Journal, compared two groups of battered women. One group included 220 women who had been killed by their partners; the other group included 343 who had been abused, but not killed.

What the researchers pinpointed was that where a history of domestic violence exists, certain other factors vastly increase the likelihood that a victim will be killed.

Battered women who have been threatened or assaulted with a gun - even once - are 20 times more likely than other battered women to be murdered. Those who have been choked are 10 times more likely to be killed.

Other factors that can increase a victim's risk are substance abuse, unemployment, depression, abuse during pregnancy, any kind of estrangement, and the presence of a stepchild. For people in the field, the study — and the danger-assessment tool it was based on — is the definitive guide for assessing risk in domestic-violence situations.

The checklist of those signs is so remarkably consistent that intake workers at domestic-violence shelters use the criteria to establish what danger a woman faces, and Phoenix police officers ask similar questions when they go out on roughly 14,000 domestic-violence calls every year.

Professor Campbell has made a checklist available for anyone to use: The checklist can be found at: http://www.dangerassessment.org and use the "Danger Assessment" menu to "View the assessment" This checklist is based on the one developed and used by professionals but does not draw a conclusion or require professional training. However, if you are or think you are in an abusive relationship, this will give you some clarity of thought.

Other Factors Fuel The Lethality:

Besides the traits of being obsessively possessive, drinking or using drugs, or being unemployed, there are other factors that increase the chances abuse will turn deadly:

Stepchildren: A stepchild increases risk, not because of anything the child does, but because his or her presence invokes jealousy over a woman's prior relationship

Abuse During Pregnancy: If there was any form of verbal or physical abuse during your pregnancy you are at greater chance of losing your life

Age Difference: There's an age difference of more than 10 years

Immigration: She's an undocumented immigrant who may fear reaching out for help because of her status or fear she'll be separated from her children

What Can I Do?:

Now that we've identified some of the personality traits and behaviors most common to abusers, let's look at things you can do to spot potential danger.

Pay attention to how he talks about and to you. Language is a powerful tool; it can also be wielded as a weapon to keep you in line and under the abusive person's "spell". A man who's expressing contempt of you while still professing his love for you is demonstrating a sign of deep anger.

Watch for patterns of intense possessiveness or jealousy. Anyone who gets angry or sulky when you want to go and have a night out with the girls, or who questions you mercilessly any time you're seen talking to a member of the opposite sex is being too possessive. Now, if you've legitimately given your partner reasons to not trust you then you probably should be managing these social situations differently.

Notice if he won't take no for an answer. An example is when the two of you have been invited somewhere and you've declined but your man will not accept your answer. He will beg, cajole, bribe, argue, sulk and otherwise continue his badgering until you surrender, he gets his way and you end up going.

Look for when he places pressure on you to change or move faster than you're prepared to. For instance, if he's pushing you to get more involved in the relationship or rushing you to move in together before you're ready. Not respecting your need to move at your own pace, trying to guilt or coerce you into something you're not ready for or wanting you to turn into someone you're not is a sign of someone who could potentially become abusive.

Pay attention to how your arguments start and, more importantly how they proceed. Do you disagree calmly while rationally expressing your feelings and negotiating a resolution that's satisfying to both of you? Does every disagreement escalate into a huge, hours-long battle? If he instantly starts pouting, yelling, or name calling, this can be a sign of bad things to come.

Note how your partner treats alcohol and drugs. Is he using alcohol or drugs to excess? Under what circumstances does he drink? Socially drinking with friends or as a crutch at the end of a long, stressful day? Does he become difficult, nasty, selfish, angry or violent when using drugs or alcohol? When sober, does he blame the alcohol or drugs for his behavior? If he becomes bolder or more confident, does this mean danger for you?

When you're around him, do you feel like you constantly need to walk on egg shells to avoid setting him off? Is he extremely prickly? For instance, can the tiniest behavior, disagreement or criticism set him/her off? If so, this man can become abusive in a relationship.

Perform a reality check by asking yourself if you're afraid of him. No matter how much you love your man or how much you've been through together, if you're afraid of your man, you have a problem that needs to be addressed.

Recognize and see physical abuse for what it is. It is absolutely never okay for anyone to push, shove, restrain or hit you for any reason. No matter how valid he makes that reason sound, it's never "for your own good" and you did nothing to "make" him hit you. Understand, there are times in most relationships where one partner or the other lashes out physically; and contextually, that may be understandable IF it is rare and is never violently directed toward you (for example, your partner is alone in the garage and throws something at the wall). Recognize the difference between someone who might momentarily lose control out of frustration and anger, and someone who uses physical violence to intimidate or subdue you.

Look for combinations of the above. Be sensible here. Just because someone does one or two of these things does not mean he is or will be abusive. What I want you to do is think about the men you are dating or in a relationship with, look at the personality traits and behaviors and try to spot the signs that may lead to a dangerous situation. Know that the personality traits may not be apparent from the beginning and the behaviors may creep in so slowly that you don't recognize them; but when you see several of those signals beginning to emerge and/or a pattern begins to form, then it's time to end that relationship.

Situational Awareness:

When you are in a new dating relationship AND your partner's moods and rhythms are unknown to you, or when a known partner's mood is suddenly different than usual, you need to become more aware of your situation including your surrounding environment. I've heard from women who were married for 10, 15, 20 years who never experienced the slightest hint of aggression from their husbands and one day he's been fired from work, comes home drunk. Her first comment is about him being late for dinner, and out of nowhere he has lashed out and assaulted her. When behavior is out of the ordinary, you need to keep your head up, eyes and ears open and focused on the situation. Stay in control of yourself and try to anticipate problems before they arise.

Document The Cycle:

Dr. Campbell suggests that you document the cycle. Mark your arguments on a calendar, include the triggers (what happened or what was said), look for consistent triggers, patterns of frequency including an increase in frequency.

When To Leave:

If anything happens that makes you afraid, trust your gut and seek help! Don't try to rationalize or justify his actions! The minute you say to yourself "He's just having a bad day." you have given him permission to abuse you.

If you have been pushed, restrained or hit at any time and your man is not in an ongoing abuse treatment program and professionals have not given clearance for you to be together, then you should not be together.

If you are in extreme danger, call the police and a domestic violence shelter, they have special intake questions that will allow them to protect you and themselves. Especially if you have ever been:

- Choked
- Threatened with death
- Shown a gun, had a gun pointed at you, even if he's only gotten the gun from the nightstand drawer and laid it on the dresser during an argument... you are 20 times more likely to die!

Address the problem early. There is help and the help is effective but the problem will NOT go away on its own. It will only get worse!

The Psychology Of Abusers:

Everyone, including researchers, therapists, abused women, non-abused women, non-abusive men and the abusers themselves all want to know what's going on inside the minds of an abuser. Let's look at some psychological causes:

PTSD - Rewiring The Brain:

Post Traumatic Stress Disorder or, PTSD, is an anxiety disorder that some people get after seeing or living through a dangerous event such as prolonged abuse, torture, natural disasters or terrorist events.

While many people believe that PTSD is an emotional condition, what really happens is that the brain rewires itself so that sufferers exhibit an over-activation of the autonomic nervous system which governs fear sensory input, memory formation and stress response mechanisms.

When in danger, it's natural to feel afraid. This fear triggers many split-second changes in the body to prepare to defend against the danger or to avoid it. This "fight-or-flight" response is a healthy reaction meant to protect a person from harm. But in PTSD, this reaction becomes damaged.

What happens is that the trauma (war, childhood abuse, rape, molestation, domestic violence, etc.) places an individual in a state of constantly having to be on guard. After a certain time, which varies between individuals, the brain gets stuck in that "on guard" state. Once stuck, the brain stays stuck, and without treatment, will stay stuck for years or even a lifetime. Even when people with PTSD know the threat is no longer there, their brain will continue to react from that stuck place with very distorted fear and flight-vs-fight responses causing people with PTSD to feel stressed or frightened even when no danger exists. An example we all hear about is the veteran who jumps under a table when he hears an unexpected loud sound such as a firecracker.

Although we most frequently hear about PTSD in military veterans, it's also found in survivors of physical and sexual assault, abuse, people who were bullied, accidents involving death and dismemberment, natural disasters, etc. Anyone can get PTSD at any age. If a child suffered abuse, or witnessed domestic violence then, normal brain growth can be disrupted and lead to problems well into adulthood.

The good news is that, over the course of our lives, our brain constantly makes new neural connections and is in a constant state of rewiring itself, so there is treatment and PTSD can be cured.

Attachment Disorder:

Attachment disorder is a broad, psychological term used to describe disorders with social relationships. Attachment researchers have learned that this disorder arises from a failure to form normal attachments to primary care giving figures in early childhood. This failure, which is a failure of the caregiver, results in the child growing up and developing distorted interpersonal expectations which create problematic relationship behaviors.

According to researchers Jac Brown, Kerrie James and Alan Taylor, in an article called "Caught in the rejection–abuse cycle: are we really treating perpetrators of domestic abuse effectively?" which was published in the Journal of Family Therapy (Brown, James, & Taylor, 2010), these researchers suggest that many men who engage in domestic violence enter a cycle of rejection and abuse that is difficult to stop.

Apparently, the cycle begins when a man who has insecure attachments from childhood and adolescent experiences enters a relationship and then encounters real or perceived rejection which leads to an inner sense of shame which he defends against by abusing his partner in order to reject the message she's sending and to soothe his sense of shame and to protect his sense of masculinity.

Respect:

In some cultures, being "respected" is the ultimate definition of being a man and any violations of what men in these cultures perceive as respect requires retribution.

A good example would be the gang culture. When a gang member is disrespected or challenged by having someone question his willingness to defend himself (he's disrespected), any failure by the gang member to retaliate with physical violence causes a loss of status within the gang. So, the last thing a gang member will stand for is having someone take away their RESPECT.

In fact, within some neighborhoods and cultures, disrespect is seen as a perfectly legitimate reason to hit someone and in street gangs, disrespect can be a reason for killing someone. In some African and mid-eastern cultures where arranged marriages exist, a woman who disrespects her husband can even be killed by her own family for "bringing shame on them."

Depending on how deeply the cultural need for respect runs, that depth can dictate the lengths one will go to protect that respect. Of course, any form of respect that has to be defended with physical violence isn't real, and it doesn't last.

Humiliation:

In his book Familicidal Hearts: The Emotional Styles of 211 Killers (Websdale, 2009), author and researcher Neil Websdale of Northern Arizona University finds that many men kill in a state of what he calls "humiliated fury" which is shame gone in to overdrive.

Shame can be sent into overdrive by him losing his job, too much drinking resulting, a DUI (which is a public humiliation for drinking that's out of control), his partner leaving him (moving out, filing for divorce etc.), flirtations of another man or essentially anything that points out that he has failed to live up to societies definition of masculinity which he finds humiliating.

According to Professor Websdale, "You can see it coming. You can log it. You can count it." Of course, what he's referring to is the increase in battering that leads up to the deadly encounter. There will be more trips to the hospital, more broken bones and more outward signs of extreme physical abuse such as swollen eyes, bruising, cut lips and broken teeth. This is also why Professor Campbell recommends keeping track of each encounter.

Obviously, shame plays a huge part in domestic violence and is why understanding shame, its roots and how your man carries his shame is such an important part of understanding your man.

Revenge Restores Balance:

Revenge plays a big part in the violence/retribution cycle. An abuser perceives some wrong against him which invokes the shame cycle and the only known course of action that can restore the emotional balance is "revenge" which comes in the form of abuse.

Throughout time, humanity has been flooded with the message that "revenge is sweet" or "she got her just desserts" and in ways it is. When researchers scanned the brains of people contemplating revenge, they found the area of the brain called the caudate nucleus, which is known to process rewards and which gets extremely active in cocaine and nicotine use, lights up when an individual contemplates revenge. Thinking about revenge feels good!

However, studies have shown that when a person pursues revenge, they actually feel worse. Not only do they feel worse but thinking about or acting on revenge causes people to hang on to the wound for long periods of time. Revenge seekers prolong their emotional involvement in their perceived wrong while non-revenge seekers tend to let go of the wrong and move on to focus on other things.

German psychological scientist Mario Gollwitzer put forth the theory called "understanding hypothesis" which states that "an offender's suffering is not enough, on its own, to achieve truly satisfactory revenge. Instead, the avenger must be assured that the offender has made a direct connection between the retaliation and the initial behavior." Through a series of experiments, Professor Gollwitzer confirmed that what makes revenge feel sweet is when the "offender" recognizes and acknowledges that what happened to them is a direct result of what they did wrong. If the "offender" does not acknowledge their wrongdoing, then justice was not served and the act of revenge goes unmet and the revenge seeker hangs on to the perceived hurt. Instead of providing closure, revenge keeps the wound open and fresh.

Another problem with revenge as a system of justice is the definition of justice is very individual. While one person may burn their partners eggs or get angry and yell, an abuser believes that violence is the only way to restore balance and justice.

Some statements made by revenge minded men are "One day, I'll get even." or "Someday, his butt will be mine."

Make Up Or Breakup?:

One question often asked is why a woman keeps going back to an abuser. Psychologists have long recognized there can be entrenched patterns of behavior that are not easily broken because the abused woman actually gets some reward from the reconciliation. Understand that the abuser has battered his mate as a means of righting that perceived attack on his masculinity or dominant role by acquiring power which thereby places the victim in the role of the accused. After the violence occurs, his rage has subsided and the remorse has set in and one or the other will attempt reconciliation. Reconciliation gives the abuser the sense that he was right while the victim is relieved of her role as the wrong doer or guilty party and this is her reward.

Does this cycle work? Of course not and the majority of non-battered woman would instantly recognize and understand this. However, battered women have been broken spiritually and mentally as well as physically. The abuse falls into a cycle as the victim becomes trained into a subservient relationship. The abuser's success comes more from attacking the emotionally weak than the physically weak. That's why it's important for you to recognize the traits, the behaviors and the signs leading up to physical violence and to remove yourself from the situation as quickly as possible.

Susan in Eugene shared her story:

"When I met my ex, he was charming, sweet, doting and attentive. He had a good job and was financially stable. Just pretty much everything a girl could want.

About 5 years into our marriage, when my oldest was 3 and the baby was 1 is when the abuse started. At first, it was just yelling when he came home and the house was messy. This just kept getting worse until one night he came home late, and I had left his dinner in the oven and was watching TV. He had been drinking and immediately started in on me and before I knew it he had grabbed me by my hair, pulled me into the floor and hit me.

From there things escalated even more. The yelling and name calling became a nightly thing. The beatings got worse. I would threaten to leave him and he would threaten to kill me and the kids.

Eventually (year 7), I ended up in the hospital with two broken ribs and a busted eye socket. And still, I continued to lie to cover up for him and to hide my shame.

More time passed with more beatings and a broken arm. He would try to beat the kids and I would have to get between them and him. Of course this meant I would take the brunt of his anger.

I couldn't keep going. I was at the end. I feared breathing.

People always ask me, 'Why didn't you leave?' I didn't leave because I was convinced that I was such a bad mother the courts would take my kids away or that he really would kill me and them.

Finally, it got to a point where dying was better than living another day the way I was. That's when I decided to leave, when I no longer cared if I lived or died. Bleeding from my nose, I called the police for the last time."

Why Women Don't Leave:

Conflict is an inevitable aspect of all human association. Conflict occurs between siblings, classmates, roommates, coworkers and domestic partners. Conflict, in and of itself, is not a bad thing but when coercion consisting primarily of intimidation, threats, force and/or violence is used as a method of conflict-resolution it is incredibly harmful to the victim on both physical and emotional levels.

For many abused women, domestic violence was significantly associated with violence in her childhood, her having no or limited education, her attitudes towards violence or her perceptions of cultural norms on women's roles.

We all know that leaving a violent relationship is crucial for a woman's safety and the safety of her children (not to mention that children who witness grow up either being abusers or being abused themselves) but for the abused, leaving is never as simple as just walking out the door.

Women feel a sense of shame and humiliation in disclosing they are victims of abuse. Leaving and going to a shelter means that everyone within both sides of the family will become aware of her situation. This can cause huge divides in families. Some women fear their brothers or fathers will exact revenge on an abuser. In traditional communities, divorced women often feel rejected and ostracized. In order to avoid this stigma, many women prefer to remain in the marriage and endure the abuse.

Beyond the emotional aspects, most abused women have been isolated so leaving means losing everything they own and becoming homeless. It means taking their children to a shelter. It means complete and total insecurity.

Can The Abuser Change?:

I believe anyone is capable of change, but men who are emotionally or physically abusive have serious psychological problems that require years of intense therapy in order to work through and resolve their issues. If your man has been emotionally or physically abusive and has not agreed to therapy, I believe you need to start making a plan for exiting.

Women want to be good partners and men really don't want to be abusive, but perpetrators of domestic violence require professional help (as do the victims). Leaving can be his motivation for change and your opportunity to change.

Restraining Orders:

The popular belief is that restraining orders don't work. Before researching this chapter I admit that, I too, shared in that belief. The fact is, in low threat cases of domestic violence, which is the vast majority of cases, restraining orders do work.

In dangerous cases, they do not! That's why the police and battered women's shelters exist and why their intake personnel are so well trained. They can help you assess your risk and guide you through the steps of leaving in as safe a manner as possible (things like leaving your cell phone behind so that you can't be tracked).

Where There Is Prey, There Are Predators:

One of the most absolute truths in life is this: "Where there is prey, there are predators!" This truth is found all through nature. A wounded mouse will easily be plucked by a sharp eyed eagle, an outcast person will find themselves bullied, a child left alone on the playground will attract a child predator, a person walking alone at night will attract a mugger.

The famous Japanese swordsman, Musashi, a man who survived

over 60 actual life and death duels and then wrote his classic text on strategy, The Book of Five Rings, had several incredibly important observations and, arguably, the most important of these is: "Make your fighting stance your everyday stance, make your everyday stance your fighting stance." What this means is be solid in how you take a stand, be clear about your convictions. If you recognize bad behavior upfront and stop it in its tracks by verbally setting boundaries or, if necessary, walking away from the relationship, you will be projecting a stance that tells predators that you are not prey and you will NOT tolerate being abused.

What Do I Do Next?:

If you or someone you know is in an emotionally or physically abusive relationship, you are encouraged to reach out to the appropriate authorities. The abuse will not end. The abuser will not change without years of therapy.

Remember:

If the level of danger is high, GET OUT! This means that if you have been choked, had a knife held to you or been threatened with a gun, you MUST get out! Get help from the police, call a domestic violence shelter and follow all of their instructions.

If your partner is a combat vet and suffers from PTSD, you must get help. His brain has been rewired to a point where normal situations cause abnormal reactions.

If your partner is suffering from substance abuse, get help. Don't be his enabler, his crutch nor his excuse.

If your partner is suffering from long term unemployment and has no other work or outlet such as volunteering, get help!

All of this is especially true if you have children!

Chapter 13

LEAVING A MAN

J UST LIKE WITH ANYTHING ELSE involving men, there's a right way and a wrong way to leave one. It doesn't much matter whether you're divorcing, breaking up from a long term relationship or just breaking things off after a handful of dates. Do it right, and you can have a long term friend and ally. Do it wrong, and he can be a huge pain in the rear every time you see him.

Why Don't Men Do The Leaving?:

According to the National Center for Health Statistics, a part of the CDC, of the marriages that end in divorce, over 70% percent of the divorces are initiated (filed) by women.

The Office of National Statistics (ONS), in the UK, shows that in 2011, which is the latest year for which numbers were available, women initiated the divorce in 66% of cases that year. This is down from 72% in the 90's.

While that seems like good news, the fact is divorce rates are essentially the same which means men are increasingly filing for divorce. So, men do leave and the trend of men initiating divorce is growing. That growth is being fueled by states which begun equalizing the distribution of assets, limiting alimony and creating child custody environments which are closer to 50/50 time share or co-parenting. These things reduce or eliminate the major barriers for men initiating divorce.

Even with these changes, still the number of men who file for divorce is far, far less than women who file. That begs the question, "Why don't men leave?" and there are two reasons for this. One has to do with how men approach relationships, and one is an anecdote which applies to men and bad situations.

The Long Road:

When a man is in a committed relationship he's, already taken the long road view. The best way to visualize this view is to imagine the stock market. The stock prices go up and down. A day will have highs and lows, as will a week, as will a month. When you put this on a graph and look at the near term, you easily see the huge swings of those highs and lows with the jagged line showing the peaks and valleys. However, if you back out and look at the stock market over the last 50, 60, 70 years, you see some peaks and valleys but overall it shows a pretty steady line upwards. Men view relationships the same way. We expect there to be highs and lows, but we also recognize that over time, the argument this week will be forgotten as will the one next week, and that when we hit the end of our lives and look back, it will be a long squiggly line that slopes downward… like sitting at the top of a playground slide and looking down. Because we take that long term view, we're less inclined to treat every argument as life and death or to overreact over trivial things. This also means that women can become very frustrated and think we don't care simply because we're not reacting the way you think we should.

The Frog And Boiling Water:

As the boiling frog story goes, if you drop a frog in a pot of boiling water, he'll jump right back out. But if you place him in a pot of cold water and very gradually turn up the heat, the frog will not perceive the danger and will stay in the water until he's eventually cooked! This story is used as a metaphor to describe the inability or unwillingness of people to react to significant changes that occur gradually, such as a worsening relationship.

Men generally don't get into boiling water relationships and if we do, we jump right back out! However, relationships can deteriorate over time, and that deterioration comes so gradually, that we don't realize the temperature is being turned up and has reached the boiling point!

The problem with trying to have discussions once the water is boiling is the man is so accustomed to the heat that he just tunes the discomfort out. (You need to use good communications methods to turn the heat down!)

Do Men Really Care If You Leave?

Leaving a relationship implies that a relationship, or rather a meaningful relationship, exists and men absolutely care about their meaningful relationships. We never want one to end. When one does end we feel a great sense of failure and shame and we grieve.

If we've only been on a few dates, we may be disappointed but we certainly won't grieve. By tomorrow or in a few days, we really won't be upset, especially if you manage the breakup well.

How Most Men Experience Grief:

This may come as a surprise to you but researchers have determined that loss is harder for men than it is for women. For eons women, society as a whole and therapist have operated under the belief that women grieve harder and longer than men.

Psychologists Wolfgang and Margaret Stroebe (a husband-and-wife team) examined all the existing research and the conclusions presented in their book "Bereavement and health: The psychological and physical consequences of partner loss" (Stroebe & Stroebe, 1987) were quite surprising. What they found is that men actually suffer more from being bereaved. Because there are more widows, it's easy to draw an anecdotal conclusion to the contrary but only because there are many more widows and because men tend to grieve internally.

Men are often times categorized as "instrumental mourners" which is a group or type of mourning in which they internalize their grief. When they act it's usually in the pursuit of accurate information, to make informed decisions, to speak of their loss intellectually and by taking action in order to solve their problems. By remaining strong, dispassionate and detached in the face of powerful emotions, by speaking of their grief in an intellectual way (we just grew apart), men tend to come across as cold, uncaring and without feeling.

In general, men tend to put their feelings into action, demonstrating our grief physically rather than emotionally. For instance, rather than telling you how much I loved my cat, Tiggy or by letting you see me cry, I busied myself with finding the perfect burial box, washing his favorite napping blanket, finding a spot in the back yard that I knew wouldn't be disturbed for years to come. By throwing myself into these time-limited tasks, I was able to recover a bit of power over the situation, and the accomplishments gave me an opportunity to be away from other family members and left alone with my thoughts. For many men experiencing a loss of relationships, those actions come in the form of increased time at work.

It's not that we men don't talk about our feelings, we do, but generally only to our closest friends and generally around shared activities like hunting, fishing, sporting events and card games. In terms of guy code, when a guy friend shares his grief with another guy, the man who is grieving can pretty much say anything he wants and the listening guy will just nod silently or agree. This is a role that women would find very difficult.

Men also cry. Sometimes in public and even then, what you see is just the tip of the iceberg. The real crying comes when we're alone, in secret or in the dark. Once a man has cried his last tear, he's put you in his past and is on his way to putting himself back together.

No matter the differences between how men and women grieve, the steps or stages are the same and the job of mourning is to confront our feelings, endure the pain and work through the emotional process of accepting the loss and realigning our definition of masculinity.

To better understand men who are grieving, it's helpful to recognize that:

- Female gender biases influence how women perceive the depth of a man's grief and his grieving process
- Just because men and women grieve differently, doesn't mean one way is better or worse than the other
- Endorsing one form of grieving over another can limit your support of someone who grieves differently than you
- No matter the approach to grieving, one must still tackle the work of processing the pain that comes from failure and loss

What looks like inappropriate behavior to a woman, is just a coping strategy to man. For instance, in an effort to numb themselves from the pain and to lower their inhibitions so they can release their emotions, some men will turn to drugs or alcohol. Other men will immediately go out and sleep with any and every woman he can find. He'll do this to recover his lost masculinity and some men will do all of these things. A man should not be judged for how he is grieving.

If a man seems more angry than sad at the loss of a relationship, he's probably angry at the situation which includes his perceived lack of fairness, the lack of respect at how the breakup process was handled, his powerlessness over the situation and the assault on his masculinity. What you don't want to do is take the man's anger personally, and you certainly don't want to react to it by escalating matters. Of course, if there is a history of domestic violence, then by all means his anger should be taken very seriously, and you should do everything you can to protect yourself and to keep your distance from him.

Also, it's very important to recognize how men grieve, which is very different than how women grieve. The masculine way of grieving is "alone and in silence" and even though men may appear to "not care" or may appear to be further along in the grieving process than they are or they may even appear to "be all right" or to have "gotten through the worst of it," you shouldn't make assumptions about what he's feeling.

Now that we know what men will experience, let's talk about how to actually break up.

How To Manage The Breakup:

Men never see the breakup coming. In his book "A Lasting Promise" (Stanley, Trathen, McCain, & Bryan, 1998, 2014) Scott Stanley, Ph.D., a Professor and Co-director of the Center for Marital and Family Studies at the University of Denver who has spent 30 year researching marriages and why they fail says there are two forms of commitment: emotional and confinement. Emotional is the love we feel for each other and confinement is the kids, mortgage, family ties, etc., and that we will stay in relationships long after the emotional commitment is gone and until the pain of staying exceeds the perceived pain of breaking all those ties. What that means is that while you are falling out of love, he's still taking the long road view. When you're ready to leave and file for divorce, for him the news comes completely out of left field. In fact, the longer the relationship has been in place, the less likely the man will see the split coming.

Frank in Knoxville tells this story:

"We were married for 48 years. 48 years! She'd never worked outside the home a day in her life. She stayed home, raised our kids, kept a good home and was a good wife and then one day she comes in all happy and tells me she's decided she wants a divorce and drops the papers on the kitchen table. I was stunned! Shocked! Angry! I'm 68 years old, still working and she wants a divorce? Since she'd never worked outside the home, she got the house, most of the savings and everything else. Two years later she'd decided that she'd made a horrible mistake and wanted me back and I can tell you there's no way in hell I would take that woman back! Not after being betrayed like that!"

Frank's story outlines two things: First, the divorce came out of left field and he felt "shocked, angry and betrayed" and; Second, after 48 years AND the fact that divorce wasn't "fair" he felt betrayed. Then when she came back after 2 years and wanted to reconcile (something divorce attorneys will tell you is not at all uncommon), she acted out of haste and something else was driving her decisions. All of these things worked to destroy every aspect of trust that Frank had for his ex-wife so there was no way he could ever take her back.

In order to have a successful breakup, you have to make sure he sees it coming. You need to have talks about the state of your relationship. You need to express that you are falling out of love with him. You need to insist on seeing a therapist and to make it clear that his unwillingness to participate is clearly telling you that he's unwilling to stay married. If you're dead set on ending the relationship, let the therapist broach the topic of ending the relationship.

Not all relationships are long term and those that aren't don't require a lot of lengthy conversations before breaking up. If you've only been out a few times, not calling can be a break-up. However, not calling is a really bad way to handle things, especially when a quick phone call can solve the problem.

Regardless of whether you're married, in a long term serious "living together" relationship, in a serious long term dating relationship or you've just gone on a few dates, how you handle the breakup determines your ability to have any form of a future friendship with the man and I can't stress enough, just how valuable an asset these friendships can be.

Respect Moves Relationships Forward:

I can't stress enough just how important it is to manage the breakup in a respectful way. There are just so many advantages in doing things right and the best and biggest advantage is how it affects your own self esteem. When you do things with kindness, honesty and respect, regardless of how he responds, you will feel good about yourself. Here are 4 good rules to follow:

Do Not Humiliate - Under no circumstances should a breakup be a humiliating experience. There should be no loud screaming, no embarrassing accusations or awkward discussions where others would "feel sorry" for the man.

Do Not Surprise! - If a breakup is coming out of left field then you've mismanaged the entire relationship. These types of surprises never end well.

Never Electronically! - You should never, ever, ever break up over social media, email or text etc. While you may want to avoid confrontation, you've turned the breakup into a very public and very humiliating experience. Not only do you hurt him but you end up looking like a complete ass in the process too. Guys have told me when they've seen women breakup over social media they immediately move those women onto the "stay away from this one" list!

Make Him 1st To Know! - While you may be angry, exasperated and "so completely over him" that you tell your friends and family thinking no one will tell him, trust me when I say this, someone will tell him (either before or after)! You tell your best friend, she tells her guy, her guy tells your guy and the whole thing takes less than 24 hours and if you don't think guys talk, you're sorely mistaken, especially when it comes to protecting other guys from pain. By letting the news filter through or by your guy hearing after the breakup "yeah, she told everyone she was leaving you" you leave your guy feeling stupid, humiliated and in a very bad place that contains you as public enemy #1.

Public Or Private:

Once you've decided to end your relationship, the next question becomes how. Face to face conversations are always best. It's respectful. However, before meeting face to face, you need to weigh the respect level vs. the risk.

The Man Puzzle

In relationships where there is a high level of respect between two partners and the risk of violence is virtually non-existent, then meeting in private is best. By private I mean a place where you won't run into friends, family and people can't overhear your conversation as this keeps the humiliation factor to a minimum.

In cases where there is no respect or there is risk of anger or violence, then meeting in public is absolutely best. If you have reason to fear for your safety, then simply don't meet at all.

Good public places are parks and very quiet coffee shops that have private places to chat. Never chose his favorite park, favorite bar or favorite restaurant because he'll always remember the breakup, and there's just no reason to ruin a good place for him.

Dan in Little Rock told this story:

I once took a date to my favorite restaurant and half way through dinner she told me "this is where my husband asked for a divorce" and she had been divorced for 12 years … 5 years longer than she was married! We never went back to that restaurant.

Set The Tone:

Be polite. If you've had enough direct and honest conversations leading up to this point, the breakup conversation won't come as a surprise and that gives you the opportunity to keep your conversation respectful and polite.

Be firm. You don't use words like "I think" as that implies that you could change your mind. Instead say things like "I've decided" as this means you have made up your mind. Being firm also means that you're direct and that you don't use weasel words. Take this example:

"It stands to reason that we'd both be happier if we weren't around each other and arguing all the time."

This statement leaves lots of room for discussion and argument. It "stands to reason" to whom? If "arguing all the time" is what's bothering you, then let's stop arguing!

Keep anger out of the conversation. If you remember back in the chapter on emotions, I discussed how women tend to break-up when angry. Don't do that! Breaking up should be thought out and done calmly.

What Do You Say?:

Finding the right words is always difficult. It's difficult for men too. If there are specific reasons that have to do with your safety, then you can say that. "You drink and drive when we're together, and I don't feel safe when I'm with you." However, unless there are very specific safety reasons, then you're much better off staying generic. Claiming they are "too messy for you" or "never take the trash out when you ask" is just petty and will lead to an argument.

Avoid the clichés. "It's not you, it's me!" If this is the best you can muster, then it really is you. Your man deserves your best, especially during this event, and your best should be nothing but complete honesty. Let him keep his dignity, and to do that, you have to be honest. Lying is really a horrible thing to do. Other horrible lies are: "I love you, but I'm not in love with you;" and "You deserve someone better than me."

Good Things To Say:

Some of the best conversations are simple, direct and honest. Here are some ideas:

After A Few Dates: *"I just don't feel a connection forming."*

Long-term Relationship: *"This relationship is not working anymore and I don't see it getting better. You're a great guy, but I want to break up."*

Divorce: *"My feelings for you have faded, and there's no way we can rekindle what we had. I want to work with you to end our marriage/relationship in a way that's fair, honest and respectful to us both."*

Bad Things To Say:

You absolutely want to avoid saying anything that attacks his masculinity. Never use his ability to provide financially, his sexuality or bedroom performance, his sensitivity or lack thereof and/or anything to do with his physical appearance (why would you attack something he has no control over?). Attacking his masculinity can escalate things into a violent situation very quickly.

Don't get into blaming. Blaming is not just mean but it comes from your own place of shame. If you need to blame him, you need to examine your own feelings of shame. If you have cheated or have some other behavior that you should own, then take responsibility and apologize for hurting him. If it's not something you should own, deflect the point away by saying "I'm sorry you feel I'm that way." If you blame him, he'll just get defensive. If he blames you and you accept the blame you'll not only appear weak and insincere, he'll feel guilty and probably get angry… and you certainly don't want to invoke his shame response.

Give Closure:

We often hear terms like "I have no idea why he left me" or "She needs closure" but what is closure and how do we give it to a man? Psychologists define closure as "an individual's desire for a firm answer which gives a peaceful resolution or conclusion to a relationship."

We give closure by giving a clear, concise and kindly worded explanation for the breakup and giving closure is the surest way to have a friendly and amicable parting.

Closing The Door:

Don't leave the door open for anything else. If at some point you reconnect and a friendship develops, that's fine. But if you break-up with the expectation that you will eventually become friends, he'll hang on to hope that there can be more, and that hope will cause him to be a pain in your butt.

Hopefully, he won't get angry. If he sees the breakup coming and is expecting the conversation, things will go much more smoothly. However, if he gets angry, let him. Don't defend yourself, as doing so will only escalate things. Unless he starts name calling, let him say what he needs to say and then be done. He'll have gotten things off his chest, and you'll both feel better in the end.

Breakup conversations should not be long and drawn out. A conversation that goes on for hours is not a breakup conversation; it's a "fix this relationship" conversation with the breakup being used as blackmail. It's highly manipulative. Keep the time allotted to a max of 30 minutes as that should be ample time to give closure.

Leave. Don't go straight home. If there's any chance he'll stop by your place later "to have another conversation," leave a note on your door addressed to him and tell him "that you do not wish to have any further conversations at this time and that his stopping by is inappropriate."

Social Media:

A good way to close out the conversation is to tell him you've not "updated your relationship status on social media yet because you wanted to talk to him first but that you'll change your status the next time you go online." He will recognize this as a very nice demonstration of your respect for him. After informing him of this, you can safely excuse yourself from the meeting.

Wait several hours before updating your status and keep your reasons private. Anyone who asks "what happened?" is really just a nosy gossip, and their questions simply don't require an answer. Take the high road and people will value you more.

Depending on your relationship and how much pain, be mindful of your social media posts by not posting about your new dates and having photos of you out the next night snuggling with a new guy. Little things can undo a lot of work. This doesn't mean you can't get on with your life; it just means be respectful.

Divorcing:

If you're divorcing, I would caution you to be very wary of using separate divorce attorneys. It's been my experience that some unscrupulous attorneys will work to inflame the situation and keep it inflamed until you can no longer afford to fight and then rush you into a fast settlement. This process will leave you broke, and you and your ex will have a deep wedge between you that can take years or decades to heal.

There is a new wave in divorcing called "divorce as friends" and I strongly encourage you to pursue this route when at all possible. If you must use separate attorneys, your attorney must be instructed to keep the inflammatory language out of the legal process and you must refrain from responding to inflammatory language used by his attorney.

If You Have Kids:

Remember, if you have kids, your ex will always be a part of their life. He will be there for every single major event including weddings, the birth of grandchildren, etc. Keeping him in your kids lives is essential to their success in life. Sons will grow up to be better men, daughters will grow up to be stronger women. With every man that I talked to who walked away from his kids, it was because his ex made his involvement unbearably painful and not just painful on the man but on the children. Judge this as right or wrong on the man's part, it takes two people to create the dysfunction and it takes two people work past it.

After The Breakup:

Time and space are the great healers and for that reason, you should plan on keeping your distance. That means no visitations, no drive-bys, no texting, no drunk texting, don't respond to any email that contains an emotional element unless your response moves the closure along to the next stage. Certainly don't get involved in protracted email exchanges. Understand that for every year you were together, it can take a month of grieving.

Be respectful in all aspects of your life. It's easy to get wrapped up in your freedom and, in doing so, cause other people a great deal of pain. This is especially true when kids are involved.

Gene in Atlanta tells this story:

"My wife and I were divorcing and after a year of battles the divorce was finally over on Thursday and I had the kids that weekend. I never told the kids anything about the divorce because they had enough battles with their mother (such as finding her in bed with two men). Sunday comes around and I took the kids back to their mothers house, the house they had grown up in and when I dropped them off I always waited until they were safely inside and before the last one was in the door I heard the screaming and crying. My ex had a number of "happy divorce" gifts and balloons out from her friends and admirers and these gifts caused so much pain for my kids that they all went into a highly emotional reaction. What she did was the height of insensitivity."

Roger in Orlando told this story:

"I had been living with my girlfriend for 4 years and she, in a fit of anger, threw me out. I was homeless. She then went around to all her friends telling them all these horrible things about me. I was unaware of this until, one day about 6 months later, I was sitting at Starbucks near my new apartment and one of her friends came up and gave me 'hell' for this, that and the other and telling me how 'I should be ashamed for treating her that way.' I sat quietly while she ranted and after she walked off I looked at the stunned crowd and said 'and that's why we're no longer together, it was massively unhealthy.' Besides that it was unhealthy, what she had told her friends were lies and half truths. It painted her in the best light and me in the worst. What little respect I had left for her evaporated in those two minutes and although she's reached out to me on several occasions, I've simply ignored her."

344

Anytime there's a breakup, people want to know what went wrong. Curiosity is powerful emotion, especially when two people seem well suited to each other. If you have one or two really close friends who would never say a word, share with them but assume that anything you say will eventually make it back to him... because, again it will!

What Happens Next?:

A new area of psychology called Evolutionary Psychology looks at how we've evolved psychologically to try and determine how and why our emotions have evolved with us. According to Brian Boutwell, Ph.D., Associate Professor of Criminology and Criminal Justice and Associate Professor Of Epidemiology at Saint Louis University who, along with colleagues, published a review paper in the March 2nd issue of the Review of General Psychology (Boutwell, Barnes, & Beaver, 2015) in which they conclude that humans are hard wired to fall out of love with one person and in love with someone else.

The breakup process which they call "mate ejection" is painful because it's a process similar to overcoming a drug addiction. This is based on brain scans done of addicts and of people "deeply in love" and noticing the same neural activity of those in love and cocaine addicts.

"Our review of the literature suggests we have a mechanism in our brains designed by natural selection to pull us through a very tumultuous time in our lives," said Professor Brian Boutwell. "It suggests people will recover; the pain will go away with time. There will be a light at the end of the tunnel."

There is light at the end of the tunnel.

Chapter 14

OUR BELIEFS HAVEN'T CHANGED

D URING MY TRAVELS AND WITH all the people I interviewed, this became my favorite exercise because, for all the great strides we THINK we've made in defining, redefining or even changing our definition of masculinity, it turns out that we've really not changed that definition at all!

On July 3rd, 1913, being unable to personally appear, President Theodore "Teddy" Roosevelt sent a speech he had recorded using a phonographic cylinder to the Boys' Progressive League in New York City which was played in his absence. The speech was known as "The American Boy" and is worth reading, as much for what it defines about men and masculinity which is still true over 100 years later, as for his explanation for what men are lacking today.

I Promise

As you read through this speech, you'll need three colors of pen or highlighters; one to mark the sections that describe your beliefs about what a man is… what you agree with; one to mark the sections about what a man isn't; one (a special color) to mark the sections you don't agree with. See how much of what you believe agrees with Teddy Roosevelt. I promise this will be one of the most enlightening things you will do.

The American Boy

"OF COURSE what we have a right to expect of the American boy is that he shall turn out to be a good American man. Now, the chances are strong that he won't be much of a man unless he is a good deal of a boy. He must not be a coward or a weakling, a bully, a shirk, or a prig. He must work hard and play hard. He must be clean-minded and clean-lived, and able to hold his own under all circumstances and against all comers. It is only on these conditions that he will grow into the kind of American man of whom America can be really proud.

> **AUTHORS NOTE:** A "prig" is a morally self-righteous person who behaves as if they are superior to others (think political extremist from either party; religious extremist or extreme atheist; racial extremist; or sexist who thinks that anyone who doesn't believe what they believe is morally deficient).

There are always in life countless tendencies for good and for evil, and each succeeding generation sees some of these tendencies strengthened and some weakened; nor is it by any means always, alas! That the tendencies for evil are weakened and those for good strengthened. But during the last few decades there certainly have been some notable changes for good in boy life. The great growth in the love of athletic sports, for instance, while fraught with danger if it becomes one-sided and unhealthy, has beyond all question had an excellent effect in increased manliness. Forty or fifty years ago the writer on American morals was sure to deplore the effeminacy and luxury of young Americans who were born of rich parents. The boy who was well off then, especially in the big Eastern cities, lived too luxuriously, took to billiards as his chief innocent recreation, and felt small shame in his inability to take part in rough pastimes and field-sports. Nowadays, whatever other faults the son of rich parents may tend to develop, he is at least forced by the opinion of all his associates of his own age to bear himself well in manly exercises and to develop his body—and therefore, to a certain extent, his character—in the rough sports which call for pluck, endurance, and physical address.

Of course boys who live under such fortunate conditions that they have to do either a good deal of outdoor work or a good deal of what might be called natural outdoor play do not need this athletic development. In the Civil War the soldiers who came from the prairie and the backwoods and the rugged farms where stumps still dotted the clearings, and who had learned to ride in their infancy, to shoot as soon as they could handle a rifle, and to camp out whenever they got the chance, were better fitted for military work than any set of mere school or college athletes could possibly be. Moreover, to mis-estimate athletics is equally bad whether their importance is magnified or minimized. The Greeks were famous athletes, and as long as their athletic training had a normal place in their lives, it was a good thing. But it was a very bad thing when they kept up their athletic games while letting the stern qualities of soldiering and statesmanship sink into disuse. Some of the younger readers of this book will certainly sometime read the famous letters of the younger Pliny, a Roman who wrote, with what seems to us a curiously modern touch, in the first century of the present era. His correspondence with the Emperor Trajan is particularly interesting; and not the least noteworthy thing in it is the tone of contempt with which he speaks of the Greek athletic sports, treating them as the diversions of an unwarlike people which it was safe to encourage in order to keep the Greeks from turning into anything formidable. So at one time the Persian kings had to forbid polo, because soldiers neglected their proper duties for the fascinations of the game. We cannot expect the best work from soldiers who have carried to an unhealthy extreme the sports and pastimes which would be healthy if indulged in with moderation, and have neglected to learn as they should the business of their profession. A soldier needs to know how to shoot and take cover and shift for himself— not to box or play foot-ball.

There is, of course, always the risk of thus mistaking means for ends. Fox-hunting is a first-class sport; but one of the most absurd things in real life is to note the bated breath with which certain excellent fox-hunters, otherwise of quite healthy minds, speak of this admirable but not over-important pastime. They tend to make it almost as much of a fetish as, in the last century, the French and German nobles made the chase of the stag, when they carried hunting and game-preserving to a point which was ruinous to the national life. Fox-hunting is very good as a pastime, but it is about as poor a business as can be followed by any man of intelligence. Certain writers about it are fond of quoting the anecdote of a fox-hunter who, in the days of the English civil war, was discovered pursuing his favorite sport just before a great battle between the Cavaliers and the Puritans, and right between their lines as they came together. These writers apparently consider it a merit in this man that when his country was in a death-grapple, instead of taking arms and hurrying to the defense of the cause he believed right, he should placidly have gone about his usual sports. Of course, in reality the chief serious use of fox-hunting is to encourage manliness and vigor, and to keep men hardy, so that at need they can show themselves fit to take part in work or strife for their native land. When a man so far confuses ends and means as to think that fox-hunting, or polo, or foot-ball, or whatever else the sport may be, is to be itself taken as the end, instead of as the mere means of preparation to do work that counts when the time arises, when the occasion calls—why, that man had better abandon sport altogether.

AUTHORS NOTE: *In the above paragraph the President talks against allowing hobbies, sports and other interests to consume us to the point of shirking our other responsibilities. That these hobbies, interests and sports should be a means to a end (entertainment, learning and fitness) and not the end itself.*

No boy can afford to neglect his work, and with a boy, work, as a rule, means study. Of course there are occasionally brilliant successes in life where the man has been worthless as a student when a boy. To take these exceptions as examples would be as unsafe as it would be to advocate blindness because some blind men have won undying honor by triumphing over their physical infirmity and accomplishing great results in the world. I am no advocate of senseless and excessive cramming in studies, but a boy should work, and should work hard, at his lessons—in the first place, for the sake of what he will learn, and in the next place, for the sake of the effect upon his own character of resolutely settling down to learn it. Shiftlessness, slackness, indifference in studying, are almost certain to mean inability to get on in other walks of life. Of course, as a boy grows older it is a good thing if he can shape his studies in the direction toward which he has a natural bent; but whether he can do this or not, he must put his whole heart into them. I do not believe in mischief-doing in school hours, or in the kind of animal spirits that results in making bad scholars; and I believe that those boys who take part in rough, hard play outside of school will not find any need for horse-play in school. While they study they should study just as hard as they play foot-ball in a match game. It is wise to obey the homely old adage, "Work while you work; play while you play."

A boy needs both physical and moral courage. Neither can take the place of the other. When boys become men they will find out that there are some soldiers very brave in the field who have proved timid and worthless as politicians, and some politicians who show an entire readiness to take chances and assume responsibilities in civil affairs, but who lack the fighting edge when opposed to physical danger. In each case, with soldiers and politicians alike, there is but half a virtue. The possession of the courage of the soldier does not excuse the lack of courage in the statesman and, even less does the possession of the courage of the statesman excuse shrinking on the field of battle. Now, this is all just as true of boys. A coward who will take a blow without returning it is a contemptible creature; but, after all, he is hardly as contemptible as the boy who dares not stand up for what he deems right against the sneers of his companions who are themselves wrong. Ridicule is one of the favorite weapons of wickedness, and it is sometimes incomprehensible how good and brave boys will be influenced for evil by the jeers of associates who have no one quality that calls for respect, but who affect to laugh at the very traits which ought to be peculiarly the cause for pride.

There is no need to be a prig. There is no need for a boy to preach about his own good conduct and virtue. If he does he will make himself offensive and ridiculous. But there is urgent need that he should practice decency; that he should be clean and straight, honest and truthful, gentle and tender, as well as brave. If he can once get to a proper understanding of things, he will have a far more hearty contempt for the boy who has begun a course of feeble dissipation, or who is untruthful, or mean, or dishonest, or cruel, than this boy and his fellows can possibly, in return, feel for him. The very fact that the boy should be manly and able to hold his own, that he should be ashamed to submit to bullying without instant retaliation, should, in return, make him abhor any form of bullying, cruelty, or brutality.

There are two delightful books, Thomas Hughes's "Tom Brown at Rugby," and Aldrich's "Story of a Bad Boy," which I hope every boy still reads; and I think American boys will always feel more in sympathy with Aldrich's story, because there is in it none of the fagging, and the bullying which goes with fagging, the account of which, and the acceptance of which, always puzzle an American admirer of Tom Brown.

> **AUTHORS NOTE:** *Fagging was a traditional practice in boarding and private schools where the younger students acted as personal servants to the older students. These younger students became known as "fags" because they were considered "less than."*

There is the same contrast between two stories of Kipling's. One, called "Captains Courageous," describes in the liveliest way just what a boy should be and do. The hero is painted in the beginning as the spoiled, over-indulged child of wealthy parents, of a type which we do sometimes unfortunately see, and than which there exist few things more objectionable on the face of the broad earth. This boy is afterward thrown on his own resources, amid wholesome surroundings, and is forced to work hard among boys and men who are real boys and real men doing real work. The effect is invaluable. On the other hand, if one wishes to find types of boys to be avoided with utter dislike, one will find them in another story by Kipling, called "Stalky & Co.," a story which ought never to have been written, for there is hardly a single form of meanness which it does not seem to extol, or of school mismanagement which it does not seem to applaud. Bullies do not make brave men; and boys or men of foul life cannot become good citizens, good Americans, until they change; and even after the change scars will be left on their souls.

AUTHORS NOTE: *In the above paragraph, the President talks about the importance of choosing good role models even in what we read. Choose role models who are strong and courageous and avoid those who extol all that is mean and bad.*

The boy can best become a good man by being a good boy—not a goody-goody boy, but just a plain good boy. I do not mean that he must love only the negative virtues; I mean he must love the positive virtues also. "Good," in the largest sense, should include whatever is fine, straightforward, clean, brave, and manly. The best boys I know—the best men I know—are good at their studies or their business, fearless and stalwart, hated and feared by all that is wicked and depraved, incapable of submitting to wrong-doing, and equally incapable of being aught but tender to the weak and helpless. A healthy-minded boy should feel hearty contempt for the coward and even more hearty indignation for the boy who bullies girls or small boys, or tortures animals. One prime reason for abhorring cowards is because every good boy should have it in him to thrash the objectionable boy as the need arises.

Of course the effect that a thoroughly manly, thoroughly straight and upright boy can have upon the companions of his own age, and upon those who are younger, is incalculable. If he is not thoroughly manly, then they will not respect him, and his good qualities will count for but little; while, of course, if he is mean, cruel, or wicked, then his physical strength and force of mind merely make him so much the more objectionable a member of society. He cannot do good work if he is not strong and does not try with his whole heart and soul to count in any contest; and his strength will be a curse to himself and to everyone else if he does not have thorough command over himself and over his own evil passions, and if he does not use his strength on the side of decency, justice, and fair dealing.

In short, in life, as in a foot-ball game, the principle to follow is:

Hit the line hard; don't foul and don't shirk, but hit the line hard!"

Chapter 15

WHAT WOMEN DON'T GET

Now that we understand a bit about how a man's inner self is shaped and where his own inner confusion comes from, we have a basis for talking about some core female behaviors that lead to relationship confusion, complexity and often times a breakup. What follows is a short list of things that men find particularly confusing:

1. Allowing chivalry and gentlemanly behavior does not diminish you as a woman. A man's willingness to open a door for you, to hold your chair or to give you his jacket when you're cold in no way diminishes you as a woman or human being. Most men will hold a door open for a man as quickly as he will for you (although admittedly, there are unspoken rules for when you do and don't hold a door open for another guy and, in business a man will extend those rules out to include women). In fact, not accepting these gestures shows a lack of graciousness on your part and leads men to describe you in unflattering terms.

2. Just because you're an independent woman (you mean adult, right?), that doesn't mean you can't have dependencies on a man. As a species, we are inherently tied to each other and our success depends on each other. Remember, men want and need to feel needed and being independent takes away his ability to be needed. If he can't feel needed, he has no reason to believe in the continuity of the relationship.

3. Men want, need and appreciate the perspective that a woman brings to his life. We need your perspective, your different way of viewing the world, your ability to find a gentler way to compromise.

4. It's not all about boobs, legs and mini-skirts. While your looks may get our attention, your brains, heart, kindness and compassion will keep it.

What Men Fear:

I have long said that when a man is in love with a woman, that woman can build a man up or shatter him at his core with just a look. Now what does that mean? What it means is that as we learn to trust you and become more intimate with you, you have more power and influence in our lives than you realize. Because of this vulnerability, we have things that we absolutely fear from our partners and these are things that you need to be aware of and, if you do these things, you need to stop them.

Ridicule. This is probably the one behavior I see at parties and around the office that makes most every guy cringe. We immediately feel sorry for the man being ridiculed and you immediately lose about half of your trustworthiness with men. I'm not talking about teasing about snoring or the laughing comment on the paunch or the other good natured fun that couples enjoy. In fact, most men probably like these things quite a bit. What I mean are the mean comments that his intelligence, masculinity or ability to provide. When you say "John's idea of foreplay is brushing his teeth!" that's one of those comments that should never be said, not just in public, but anywhere.

Not being understood. We all know and recognize that men are far less adept at expressing themselves than women. It doesn't mean we don't try, it just means we're not as good at it. Women who are successful with men, put forth the extra effort to understand what their men are trying to communicate.

A fight. There is probably nothing a man hates more and fears more than a fight. Very few men like fighting with their women, and I would venture a guess that 100% of them would choose almost anything other than a fight. Learn to not fight with your man, and if you must have a fight, learn to fight fair!

Rejection. As we discussed in the previous section, rejection cuts a man straight to his core. Does that mean you need to always give in to your man? Of course not. There are just ways of handling rejections so that men don't feel rejected.

Being seen as a failure. We want to please you. We want you to respect and admire us. Being seen as a failure in your eyes is devastating to us.

Not being valued by you. There are lots of ways to value a human being. You can value their ability to fix anything or their ability to trade stocks or how they handle a homeless person or how they handle themselves in a courtroom. All of those things are important to a guy but most important is how you value him as your partner. Learn to let him know that you value him.

Not able to make you happy. This has already been said several times in this book and more times than can be counted in the history of mankind. A man in love will live to make you happy and he fears failing at that.

Abandonment. Whoa! Wait a minute! Isn't that a rather infantile fear? Don't kids have abandonment issues? Why, yes. Yes they do. That doesn't mean that a fully functioning man in a loving relationship can't and doesn't have that fear. They do.

Disrespect. Disrespect can take many forms. Anything from the ridicule mentioned earlier all the way up to and including infidelity. Disrespect, or perceived disrespect is one of the fastest ways to end a relationship with any man so it pays to understand how and when he feels disrespected and for you to find ways to compromise or to avoid those situations all together.

She's going to change me. Most every man in existence knows that he'll have to make some changes in order to be in a relationship with a good woman. So this isn't about the whole seat up/seat down argument. What we're talking about is asking a man to change a core component of his being to something he's not or, worse, he doesn't like. While his need to please you is quite overwhelming, and while he may go through the motions of changing in order to please you, asking for core personality changes will ultimately come back and bite you.

Keeping It Simple

The #1 rule with all men is: keep it simple! Men hate complexity. No matter what our jobs are, we deal with complexity all day long so we don't want complex relationships. If our friendships with our men friends were complex, well, they'd not be our men friends. Complexity is the fastest way to kill a relationship with a man. You have to learn to keep a man's life simple.

Here is an example:

Example:

Monday:

> **She says**: *"Honey, would you like to go to Joe's Restaurant" for dinner on Thursday?*
>
> **He says:** *(thinking to himself: I hate Joes, the food is horrible, the service is slow and it's expensive) "You know I don't like that place but if you really want to, I guess I could stomach it one more time."*

Tuesday:

> **She says:** *"Oh Honey, I hope you don't mind but I invited Emily to join us."*
>
> **He says:** *(thinking to himself: Oh God, not her! She never shuts up!) "Really? That doesn't sound at all fun to me."*
>
> **She says:** *"Oh come on. It will be nice and besides, all you have to do is sit there and she and I will keep each other entertained."*
>
> **He says:** *(not one word)*

Wednesday:

> **She says:** *"Oh Honey, Emily's boyfriend Jack is going to be joining us for dinner tomorrow night."*
>
> **He says:** *(thinking to himself: That guys a total jackass this is*

soooo gonna suck!) "You know I hate him."

She says: *"Emily says he's been in therapy and he's really changed. Come on, it will be fun!"*

Thursday:

He says: *(thinking to himself: This is way too complicated and there is no way I'm spending my evening at a restaurant I don't like with people I can't stand and I'll probably get stuck with the check to boot!) "Honey, I hate to do this at such short notice but I have to work late tonight."*

The Balloon Principle:

Now, I'm going to ask you to draw upon your imagination while I explain this very basic principle of how of how men decide to stay in or leave a relationship. It's amazingly simple (as are we men) and I'm sure you'll find some amusement in it.

First, imagine one of those long balloons, like the kind they make balloon animals with but bigger around.

Next, I want you to use a marker and draw two rings around the balloon so that there are three separate but equal sections.

Finally, in the first section I want you to write "Great Sex"; in the second section I want you to write "Feel Good" and in the third section write "Simple".

Balloon illustration: (Feel Good | Simple | Great Sex)

What each section represents are the sections or areas of a mans relationship. "Great Sex" is pretty obvious. It's what your man thinks is Great Sex (which can be very different from what you or your ex-boyfriend considered Great Sex). "Feels Good" is how a man feels about himself while in a relationship with you. "Simple" is the complexity of the relationship. All men want simple relationships but, not being complete idiots, we're willing to make sacrifices. Let me explain:

What I want you to do now is to squeeze the section called "Great Sex" which is like taking "Great Sex" away from the relationship. Notice how the other two sections (Simple and Feels Good) get bigger? Great Sex is gone but the relationship has more "Simple" and more "Feels Good". A man is willing to make trade-offs. We'll take mediocre sex as long as the relationship is "Simple" AND we "Feel REALLY Good" about ourselves.

Now, release "Great Sex" and squeeze "Feels Good" so that you're taking "Feels good about himself" away and notice how "Great Sex" and Simple just got bigger? A man will sacrifice feeling good about himself if he's getting lots of great sex AND the relationship is simple.

Now, squeeze "Feels Good" and "Simple" so that all's remaining is a really huge and bloated "Great Sex". If you imagined this correctly, the balloon would have popped at this point! What this means is that no matter how good any one part is, if the other two parts are gone, no man will stick around!

Men will sacrifice any one of "Feeling Good", "Simple" or "Great Sex" but will not stay in a relationship where any two are missing. Take away any two and your man is gone!

Chapter 16

QUESTIONS FROM WOMEN

DURING MY TRAVELS AND WITH all the women I interviewed, there were certain questions that came up time and time again. In this chapter I'm going to cover the most common of those questions.

While some of the questions have been answered elsewhere in this book, some are new and, frankly, my answers below are raw.

1. How do you know when a man is really interested in you if he never expresses his feelings?

There are lots of ways of expressing feelings... spending time with you when he could be at a ballgame is expressing his feelings. Fixing something for you is expressing his feelings. Making sure the lawn is perfect is expressing his feelings. Men have a lot of ways of expressing their feelings. Look at his actions first. Is he doing the right things?

Questions From Women

2. Why do men think it's okay to cruise the Internet and contact women for chatting, etc. when they say they are committed to you?

They are lying to you. But the bigger question is this: Why would you allow yourself to be treated that way?

3. If a man cheated in his marriage, and is now dating you, does this mean that chances are good he will also cheat on you?

Cheating is never a good sign and, in my mind, there is never an excuse good enough to justify it so I consider cheating of any nature to be a warning sign. Having said that, I will now tell you what my research says: When a man cheats, it's usually because his needs were not being met and those unmet needs have created emotional issues that he's incapable of dealing with. This doesn't mean his needs are realistic nor does it mean the emotional issues are his, it could be his partners issues that he is incapable of dealing with.

If I were confronted with a known cheater, I would keep my panties on until I was able to fully discern what the problem is/ was. Was it him or was it truly his ex.?

4. Should women see red flags if he doesn't take you to his local hangouts, introduce you to family, etc.?

I dated a woman for three years (and was actually engaged to her) and there were two things she never got: 1) My secret watering hole where I could go and hang with friends, and 2) she never heard me fart. Sometimes we just need our own place and our own space. If our needs are being met, then the local hangouts will be yours as well.

363

5. Is there a prescribed time frame when women might be let into men's inner circle?

It depends. It depends on how hot the woman is, how good he thinks she will mesh with his friends, how rough his friends will treat her (some friends think by virtue of your presence, you can hang!), his ultimate intentions and how long he thinks she might be around.

Unless you are a trophy, most men want to know the relationship is stable before they introduce you to their friends. Either that, or they throw you to the wolves and see how you sink or swim... that can really test a woman's mettle.

6. How do women know when they've been listened to and heard so they don't beat a dead horse?

If you learn to speak to a man correctly, you will always know you have been heard. However, being heard does not mean compliance (make sure you know the difference). Asking me to put the toilette seat down will get you heard but I will not change my habits, and I will not put it down unless I need it down.

7. Is it best to wait for men to make the first moves (virtually or real time) to indicate interest? If women do, do men think less of them?

Welcome to a man's world! Women wanted ERA, and this is one area where you're finding just how painful this process is. Now, to answer the question: It depends on the man. Some men are old fashioned and like to be the pursuer, while others (like me) are more into equality and are appreciative of a woman reaching out.

8. Why is it that men do not have the need to give closure in relationships?

We want things simple. We don't want to be hurt nor to hurt you. This is why we basically use the old "it's not you, it's me" breakup phrase. Here is a list of direct translations as given to be by men (warning, these aren't nice but they do reflect their pain and frustration):

A. There is nothing wrong with you, but you are not what I am looking for

B. You drive me nuts because you can't accept what I say at face value (e.g. it's not you, it's me!)

C. The list of things wrong with you is so long, I don't have time to go over them all

D. I am SO done with you that I am not willing to spend any more time on the subject

E. If I don't give you anything to go on, you and your girlfriends will spend far, far less time dissecting this, and you'll move on to a new relationship quicker (and therefore leave me alone)

F. If I hurry this up, I can make my Tee time, ball game, poker night etc.

G. The last thing in the world I am willing to do is to give you a list of things to fix so that I have to be stuck with your ass for another 'x' years

H. Last thing in the world I am gonna do is listen to another one of your lectures about how I am wrong and you are right

I. I really wanna hurry this up so I can get to my new girl friends' house because she's fun!

J.   It's really gonna end up being my fault anyway so why bother getting in to all this.

Don't take these personally. Just understand there are a whole lot of reasons, translations and frustration in those statements and when you hear "it's not you, it's me" that it's best to let sleeping dogs lie.

9. How can men just eradicate women from their lives in a single heartbeat and just appear as they never think of them again after being in long term relationships?

They can't. They don't.

However, the person ending the relationship typically grieves while still in the relationship, and, eventually, they reach a point where enough grieving has been done that it's no longer worth staying in the relationship, so they walk away and it does appear as though the person never cared.

10. Why is it that most men tend to prefer women 10 or more years their junior?

We don't. We want to feel proud of the woman we are with. It makes us feel good about ourselves. It's an unfortunate reality that some women don't take very good care of themselves (not that men do either). What men are saying here is take better care of yourselves, be more active, be more interesting!

11. Should women wait for men to say "let's be exclusive?" or is it ok for women to introduce this topic?

I think it depends... what signs is he giving you? What are your own needs? How and when will you introduce this topic? On the way to a party to meet his friends? Your friends? After you have been having sex for 6 months?

12. What can women do to keep men interested in them sexually?

Lose the "only bad girls do that" attitude. Truth is, if only bad girls did stuff, we would have died off as a race a long, long time ago... Oh, and stop reading those women's magazines and ask him what turns him on! Learn to flirt... learn to text him and tease him... he'll let you know what he wants to do with and to you.

13. How do women know it's over when men won't tell them? If she's left to read the signs, what signs should she look for?

Withdrawal defined as time, involvement, communications... if he's all of a sudden going back to playing golf on Saturdays, and he's stopped making plans and talking about the future, then you are headed for trouble.

14. Why do men lie?

It can be any number of reasons from insecurity to simplicity but you can break it down to one of these four basic reasons:

1. He doesn't want to hurt your feelings. If you're a woman who gets upset when he tells you the truth, you're essentially training him to lie because telling you what you want to hear and keeping the peace is far, far easier than dealing with the waterworks. Cowardly? Absolutely! But remember, men live in the mindset of long views and wins and losses, victories and defeats. With no perceived upside, why would your man tell the truth when all it will do is create unneeded drama in his life?

2. He likes things simple. I've covered this in several places in this book. If the lie is essentially harmless versus being truthful which will bring out your wrath, why be honest? Men will always take the easiest path.

3. No benefit in being honest. Like I said earlier, a man will always look at the long view and is generally pretty good at picking his battles. If you want the truth, you have to change the way you react and you have to not expect change to happen immediately. It's not just your programming you have to undo, it's his mother, sisters, previous girl friends, your mother, sisters, your Aunt Betsy etc.

4. He is insecure and doesn't believe he can keep you without building himself into something he's not. My personal advice is that if you learn he's lying out of insecurity, then walk away. The relationship has nowhere to go but down hill.

15. Why do men settle?

There are two kinds of settling: 1) Accepting someone less than one is capable of attracting or keeping and; 2) to settle as in "to be settled down"?

To settle, as in accepting someone less than one is capable of... 3 things: 1) your insecurity... he may feel he's got someone better than he could normally get. 2) Having the upper hand gives him some control; 3) It's comfortable. Settle down: He's comfortable, the sex is good, he likes who he is when he's with you, he feels loved.

16. Why would a man NOT want to ever get married?

There are several reasons for this:

It could be code for "you're not the one" or, at least, "you're not giving me what I need." Or, it could be something much deeper.

For Instance, some younger men I interviewed had no desire to ever marry. They had seen their fathers financially devastated and sleeping in their cars and swore they would never be in that position. On the flip side, many older men whose kids are grown have said they simply see no reason for marriage.

17. Can a previous relationship ruin a man?

While every relationship leaves its scars, the severity of those scars is dependent on the man and how much healing he has accomplished.

18. Why do some men not open doors or do all the other things that a gentleman does?

For most men, this is a very confusing area. On the one hand, if you act gentlemanly, you risk being labeled sexist. On the other hand if you don't do those things, you're a Neanderthal. I, personally, have been yelled at for holding a door for a woman who was a few steps behind me. Somehow, my politeness offended her.

If you ask most men, they don't think anything about holding a door open for anyone behind them, man or woman, and most of us will tell you that about 95% of the men will say thank you while less than ½ the women will.

If gentlemanly behavior is important to you, then ask for it and encourage it by being appreciative. If your man has stopped opening doors tell him how much you miss him doing that and then show appreciation when he does.

19. Why Do Men Like Sports?

Man's love affair with watching organized sports can be traced back 1000's of years to the arenas in Rome where gladiators fought lions, tigers, bears and each other. Fans picked and rooted for their favorite gladiator. These were modern, civilized men sitting in the seats.

Sports then, as they are now, are the modern day version of tribal battles with the winner gaining pride and bragging rights in their chosen team. My city is better than your city. My tribe is better than your tribe.

Sports fulfill some of mans biological needs: First, is the thrill of the chase (in this case we're chasing a championship); Second, is the thrill of the battle; Lastly, by nature, men are competitive and sports play on our competitive nature (even though we may not be doing the competing).

Man has always fought for survival, after all, and the history of our tribal minds, of our capacity to test wills, and ultimately, of our drive to compete, has fueled modern sports.

According to a 1998 study in Physiology & Behavior, when a guy watches his team win, he actually has an increase in testosterone levels.

Viewing combative sports also helps men identify with traditional ideals of masculinity like domination, risk taking, and competition, explains Douglas Hartmann, Ph.D., Associate Professor of Sociology at the University of Minnesota. "In fact," he says, "the less physically competitive his daily life is, the more sports can become a means toward achieving those ideals, at least in his mind."

The drafting of new players feeds hope. Hope that past mistakes will be corrected, hope that the new players will bring that winning season. It keeps players connected to the sport.

Men bond by doing things together that have an emotional significance and by tracking sports, watching games and celebrating together, male friendships are forged and bound.

Chapter 17

REQUESTS FROM MEN

A s I CLOSED EACH GROUP interview session with all these great guy participants, I would ask them what things they wish women knew or they wished women would do more of. After awhile you realize there's a fairly consistent pattern. Here are the most often stated requests from men.

Work As A Team:

That doesn't mean you're both doing the same things at the same time. It means you both have the same end goal in mind. It doesn't matter who the primary bread winner is or who the primary care giver is to the kids or when those roles get temporarily flipped. What matters is that he knows you're on HIS team and that you have talked about your strategy and who is responsible for which role at which time.

Play As A Team:

Many couples who "grow apart" do so because they stop spending time together doing fun and interesting things that they both enjoy. It's important to support each other's interest and to develop fun things to do that you both enjoy.

Privacy Rules The Day:

Ultimately, your love and your relationship are private. If you share intimate details with your mom or your best friend and that gets back to your man, you will have destroyed an essential part of your trust. Keep things private that should stay private.

Go At Your Own Pace, Let Him Go At His:

Everyone has a different pace for everything. Some people believe in love at first sight, and others take years to make a decision. Likewise, some people can get over an argument in an instant while others take days. No matter what it is, go at your own pace AND let him go at his.

Keep The Spark Alive:

Dating for a long time? Married? Kids? Doesn't matter. If you don't work to keep the spark alive, the spark will die. Keep it sexy. Keep it interesting. Keep it simple!

Appreciate Your Man:

Yeah, he may have forgotten to get the milk on the way home, but he also just worked a 14 hour day and filled your tank with gas so you wouldn't have to do it in the morning. It doesn't matter how little you think he does, be appreciative and you will get more... maybe not overnight... but you will, and you will get more than you could imagine!

Accept His Differences:

Your man may have a completely different outlook and may do things completely differently and those differences may annoy you beyond hope and reason. Remember, one of the top needs of men is to be unconditionally accepted and when that happens, you get it 10 x back.

Have Fun:

You don't like to fish? Go anyway and learn to bait the hook! You think he'll be annoyed that you squeal from the worms? Not really. Despite what his face might show, he'll laugh and, more importantly, he'll appreciate your being the good sport. Just don't nag. Nagging makes you complicated and the time spent with you becomes unenjoyable and will more than erase the good points you would get from doing what he loves. Be fun!!!

Make Time For Each Other:

Dating should never stop and neither should your commitment to spend quality time with each other. Set aside one day a week (Friday, Saturday or even Tuesday) and don't let anything interfere with that time. No money? Stay home, rent a movie, cook something easy that doesn't tie you to the kitchen... the important thing is to spend time together... after all, you made time when you were first dating, you should be able to make time now! (and don't let him back out either!!!!)

Don't Be Afraid To Show Affection:

One of the strongest statements is "Mine!" "That man is MINE!" "That's MY boyfriend/fiancé/husband!" One of the surest and fastest ways to show MINE is the public display of affection (PDA) so don't be afraid to show those PDAs! (And be minimally wary and certainly understanding of the man who wants no PDAs!)

Be The Launch Pad:

Tough times are tough for a reason. They're not easy and they're not pretty but do you know what tough times are? Growth! What happens with growth? Something new is born! Be the place where he can grow and something new can be born. I know this is contradictory but the reality is this: When you are his launch pad, you are also where he will land. That support structure is important! Don't under estimate it! Ever!

Sex Is Important:

It's primal and necessary because sex help keep intimacy intact. Once a couple stops having sex, intimacy diminishes and like a person dying where one organ shuts down after another, so it goes with the relationship. When intimacy starts fading, so do communications, trust and your commitment to each other. Remember, women need emotional closeness in order to have sex while men need sex in order to have emotional closeness.

Support His Career:

Your career is no less important to you than his is to him. Often power struggles develop and arguments ensue and one partner ends up feeling less important and when that happens, you have BIG problems. Remember, men are hard wired to want to protect and care for you and when you take that away from him, you will evoke a whole set of feelings (such as being unwanted or unneeded) which lead to a whole set of bigger problems. More often than not, it's a matter of communications, compromises and setting priorities. Learn to think and always talk through the consequences of him missing opportunities to support you and you missing opportunities to support him.

Never Stop Dating:

Did I mention this already? Then this one MUST be important! Yeah, money gets tight, schedules get busy, we have kids, bosses and 1000's of other things going on but no matter what happens, you should never stop dating. Every week you should set aside time to date each other and by date, I don't mean sit in different rooms and watch different things on TV. I mean spend time together doing the same thing. It doesn't have to be expensive, an old movie and some popcorn can be just as awesome as a big dinner out with dancing. In fact, with many guys, it may be the preferred! I should also add that date night is NOT the time to bring up relationship issues. It's the time to connect and be a happy couple!

Keep The Foundation Strong:

Relationships built on solid ground will last longer than those whose weren't and just because the original foundation was solid doesn't mean it can't get cracks from settling. Constant work is required in order to keep that foundation solid. Remember, the stronger the foundation, the bigger the castle that can be built on it.

Communicate Constantly:

Stay in touch! Know what's going on with each other, how it affects each other and how each of you feels about it. Discuss everything. This doesn't mean nag your man or question everything he does. It means communicate effectively and often. The more you communicate by listening effectively and not judging, the more he will open up, and the more he opens up the easier this all becomes!

Trust His Judgment:

You each come to the table with different experiences, and both of you could enter the same situation and choose a different course of action. It doesn't mean that either way is right or wrong, just different. Learn to trust his judgment and if he learns a hard lesson, then that's a part growth and your support is part of being on the same team! Obviously, if you KNOW his choice will end in disaster, you MUST speak up because that is also a part of being on the same team.

Timing Is Everything:

Know when to bring up a subject, when to let things cool off, when to step up and be supportive and when to pack his lunch and send him off fishing with the guys. Timing is an art form and it's an art worth learning.

Growing Is Good:

When growing, you have two choices; you can either grow together or grow apart. Former First Lady Barbara Bush has been married to former President George Bush for sixty-nine years, and she said "I think we grew together. We always turned to each other," she said. Think for a moment about what that means… when either of them came to a fork in the road, they discussed it, discussed how it affected each of them, their family and their goals and, TOGETHER they made a decision and moved on. They grew TOGETHER.

Break Some Rules:

You can read 1,000 relationship books, and every book will say do this and don't do that. In the end, however, it's your relationship so it's up to you to do what works for you. Talk to your man and have your own agreement. If that agreement falls within standard advice, then great; if it doesn't but you're both happy with your choices, then by all means break the rule!

Learn To Laugh:

Relationships come with their own sets of problems and, on some occasions, their own drama and guess what? It's all normal! Learn to find the humor in the good and the bad and learn to laugh about those things. Don't take everything so seriously or so personally, but also don't laugh at your partner's expense.

Be Appreciative:

Have I mentioned this already? When your partner supports you, your cause, your career or anything else, BE APPRECIATIVE! Women who are appreciative towards their man, have men who are more willing to do more, try harder and exceed in making their women happy!

Be Thoughtful:

Breakfast in bed? It doesn't have to be just on special occasions and, in fact, two plates are just as easy to make as one. Put special notes in his pockets or open a cold beer when he puts the lawn mower up. It doesn't take much effort to be thoughtful, but it does take practice! Find a way to be thoughtful each and every day!

BIBLIOGRAPHY

Allesen-Holm, B., Bredie, W., & Frøst, M. B. (2008, December 18). *Girls Have Superior Sense Of Taste To Boys.* Retrieved from ScienceDaily: www.sciencedaily.com/releases/2008/12/081216104035.htm

Amen, D. D. (1999). *Change Your Brain, Change Your Life.* Harmony; Reprint edition.

Baron-Faust, R. (2000, July 28). *A woman's heart: a mystery of science.* Retrieved from www.medscape.com: http://www.medscape.com/viewarticle/782902

Boutwell, B. P., Barnes, J. P., & Beaver, K. M. (2015, March). Just Slip Out the Back, Jack. *Review of General Psychology* .

Briere, J., & Elliot, D. (2003). Prevalence and psychological sequelae of self-reported childhood physical and sexual abuse in a general population sample of men and women. . *Child Abuse & Neglect* , 1205–1222.

Brown, J., James, K., & Taylor, A. (2010). Caught in the rejection–abuse cycle: are we really treating perpetrators of domestic abuse effectively? *Journal of Family Therapy (32)* , 280–307.

(2011). *Children's Living Arrangements and Characteristics.* Washington, D.C.: U.S. Census Bureau.

Civitas. (2009, March). *How Do Fathers Fit In?* Retrieved from civitas.org.uk: http://www.civitas.org.uk/hwu/fathers.php

(2010). *CPS Involvement in Families with Social Fathers.* Princeton, NJ and New York, NY: Bendheim-Thomas Center for Research on Child Wellbeing and Social Indicators Survey Center.

Doty, R., & Cameron, E. L. (2009). Sex Differences and Reproductive Hormone Influences on Human Odor Perception. *Physiology & Behavior , 97* (2), 213–228.

FAQ. (2010). Retrieved from http://www.kinseyinstitute.org/: http://www.kinseyinstitute.org/resources/FAQ.html

Fisher, T., ZT, M., & MJ, P. (2012). Sex on the brain?: an examination of frequency of sexual cognitions as a function of gender, erotophilia, and social desirability. *Journal of Sex Research ,* 69-77.

Geary, D. C. (2010). *Male, Female: The Evolution of Human Sex Differences, Second Edition.* Amer Psychological Assn; 2 edition (November 2009).

Glenn, N. P., & Whitehead, B. D. *MAMA SAYS: A National Survey of Mothers' Attitudes on Fathering.* National Fatherhood Initiative.

Guarnaschelli, J. S. (2010, Feb.). *Turning Shame To Gold: Men Feeling Shame, Men Healing Shame.* Retrieved from onthecommon ground.org: http://www.onthecommonground.org/readingroom/ HEALING_SHAME_PART_I.pdf

Harlow, C. W. *Education and Correctional Populations.* Washington, D.C.: U.S. Department of Justice.

Howard, K. S., Burke, L. J., Borkowski, J., & Whitman, T. L. (2006). *Fathers' influence in the lives of children with adolescent mothers.* Journal of Family Psychology.

Johnson, P. M. (2008). Typology of Domestic Violence: Intimate Terrorism, Violent Resistance, and Situational Couple Violence. In P. M. Johnson, *Typology of Domestic Violence: Intimate Terrorism, Violent*

Resistance, and Situational Couple Violence (p. 168). Northeastern University Press.

Koehler, R. (2013, 12 19). *The code of shame.* Retrieved from Chicago Tribune: http://www.chicagotribune.com/sns-201312181800--tms--rkoehlerctnbk-a20131219-20131219,0,2348546.column

Lurito, J., Phillips, M. M., Dzemidzic, M., Lowe, M. J., Wang, Y. M., & Mathews, V. (2000). Men Do Hear—But Differently Than Women, Brain Images Show. *86th Scientific Assembly and Annual Meeting of the Radiological Society of North America (RSNA).*

Neuhoff, J., Planisek, R., & Seifritz, E. (2009). Sex differences in auditory motion perception: looming sounds are special. , 35,. *Journal of Experimental Psychology: Human Perception and Performance , 35,* 225 – 234.

Pollack, W. (1998). *New Psychotherapy For Men.* John Wiley & Sons.

Salisbury, E. J., & Department of Criminal Justice, U. o. (Eds.). (n.d.). *Criminal Justice & Behavior , 403-26.*

Sokhi, D. S., Hunter, M. D., Wilkinson, I. D., & Woodruff, P. W. (2005). Male and female voices activate distinct regions in the male brain. *NeuroImage , 27* (3), 572-578.

Stanley, S. M., Trathen, D., McCain, S., & Bryan, B. M. (1998, 2014). *A Lasting Promise.* John Wiley & Sons, Inc.

Stroebe, W., & Stroebe, M. S. (1987). *Bereavement and health: The psychological and physical consequences of partner loss.* Cambridge University Press.

The eyes have it: Men and women do see things differently. (2012, September 3). Retrieved from Biomed Central Limited ScienceDaily: www.sciencedaily.com/releases/2012/09/120903221050.htm

The Partnership Attitude Study. (2012, May). Retrieved from drugfree.org: http://www.drugfree.org/wp-content/uploads/2012/05/PATS-FULL-Report-FINAL-May-2-PDF-.pdf

Thompson, M. P., Kingree, J. B., & Desai, S. P. (2004, April). Gender Differences in Long-Term Health Consequences of Physical Abuse of Children: Data From a Nationally Representative Survey. *American Journal Public Health* , 599-604.

Websdale, N. (2009). *Familicidal Hearts: The Emotional Styles of 211 Killers.* Oxford University Press.

Wedekind, C., Seebeck, T., Bettens, F., & Paepke, A. J. (1995, June 22). MHC-Dependent Mate Preferences in Humans. *Proceedings: Biological Sciences* , 245-249.

Wilcox, W. B. (2012). *The State of Our Unions 2012.* Charlottesville, VA 22904-4766: National Marriage Project.

INDEX

Index